French Politics, Society and Culture Series

General Editor: Robert Elgie, Paddy Moriarty Professor of Government and International Studies, Dublin City University

France has always fascinated outside observers. Now, the country is undergoing a period of profound transformation. France is faced with a rapidly changing international and European environment and it is having to rethink some of its most basic social, political and economic orthodoxies. As elsewhere, there is pressure to conform. And yet, while France is responding in ways that are no doubt familiar to people in other European countries, it is also managing to maintain elements of its long-standing distinctiveness. Overall, it remains a place that is not exactly *comme les autres*.

This new series examines all aspects of French politics, society and culture. In so doing it focuses on the changing nature of the French system as well as the established patterns of political, social and cultural life. Contributors to the series are encouraged to present new and innovative arguments so that the informed reader can learn and understand more about one of the most beguiling and compelling of all European countries.

Titles include:

Gill Allwood and Khursheed Wadia
GENDER AND POLICY IN FRANCE

Sylvain Brouard, Andrew M. Appleton, Amy G. Mazur (*editors*)
THE FRENCH FIFTH REPUBLIC AT FIFTY
Beyond Stereotypes

June Burnham
POLITICIANS, BUREAUCRATS AND LEADERSHIP IN ORGANIZATIONS
Lessons from Regional Planning in France

Tony Chafer and Emmanuel Godin (*editors*)
THE END OF THE FRENCH EXCEPTION?
Decline and Revival of the 'French Model'

Jean K. Chalaby
THE DE GAULLE PRESIDENCY AND THE MEDIA
Statism and Public Communications

Pepper D. Culpepper, Bruno Palier and Peter A. Hall (*editors*)
CHANGING FRANCE
The Politics that Markets Make

Gordon D. Cumming
FRENCH NGOs IN THE GLOBAL ERA
France's International Development Role

David Drake
FRENCH INTELLECTUALS AND POLITICS FROM THE DREYFUS AFFAIR TO THE OCCUPATION

David Drake
INTELLECTUALS AND POLITICS IN POST-WAR FRANCE

John Gaffney
POLITICAL LEADERSHIP IN FRANCE
From Charles de Gaulle to Nicolas Sarkozy

French Politics, Society and Culture
Series Standing Order ISBN 978–0–333–80440–7 hardcover
Series Standing Order ISBN 978–0–333–80441–4 paperback
(*outside North America only*)

You can receive future titles in this series as they are published by placing a standing order.
Please contact your bookseller or, in case of difficulty, write to us at the address below with
your name and address, the title of the series and the ISBN quoted above.

Customer Services Department, Macmillan Distribution Ltd, Houndmills, Basingstoke,
Hampshire RG21 6XS, England

The End of the French Exception?

Decline and Revival of the 'French Model'

Edited By

Tony Chafer
Professor of Contemporary French Area Studies, University of Portsmouth, UK

Emmanuel Godin
Principal Lecturer in French Studies, University of Portsmouth, UK

First published 2010 by
PALGRAVE MACMILLAN

Palgrave Macmillan in the UK is an imprint of Macmillan Publishers Limited,
registered in England, company number 785998, of Houndmills, Basingstoke,
Hampshire RG21 6XS.

Palgrave Macmillan in the US is a division of St Martin's Press LLC, 175 Fifth
Avenue, New York, NY 10010.

Palgrave Macmillan is the global academic imprint of the above companies
and has companies and representatives throughout the world.

Palgrave® and Macmillan® are registered trademarks in the United States,
the United Kingdom, Europe and other countries

ISBN 978-0-230-22078-2   hardback

This book is printed on paper suitable for recycling and made from fully
managed and sustained forest sources. Logging, pulping and manufacturing
processes are expected to conform to the environmental regulations of the
country of origin.

A catalogue record for this book is available from the British Library.

Library of Congress Cataloging-in-Publication Data
    The end of the French exception?: decline and revival of the 'French
    model' / edited by Tony Chafer, Emmanuel Godin.
        p. cm. – (French politics, society and culture series)
    ISBN 978-0-230-22078-2 (hardback)
      1. France–Civilization. 2. National characteristics, French.
    3. France–Social life and customs. 4. France–Politics and government.
    I. Chafer, Tony. II. Godin, Emmanuel.

    DC33.8.E64 2010
    944.084–dc22   2010004781

10   9   8   7   6   5   4   3   2   1
19   18   17   16   15   14   13   12   11   10

Printed and bound in Great Britain by
CPI Antony Rowe, Chippenham and Eastbourne

*In memory of Douglas Johnson,
lifelong observer of 'la France exceptionnelle'*

Contents

List of Tables and Figure

Tables

Figure

Notes on Contributors

David Bell is currently located in the School of Politics and International Studies at the University of Leeds. Amongst the more recent publications are a biography of François Mitterrand and articles on the French left (Socialist and extreme left). He is currently working on a study of the contemporary French Socialist Party with Byron Criddle.

Tony Chafer is Professor of Contemporary French Area Studies and Director of the Centre for European and International Studies Research at the University of Portsmouth, UK. He has published widely on Franco-African relations in the late colonial and post-colonial era and is the author of *The End of Empire in French West Africa: France's Successful Decolonization?* (2002). He is currently undertaking a research project on Franco-British Cooperation in Africa with Gordon Cumming (Cardiff University), the main findings of which will be published in a book entitled *From Rivalry to Partnership? New Approaches to the Challenges of Africa* (forthcoming 2011).

Sue Collard has been a Lecturer in French at the University of Sussex since 1986, and has since 2003 been attached to the Sussex European Institute as a Lecturer in Politics and European Studies. Her teaching interests have mainly spanned 19th and 20th century French history, as well as politics and society in France since 1945, but also include the making of contemporary Europe. Her research interests have centred on various aspects of the Mitterrand presidency, and most specifically, the politics of the 'grands travaux'.

Hugh Dauncey is Senior Lecturer in French in the School of Modern Languages at Newcastle University. He works principally on French public policy in relation to popular culture, especially sport, music and the media. He is currently working on a social and cultural history of French cycling, and has edited and co-edited a number of books on the 1998 World Cup, the Tour de France, French popular culture, popular music in France, and comparative sociological perspectives on the study of popular music in France and the UK.

Helen Drake is Senior Lecturer in French and European Studies at Loughborough University, UK. She is the author of *Jacques Delors*:

Perspectives on a European Leader (2000) and editor of *French Relations with the European Union* (2005). Her currrent interests include 21st century Franco-British migration.

Emmanuel Godin is Principal Lecturer in French and European Studies at the University of Portsmouth. He is currently working on the extreme right in Europe with Brian Jenkins and Andrea Mammone and preparing a monograph on France and the French since 1968 to be published by Reaktion Books in 2011.

Aboulaye Gueye holds a PhD from the Ecole des Hautes Etudes en Sciences Sociales in Paris. He is Associate Professor at the University of Ottawa. Currently he is a Sheila Biddle Ford Foundation resident fellow at the W.E.B. DuBois Institute for African and African American Research, Harvard University. He has authored and edited several books among which *Les intellectuels africains en France*, and many articles.

Robert Harmsen is Professor of Political Science at the University of Luxembourg, and was previously Senior Lecturer and Director of Research in European Governance and Gender at Queen's University Belfast. His publications include the co-edited (with Menno Spiering) volume *Euroscepticism: Political Parties, National Identity and European Integration* (2004), as well as numerous chapters and articles examining the evolution of national European debates in Britain, France, and the Netherlands.

Nick Hewlett is Professor of French Studies at the University of Warwick. He is author of: *Badiou, Balibar, Rancière. Re-thinking Emancipation* (2007); *Democracy in Modern France* (2003) and *Modern French Politics. Conflict and Consensus since 1945* (1998).

Raymond Kuhn is Professor of Politics at Queen Mary, University of London. He has written widely on French media policy and political communication, including a single authored study *The Media in France* (1995).

Margaret A. Majumdar is Visiting Professor of Francophone Studies at the University of Portsmouth. Her publications include *Post-coloniality: The French Dimension*, 2007; *Transition and Development in Algeria: Economic, Social and Cultural Challenges*, 2005 (with M. Saad); *Francophone Studies: The Essential Glossary, 2002; Althusser and the End of Leninism?* 1995.

Susan Milner is Reader in European Studies at the University of Bath. Her research interests cover employment and social policy in the EU. She is particularly interested in cross-national comparative research and has recently published the results of a study carried out with Abigail Gregory (Salford University) on fathers and work-life balance in France and the UK.

Martin Schain is Professor of Politics at New York University. His most recent books are *The Politics of Immigration in France, Britain and the United States: A Comparative Study* (2008) and *Comparative Federalism: The US and EU in Comparative Perspective* (2006). He has also published on politics and immigration in Europe and the United States and the politics of the extreme right in France. He is the founder and former director of the Center for European Studies at NYU and former chair of the European Union Studies Association. He is co-editor of the transatlantic scholarly journal, *Comparative European Politics*.

Natalya Vince received her PhD in 2008 from the University of London (Queen Mary) for her thesis 'To be a moudjahida in Independent Algeria: Itineraries and Memories of Women Veterans of the Algerian War'. Her research interests lie in 20th century French and North African history, politics and society. She is currently a lecturer in the School of Languages and Area Studies at the University of Portsmouth.

Acknowledgements

The editors gratefully acknowledge the support of the Centre for European and International Studies Research at the University of Portsmouth for funding the workshop from which this volume emerged.

Introduction

The notion of the 'French exception' can be conceived in two different ways. First, it can be understood as an evolving set of politically loaded *discourses*, which is often exploited by political leaders, commentators and intellectuals with a specific political agenda. Alternatively, it can be an *analytical tool* that is used to decipher certain specific economic, political and social issues. In this latter sense it provides a framework of analysis that has been adopted by commentators on contemporary France in an effort to establish what it is that makes the 'French model' stand out as 'different' from other countries. Each of these ways of conceiving French exceptionalism is in some respects problematic, as we shall see, and the distinction between them is in any case not as clear-cut as this might appear to suggest, not least because academics do not simply and dispassionately test hypotheses, they also take sides in the issues and debates they analyse. Nonetheless, the distinction is a useful one for understanding the different ways in which the term 'French exception' is used. Thus, in the first chapter Sue Collard shows how the term became common currency after the publication, in 1988, of an influential book by François Furet, Jacques Julliard and Pierre Rosanvallon: *La République de centre. La fin de l'exception française.* She shows how they framed and defined the notion of French exceptionalism in order to construct a specific discourse about the 'end of the French exception': 'We are all agreed: we are at a turning-point ... an era is coming to an end ... What we are living through is quite simply the end of French exceptionality' (Furet *et al* 1988: 11). This was a development that they welcomed as it meant that France was finally coming into line with the rest of the Western world and it was this process of 'normalisation' that they set out to describe. Collard shows how their discourse of the 'end of the French exception' was challenged by various groups of intellectuals, notably by the Fondation Marc Bloch and the Fondation Copernic, and she goes on to show how the discourse of French exceptionalism has again changed in the aftermath of the 2008–9 global financial and economic crisis. The next ten chapters are then organised thematically in four sections, each of which sets out to examine an area in which France has regularly been claimed to be 'exceptional': the major role of the state, political and ideological polarisation, citizenship and the republican model, and French 'universalism'. In each case, these areas of claimed French exceptionalism are treated as hypotheses rather than empirical truths and the authors seek to evaluate to what extent such hypotheses make sense and whether they provide a useful tool of analysis. At the same time they also, where appropriate, examine the discourse of French exceptionalism in the area under study, in order to show how the claim to exceptionalism emerged and has evolved and to assess the continuing relevance of a discourse of exceptionalism in this area. In Chapter 12 the central focus, as in the first chapter, is on the discourse of the French exception, but treated here as a 'performative discourse' (p. 223) viewed from outside France: Abdoulaye Gueye explores the French exception from the perspective of African writers and thinkers as a journey into the 'Other's imaginary and intellectual territory' (p. 223). Finally, Chapter 13 assesses the impact of the early Sarkozy presidency on French exceptionalism.

Before going on to discuss the discourse of French exceptionalism, it is important to note that there has been a semantic shift in the use of the term 'the French exception' which is today used by commentators and journalists more or less interchangeably with 'the French model'. The latter term also refers to aspects of what is claimed to be 'exceptional' about the French republic's socio-economic and political model, but the change in usage is nonetheless significant. Whereas the 'French exception' was a contested term that was often used by its detractors in France and abroad to denounce its 'archaism' and to call for 'modernisation' and 'normalisation', which was usually taken to mean freeing up the labour market, cutting taxes and reducing the 'burden' of an overbearing and overly expensive welfare state, defenders of the 'French model', in contrast, stressed the success of a distinctive 'French model' and portrayed instead a positive image of an economic and social system that provided a desirable, and at times of crisis vital, bulwark against the ravages of liberalisation *à l'anglo-saxonne*.

The discourse of the 'French exception'

In the spring of 2009, *The Economist* carried a front page feature with Nicolas Sarkozy standing on a podium looking down scornfully on the German Chancellor Angela Merkel, who is standing on the ground, and British Prime Minister Gordon Brown, whose eyes peer out from a manhole down which he has apparently fallen; the headline is 'Europe's new pecking order'. Sarkozy's picture carries the caption 'Le modèle français', Merkel's represents 'Modell Deutschland' and Brown's 'The Anglo-Saxon model'.[1] What a difference two years makes! In May 2007 Nicolas Sarkozy was elected on a promise of '*rupture*' from the 'French model' and a pledge to put an end to the 'French exception', which was interpreted by commentators at the time as meaning that he intended France to break away from its traditional model and to move to embrace the more liberal 'Anglo-Saxon model'. In stark contrast, two years later, the president's spokesman was publicly lauding the virtues of the French model: 'The French model is the model of a one and indivisible Republic, in which everyone has the same rights and the same duties ... it is the constantly renewed will to live together. At the centre of the French model is the integrational strength of the "*service public*"' (Guaino 2009).[2] With the meltdown of the global financial system in 2008–9, thanks to casino capitalism *à l'anglo-saxonne*, the French model of a voluntarist state, greater regulation and social solidarity has come back into fashion and is presented, including by President Sarkozy himself, as a desirable and necessary bulwark against the excesses of 'Anglo-Saxon', neo-liberal, free market economics: 'the global crisis once again creates circumstances that are favourable to the French aspiration to make the economy serve the people and not the opposite ... At the very moment when the necessity to regulate globalisation and the markets imposes itself, the French model once again has a chance to prove its worth ... The crisis has brought the French model back into fashion' (Sarkozy 2009a).

Thus the debate about the French exception has moved on considerably in recent years. In the 1980s, as Collard shows in her chapter, the 'French exception' was seen by many commentators as a millstone round the neck of France, from which it needed to be liberated – and the best way of doing this was to break away from the political tradition derived from the Revolution. This was essentially what was advocated by Furet *et al* (1988) in *La République du centre*. However, as Collard also points out, it was unclear what exactly they were advocating in its place, apart from 'modernisation' and economic liberalisation, which was in any case already happening under governments of both left and right. With the successful launch of the euro and accelerating European integration, there appeared to be increasingly less space for a continuing 'French exception'. The Fondation Saint Simon that had done much to launch the idea of the 'end of the French exception' was wound up and intellectual interest in the question, with one or two notable exceptions (cf. Lindenberg 2002), subsided. In popular and journalistic parlance, on the other hand, Collard shows that the notion of a 'French exception' continued to be used to point to a whole range of areas in which France is perceived to be different from other countries, from road safety to gynaecology, from its trade unions to its banking system. However, the global economic and financial crisis of 2008–9 rekindled intellectual and political interest in the 'French exception', which was now referred to as the 'French model' and presented as a desirable alternative to the excesses of economic neo-liberalism. As a result, the 'French model' is no longer perceived as a burden, but rather as a potential blueprint for Europe, and indeed the rest of the world, to follow; in particular, a reinvigorated, interventionist state '*à la française*' has come to be seen as essential in the short to medium term to stabilise the global financial system and relaunch economic growth and in the longer term as a necessary defence against the recurrence of such an economic meltdown in future. Moreover, the terms of the debate about the 'French model' have fundamentally changed: before 2008–9, detractors of the French model used the word 'reform' as code for urgent and fundamental change in the economic and political system; post-2008–9 reform means repairing the system so that it works more effectively to protect people against the ravages of economic liberalism; before 2008–9 public debt was a financial burden to be borne by coming generations, post-2008–9 it was presented as the necessary springboard for renewed economic growth and an investment for the future.

However the discourse of French exceptionalism is not just about public policy. It raises and encapsulates wider concerns about 'French identity'. In *La République de centre: la fin de l'exception française*, Julliard, Rosanvallon and Furet sought to bury the heritage of the French revolution – Jacobinism, *dirigisme* and a culture of political polarisation – and looked forward to the emergence of a new consensus that would at last contribute to the appeasement of French political life. But one scion of the Revolution refused to be buried quietly: the Nation, whose republican identity in a global, post-colonial world has become a source of new and major conflicts rather than consensus. This emerges as a theme in this volume in the chapters by Robert Harmsen, Martin Schain, and Natalya Vince. The electoral strength of the French extreme right polarised the debate about immigration, Europe and national identity and ensured that it remained at the forefront of the policy agenda (Fysh and Wolfreys 2003; Schain 2006). The endemic economic and social exclusion of French citizens *issus de l'immigration* questioned the ability of the republic to turn immigrants into Frenchmen as much as its equalitarian credentials, whereas re-examinations of its colonial past suggested that historically and to this day, republicanism and racism are far from being mutually exclusive (Bancel *et al* 2003). The debate about the nature, objectives and outcomes of the republican model became polarised not so much along the traditional left-right axis, but between those who thought that the republic ought to promote equality and those who thought that it ought to promote diversity, as exemplified by the argument in 2003 surrounding the nomination of Aïssa Dermouche as *préfet issu de l'immigration* [a prefect issued from immigrant stock] (for Jacques Chirac) or *préfet musulman* [Muslim prefect] (for Nicolas Sarkozy) (Bezat 2003) and more generally by the multilayered controversy about the nature and meaning of republican *laïcité*. Thus, French national identity remains a contested subject, contrary to what Pierre Nora postulated in *Les Lieux de mémoire* (Nora 1984).

* * *

As we saw above, the 'French exception' has become part of a variety of political discourses, in France and abroad, that was widely used by its detractors to call for 'modernisation', 'normalisation', and/or the alignment of French economic and social policies with those of other Western democracies. Conversely, the 'French model' has been enthusiastically endorsed by a variety of actors, from left-wing, 'sovereignist' republicans to Gaullist standard bearers, from trade-unionists to sections of the extreme right and the extreme left, from film-makers to medical staff, who for very different reasons warn against the dangers of liberalisation *à l'anglo-saxonne*.

In a stimulating book published in 2006, Culpepper, Hall and Palier challenged one feature of French exceptionalism. They questioned the notion that France is a *'société bloquée'* (stalled society), arguing that France has, like other Western countries over the past 25 years or so, undergone dramatic economic and social changes due to global and European constraints. Free market mechanisms – privatisation, deregulation, greater labour market flexibility, increased differentiation of wage rates, to name a few – have now changed the way objectives are chosen, decisions are made and redefined the prevailing hierarchy of societal values. If the State has not entirely withered away, it has nevertheless lost its monopoly on decision-making to global markets, decentralised local authorities and the EU. The result is that the everyday life of the French, like that of their Western and European neighbours, has been profoundly altered, a far cry from the caricature of a society gripped by *immobilisme*. Yet, what seems to be *bloqué* is the enduring inability of French political actors to contrive a convincing political discourse to explain and legitimise such changes: 'liberal measures are often presented as a necessary, if slightly distasteful, response to the imperatives of the global economy' (Culpepper *et al*: 17). The political consensus that has emerged about the way to conduct the business of the country has essentially been a consensus by default – *faute de mieux* – and cannot be compared to wider neo-liberal projects, such as those articulated first by Thatcherism and then, in its benign version, by Blairism (Godin 1996). In 1999, a disillusioned Rosanvallon complained: 'We have gone too far. The culture of government has become a culture of management [*culture de gestion*]' (Aeschimann and Riche 2006). For different reasons, the mainstream left and the Gaullist right have found that this *culture de gestion* undermines their own political appeal: the distortion between market-oriented policies that have been pursued on the ground and a mostly incantatory political discourse suspicious of – or at least unenthusiastic about – global, free-market capitalism, has fuelled a growing form of cynicism towards left and right governing parties, resulting in higher levels of abstention and increasing support for marginal or extreme parties. In this framework, the French exception is less a matter of policy but expresses rather the reluctance, embarrassment and inability of the governing parties to engineer a discourse legitimising the sort of global changes facing French society. The rhetorical opposition between a 'French' and an 'Anglo-Saxon' model may conceal a degree of policy convergence in some sectors, but it also reveals French anxieties about what is perceived as an alien, inimical model. As Peter Hall (Culpepper *et al* 2006: 17) has argued, in France change has not been so much 'accepted' as 'endured', as shown by the recurring and diverse forms of social unrest mounted against reforms deemed to 'undo' the French social model – from the Juppé reforms in 1995 to the Contrat Première Embauche fiasco in 2006 – or indeed by the rejection of the European Constitution Treaty in the 2005 referendum.

Several chapters explore and evaluate how, in French politics and society, various actors have constructed the notion of the French exception in specific ways, ascribed certain value(s) to it and mobilised, developed or modified it for specific reasons. In this volume, these discourses will be contextualised and analysed. For instance, the exceptionalism of the 'French model' has, as Hugh Dauncey, Martin Schain and Natalya Vince show, frequently been 'talked up' in French political discourse, highlighting what is supposedly still 'exceptional' about France when in reality French policy and practice are in many ways converging with that of its European neighbours. Contributors to this volume also provide examples of how the discourse of French exceptionalism has been transposed in different ways to the European level. For instance, Sue Milner shows how 'the European policy level has allowed political leaders to develop a double discourse of protection and reform' (p. 70). Thus French politicians have argued that the best way of preserving the French model and retaining as much as possible of the institutional specificity of its system of social protection is to undertake a process of reform that corresponds to EU requirements. In a quite different setting, Hugh Dauncey shows how the notion of a 'cultural exception' was promoted during the Uruguay Round of multilateral trade negotiations between 1987 and 1993 to justify a protectionist stance on French cultural products. He then goes on to show how, during the later 1990s and early 2000s, the defence of the 'cultural exception' was transformed into a discourse promoting 'cultural diversity'. The former came to be seen as too defensive in its implication of the need to 'protect' French culture, whereas the latter was seen as emphasising the positive role of cultural policy in general and thus more likely to gain the support of other countries, especially within the EU. This modification of the discourse of exceptionalism was essential if France was to win the battle to ensure that cultural products were treated differently from other products, since it is the European Commission that represents the member states in international trade negotiations. The 'Europeanisation' of the French exception is also a theme of Helen Drake's chapter, in which she shows that France has a specific set of strategic objectives in Europe that 'revolve around the ambition for a European entity that is a *powerful* world actor, that is constructed by a *political* process, and which has a distinct *identity* in the global capitalist system' (p. 187, author's emphasis). What is immediately striking about these objectives is that they mirror closely traditional French national concerns with '*rang*' (rank), with the construction of the nation as an essentially political process and with the defence of a 'French social model' that is a key element of France's identity distinct from the more free-market, 'Anglo-Saxon' model. Thus Europe, or more specifically the EU, has become a key arena for the promotion and defence of the French exception. Drake suggests however that the referendum vote of May 2005 shows that the French are no longer convinced by the discourse of exceptionalism constructed by French elites and that 'there is a growing gap between their rhetoric on Europe and the realities faced by French citizens' (p. 198). In a similar vein Robert Harmsen warns that 'the Europeanisation of national exceptionalism … appears … unlikely to live up to its superficially beguiling promise' (p. 117) more starkly, Drake concludes by describing the politics of exceptionalism as 'a discursive house of cards' (p. 201) that 'reach[es] into the essence of French identity itself' (p. 201).

Like Drake, Gueye links the 'French exception' to the issue of identity. He distinguishes three dimensions to the discourse of exceptionalism: its embedding in the Enlightenment idea of progress, its relational dimension that requires it to be defined in opposition to an Other, be it a nation, a people or a larger constituency, and finally its implied tutelage over, or responsibility for, the Other (p. 224). In these respects the discourse of exceptionalism is clearly linked to the French republic's self-proclaimed 'civilising mission' and Gueye shows how its effectiveness as a discourse has depended on it being articulated and promoted by institutions vested with the authority and power to legitimise it. It is also, as he points out, a 'discourse of [French] self-identification' (p. 233). This raises interesting questions about the future of the discourse of French exceptionalism in the context of intensifying debates within France about the nature of French identity in an increasingly multicultural and globally interconnected society, embedded within an increasingly integrated European Union. Indeed one explanation for the continuing vitality of the discourse of the 'French exception' may be nostalgia for a Golden Age of French power and '*rayonnement*' that has now passed; in this purview it is the discourse of a middle-sized power that still thinks of itself as a major world power (*Le Monde* 2002).

The 'French exception' as an analytical tool

As Nick Hewlett (2005: 3) has pointed out, whether we think that the notion of the French exception as an analytical framework, is 'inaccurate or even trivial', we have to admit that it has permeated an enormous number of academic works. For instance, David Bell in *French Politics Today* (2002: 3) argues that studying the 'exceptional' nature of French political culture could be useful since an understanding of 'the history of French politics will help explain why France is different'. This is carefully qualified as he also points out that France shares many common traits with other Western liberal democracies. Nevertheless, the questions that Bell puts forward in the course of this book suggest that the notion of 'the French exception' is a useful starting point to ask interesting questions: What is distinctive about the French economy' (*ibid*: 39), 'the French Left' (*ibid*: 78) and 'French foreign policy' (*ibid*: 240). If the notion of French exception is not explored as such, it often provides a backdrop to the analysis. For example, David Howarth and Georgios Varouxakis (2003: x) use the notion of the French exception as the starting-point for a discussion about whether the tradition of political and ideological polarisation in France is now coming to an end. In their conclusion, they underline France's claim to universalism and point out that what makes it different is that it is the only country that 'offers its "sister-republic", America, a mirror image through which to see itself better, and the rest of the world an alternative way of living and thinking than that of the *hyperpuissance*'. (*ibid*: 211).

As an analytical tool, the notion of the French exception has its roots in a distinctive republican model, attaching central importance to the prestige of the State, the primacy of politics and the active propagation, at home and worldwide, of certain values that are perceived, rightly or wrongly, to be enlightened and progressive. Thus, the 'French exception' could be defined by four core elements. First, the French State, in its *Jacobin*, *dirigiste*, republican or protectionist guise, is supposed to dominate civil society and to play a more powerful role than in any other Western democracy. Second, France is a country divided against itself, where domestic conflicts are more polarised than in other Western countries. It displays a degree of political radicalism which ensures that debates are highly politicised and issues are solved, if at all, through confrontation, not negotiation. Third, the French republican model only recognises individuals and not communities within the nation-state. Thus the existence of minority groups, whether religious, ethnic, regional or, linguistic, is not acknowledged. The 2004 decision to ban the wearing of religious symbols such as the veil in schools is testimony to the continuing durability of this model. Fourth, France has long seen itself as the repository of values inherited from the Enlightenment and the French Revolution. Its mission is to diffuse them universally. From the Napoleonic conquests to colonial expansion, from the Gaullist refusal of the Cold War divide to the development of *Francophonie*, France has presented itself as a model to follow for the rest of the world. In this respect, it shares the same ambition as the US and this might help to explain the periodical outbursts of anti-Americanism in France.

Two important points need to be made at this point. Firstly, within academic discourse, such characteristics are treated as hypotheses rather than empirical truths. Indeed, academics – and this is the second axis of the debate about the 'French exception' as an analytical tool – have long tried to evaluate critically whether and to what extent such hypotheses make sense at all. Secondly, until the mid-1980s, the assessment and evaluation of such hypotheses did not make, or indeed require, any explicit reference to the notion of the 'French exception'. Indeed, the role played by the State, the polarised and radical nature of French society as well as the willingness to promote French *rayonnement* on the international stage, were used to described France's attempt to overcome the humiliation of defeat and occupation in 1940 and embark on a largely state-led programme of modernisation from 1945 onwards.

To take the first of these hypotheses, the centralising proclivities of the French State, its impulse to concentrate power and propensity to denigrate regional particularisms have often been critically re-examined by social scientists. Pierre Grémion's seminal work on the French prefects (1974), for example, highlighted the relations of complicity, rather than of domination, between local elites and the representatives of the central state, leading to a more subtle reassessment of the idea and practice of centralisation. In a similar vein, Dupuy and Thoenig (1985) have described the French state apparatus as being rather fragmented, marred both by inertia and internal conflicts, a description far removed from the image of an all powerful and effective bureaucracy. Likewise, Vincent Wright (1992: 334–5) has shown that our traditional view of republican centralisation, both as a concept and a practice, should be empirically reassessed.

In this volume, several chapters challenge the notion of a dominant and powerful French State. Sue Milner, Hugh Dauncey, Martin Schain and Helen Drake depict a French State increasingly forced to negotiate a passage between pressures 'from above' (globalisation, Europeanisation) and 'from below' (civil society, public opinion) and, in the case of immigration and social policy, for example, to undertake cautious and timid reforms that represent the limit of what is politically achievable. In a rather different vein, Nick Hewlett analyses the efforts of President Sarkozy to recentralise power through a 'style of rule that may aptly be described as "personalised, authoritarian and populist"' (p. 39). In this, he revives a tradition of leadership that has a number of precedents in French history, from Napoleon to De Gaulle. Raymond Kuhn then shows in his chapter how this personalised style of rule has been combined with a very 'un-French' blurring of the boundaries between the public and private lives of the president. In the concluding chapter we return to the question of the state in order to show how the weakness of a liberal political culture in France, which the Fondation Saint-Simon both deplored and tried to remedy, has made it difficult to build powerful neo-liberal arguments that legitimise changes with the strength of moral arguments, in the way that Thatcherism did in the UK for example (Jobert 1994; Godin 1996). Sarkozy made clear his commitment to economic neo-liberalism during his 2007 presidential election campaign but, as we point out, the implementation of his neo-liberal economic agenda is constrained by the strength of France's *dirigiste* legacy.

The emergence of a *'consensus mou'* ('soft consensus') among the main parties of government and the marginalisation of other voices with a more radical agenda are at the heart of the debate about the French exception in domestic politics. The fact that the Parti Communiste Français (PCF) is a spent-electoral force (it only gained 1.93 per cent of the votes in the 2007 legislative elections) is often taken as evidence that France is on the road of normalisation. Indeed, the electoral collapse of the PCF represents a dramatic change in the French political landscape. In this volume, David Bell reveals that what distinguished the PCF from other Communist parties in Western Europe was not so much its subservience to Moscow, but its electoral success. It monopolised most of the space to the left of the political spectrum, leaving little room to its right for the development of a reformist, social democratic party, or to its left for the development of other extreme left parties. However, the Party failed to adapt to the socio-economic realities of late 20th-century France and went into long-term decline (Martelli 2008). Bell argued in the previous edition of this book that this success could be explained in large part by the PCF's ability to exploit in its political discourse radical and nationalist republican themes inherited from the Revolution: 'It is the Revolution that is the key to "exceptionalism" on the French left.' (Bell 2005: 56). However, if Communism is ideologically discredited today, this is not necessarily the case for radical left politics, which have seen something of a revival in recent years, and Trotskyite parties now occupy the 'space' on the political spectrum previously occupied by the PCF: 'Trotskyism has maintained the flame of Revolution even after the Communist Party has allowed it to dwindle' (p. 102). The relative success of the French extreme left in the 2007 presidential and 2009 European elections provides evidence of the continuing vitality of the revolutionary tradition in France.

Robert Harmsen studies a different type of challenge to the mainstream *'consensus mou'* in French politics. In his chapter he shows how the pro-European stance of the main parties of government has been challenged by the emergence of left and right-wing Euroscepticisms, both within and outside these parties. These can be seen as representing a new manifestation of political polarisation insofar as, as Harmsen shows, the challenges they represent to this 'European consensus' are increasingly divergent. Whereas in the early 1990s the Euroscepticisms of both left and right were imbued with 'the strong presence of a Republican discourse of national exceptionalism' (p. 106) and protection of national sovereignty, they have subsequently diverged. Thus, right-wing Euroscepticism has become 'increasingly marked by "particularist" defences of national traditions' (p. 110) and of a French 'way of life' (p. 113), while left-wing Euroscepticism now largely takes the form of an 'intensified critical engagement with the European project itself ... [that seeks] to recast the EU in more social and democratic terms as a rampart against neo-liberal globalisation' (p. 114).

The exploration of France's republican model of citizenship, that recognises only individuals and not communities within the nation-state, has been a leitmotif of studies of what is exceptional about the French political model (cf. Rosanvallon 2004). However, as Martin Schain points out, 'the French republican model of integration, while different from approaches to integration in some other countries, Britain and the United States in particular, has never been strikingly exceptional in practice' (p. 141). While the republican model has shaped the way that policy is developed, it has not prevented the adoption of policies that target particular groups or reinforce ethnic identities, nor has it prevented the creation of pilot programmes of affirmative action. Each of these initiatives can be seen as representing compromises with 'Anglo-Saxon' multiculturalism. In a similar vein, Natalya Vince shows that in practice the French republican model of *laïcité*, which is often contrasted with the 'Anglo-Saxon' model of multiculturalism, shares many characteristics with the latter: 'the United States and United Kingdom have always required that individuals and groups respect the law of the land, which is based on mainstream social and cultural norms' while at a local level 'in France new cultures have been accommodated and differences negotiated', as evidenced by the provision by town halls of prayer spaces and Muslim cemeteries (p. 159). In fact, the supposed 'exceptionality' of French *laïcité* has often been instrumentalised by both its supporters and defenders in order to legitimise particular political and ideological stances in relation to organised religion and in particular, recently, in relation to Islam.

The republican 'model' of *laïcité* is also one element of the French claim to universalism, insofar as it encapsulates political, social and cultural values defined by the state that are deemed to be universal in their application. Indeed, France has long presented itself as a 'universal' model for other countries to follow, both within Europe and beyond (Keiger 2001: 18). The chapters by Harmsen and Drake show how France has sought to 'project' its national influence onto the European stage and to get the EU to uphold its social model. Similarly Africa, as Chafer and Majumdar demonstrate, has also been a privileged arena for the projection of French universalist ideology and values. Here it found expression notably in France's self-appointed civilising mission, that sought to bring the progressive, 'universal' values of French republicanism and modernity to Africans. This notion of France as a force for civilisation and progress in Africa has continued to underpin French policy in Africa in the post-colonial period, although as Chafer and Majumdar show, there is an increasing disjunction between the idealist and universalist rhetoric that continues to provide much of the rationale for the Franco-African 'exceptional relationship' and its underlying realities. As president, Sarkozy has sought to close this gap by promising a '*rupture*' [break] with the corrupt practices of '*la Françafrique*' and a refoundation of Franco-African relations on a more 'normal' state-to-state footing. However his ability to follow through on this promise has been inhibited by the weight of the past and a nostalgia among parts of France's governing elites for the 'old way of doing things'. Indeed nostalgia for a Golden Age of French political and cultural influence may be part of the explanation not only for France's 'exceptional' relationship with Europe and Africa but also for the 'cultural exception'.

Challenges to the French exception

The political debate about the end of the French exception has led academics to seek to interpret recent shifts in the discourse of exceptionalism and to formulate new hypotheses, in an effort to understand the changing nature of the 'French exception' within a polity that is increasingly embedded within, and in some ways constrained by, the processes of economic globalisation and European construction (Schnapper 2002). These external pressures offer new opportunities for comparative analysis and the comparative method is in this respect very useful (Hague and Harrop 2001). It does not however presuppose that convergence is the necessary or likely outcome of the forces of globalisation or Europeanisation: the resilience of national cultures and strength and flexibility of specific institutional arrangements need to be taken into account in order to understand how each nation mediates such general trends.

The processes of Europeanisation and globalisation also help to generate new questions: to what extent, for instance, has 'French *politics* [acquired] a European character, since much of French *policy* – in both domestic and foreign policy areas – is made *jointly* within the EU' (Guyomarch *et al* 2001: 2)? Conversely, to what extent has France been able to influence European developments and shape the EU to its own liking (Guyomarch *et al* 1998)? Is there still room today for the successful development of a voluntarist economic or social or immigration policy at the national, or indeed European, level? To what extent has France espoused the rhetoric of economic neo-liberalism without adopting and internalising its practices and norms (Culpepper *et al* 2006)? Faced with similar dilemmas, different polities do not necessarily produce the same answers.

Comparisons with other countries can again be useful here. What emerges is a complex picture, with Europeanisation placing constraints on the action of national governments, but also, for economically developed nations such as France, providing new areas of opportunity and arenas for intervention. In the areas of social and cultural policy, for instance, while the EU has limited the ability of French governments to pursue policies that are significantly out of line with other member states, it has also created new opportunities to legitimate policy reforms within the domestic polity (in the case of social policy) (Milner) or to mobilise other member states in support of French policy priorities (in the case of cultural policy) (Dauncey). Drake shows how the EU has placed limits on French exceptionalism that are, paradoxically, in large part a direct product of France's 'exceptional relationship' with Europe. In other words, France made a major strategic choice to lead the process of European construction but was then caught between two contradictory logics: its ambition to create a Europe that is a powerful world player on the one hand, and its desire to protect French national sovereignty and its consequent defence of an intergovernmental conception of Europe on the other. Similarly within the constraints vs. opportunities paradigm, Chafer and Majumdar show how France's 'exceptional relationship' with Africa has been criticised and has come under increasing challenge, both internally and externally. They then go on to demonstrate how the multilateralisation and 'Europeanisation' of French African policy has offered new opportunities to pursue and legitimise an interventionist policy on the continent (Charbonneau 2008a). Arguing from a different perspective, outside the constraints vs. opportunities paradigm, Vince sees French policy convergence with that of other member states in the field of secularism as resulting not from a 'European influence' on France, but rather as the product of common concerns about national security and a shared desire to maintain diplomatic dialogue with the Arab world.

With respect to globalisation, it is in many ways a similar story of constraints and opportunities. The central role played by the market place plays a key role in defining the parameters for political intervention and actions at national level (Culpepper *et al* 2006). However this has not prevented France from pursuing a protectionist agenda, at the level of the EU, in defence of its agriculture and its cultural products, and its political leaders, at least in their rhetoric, frequently express reservations about an out-and-out neoliberal, free market economic agenda for the EU, as for example in 2007 when President Sarkozy intervened in negotiations over the Lisbon Treaty to argue for the removal of the commitment to 'fair and free competition' from the statement of the EU's founding principles. Yet France has, in contrast, supported its state-owned and partly state-owned companies, such as EDF and France-Telecom, as they have moved to take control of large public utility companies in other member states that are less protected from predatory takeover by national legislation than is the case in France (Maclean 2002: 224–6). Beyond its borders it has also actively promoted a neo-liberal economic agenda, by for example supporting the structural adjustment programmes of the IMF and World Bank and demanding the dismantling of barriers to free trade in Africa (Chafer 2008). Moreover, it is not the forces of globalisation *alone* – such as commercial pressures and technological change – that can provide us with complete explanations of the processes of change. As Kuhn shows in his chapter, we can only appreciate how the blurring of the dividing line between public and private in journalism and political communication in France has come about if we take into account *both* the impact of commercial pressures and technological change *and* the special relationship – interdependent and often complicitous – that exists between politicians and journalists in France.

So, while Europeanisation and globalisation are key factors shaping the parameters within which national policy is made, they do not *determine* policy. Policy-making takes place within national contexts that are defined by history (existing institutions, national norms and cultural values, etc) and by the preferences and relative power of political and socio-economic actors within the domestic polity. What is interesting within the framework of this book is to seek to understand how the French national polity has responded to these external pressures: what, if anything, makes French responses 'exceptional', or at least different, compared to those of other countries? How are we to understand these differences? And how might this analysis lead us to rethink or modify our hypothesis of French exceptionalism? These are the key questions addressed by contributors to this volume.

Tony Chafer and Emmanuel Godin
Southsea, Portsmouth July 2009

Notes

1   Front page of *The Economist*, 9–15 May 2009.
2   Henri Guaino is Nicolas Sarkozy's personal advisor and main speech-writer.

1

The French Exception: Rise and Fall of a Saint-Simonian Discourse*

Sue Collard

What, if anything, makes the French claim to exceptionalism more convincing than others such as the American, the German or the British (Lipset 1996; Adams and van Minnen 1994; Madsen 1998; Gauzy 1998; Colley 1992)? Aren't all nations in some respect exceptional? What exactly is the French exception? These questions lie at the heart of all the chapters in this volume, but in contrast to other contributors, my approach is not to seek the answers through a scholarly demonstration of the ways in which French history, politics and culture have combined to produce a particular set of events, traditions and discourses that are allegedly different from those of any other country, or to undertake a comparative study of particular policy areas in order to highlight parti-cular aspects of divergence or convergence. Rather, I shall first of all seek to show that what has made the case for the French exception so much more convincing than any other is the manner and extent to which the expression 'French exception' and the concepts that it denotes came to pervade public discourse in France. It is this that makes the French exception so exceptional. Secondly, I shall show how a group of centrist and centre-left intellectuals, politicians and business people with a spe-cific political agenda of their own orchestrated and promoted the notion of the 'end of the French exception' during the late 1980s and 1990s. Finally, I shall show how, in the first decade of the 21st century, intel-lectual debate surrounding the concept has continued under other guises, whilst the expression 'French exception' continues to feature widely in both general and academic discourse in France, albeit somewhat less prominently.

The discourse of French exceptionalism: origins and uses

Academics and journalists, both within and beyond the borders of the Hexagon, have adopted the notion of the French exception as a useful framework for their analyses of contemporary France, usually to evaluate manifestations and degrees of change, either on the 'before and after' model of 'France then' compared to 'France now', or as a means of comparing particular policy areas in France with those of other Western democracies.[1] They have largely taken their cue from the political debates that have dominated the agenda over the past 20 years and which, for reasons to which we will shortly return, have had as their underlying focus the question of whether or not the 'French exception' still exists, if it ever did, and if so, in what form. In these debates, the concept usually takes on connotations that are either positive (the defence of culture or of *'le service public'*), or negative (resistance to reform), depending on the issue and author's position. Indeed the expression has become so widely accepted as a dimension of the political landscape that its origin is seldom questioned. Rather, it is naturally 'understood' by any scholar, journalist or observer of France, since it evokes a whole host of features that can easily be identified with it: the propensity towards conflict and political turmoil rather than consensus and reform, the traditional divide between Right and Left, the uniquely important role of the central state, France's vision of itself as the repository of values inherited from the Enlightenment and the French Revolution and its mission to diffuse these values universally, and the construction of a republican model that recognises only individuals and not communities within the nation-state. Indeed, in the very extensive literature analysing France over the past couple of centuries and beyond, going back as far as Montesquieu, de Tocqueville and Michelet, France has often been described in terms which emphasise its singularity, its originality, its specificity, its exemplarity and even its 'hexagonalité' (Montesquieu 1961; de Tocqueville 1928 and 1966; Michelet 1963; Hoffman 1963; Wyplosz 2000). These rather mystical representations of France were successfully tapped into by De Gaulle in the 1960s when he set about 'restoring' French grandeur on the basis of a position of national independence that was totally at odds with the collective security policies of its neighbours. His gamble that to restore greatness necessitated an ambitious set of policies matched by bold rhetoric was clearly successful, in the sense that accounts of the Gaullist period published in recent years often emphasise that these were indeed the glorious years of the French exception, even if the analytical framework most commonly adopted to describe them in the earlier literature was usually that of modernisation rather than exceptionalism (Hoffman 1963; Cerny 1980). So the concept of French exceptionalism is familiar to all observers of France and has been much commented upon.

However, the origin of the expression has been unclear, and was in fact only first coined in 1988, as the sub-title of the book which paradoxically was announcing its demise: *La République du centre. La fin de l'exception française* by François Furet, Jacques Julliard and Pierre Rosanvallon.[2] *La République du centre* is in fact a collection of three essays, all of which contribute to the central theme that is best summed up in Furet's preface: 'we are all agreed: we are at a turning point ... an era is coming to an end ... What we are living through is quite simply the end of French exceptionality' (Furet *et al* 1988: 11). He went on to describe how France had had an unparalleled history, marked by the early development of the state and by a series of revolutions, so that until recently it occupied a unique position amongst other nations, which it saw as being exemplary. Indeed, it was this claim to the exemplarity of the French model that made France exceptional, rather than any differences it may have had in comparison with other nations (*ibid*: 54). France, he explained, has traditionally had a particular way of orchestrating its national dramas, of celebrating its contradictory passions and conducting its politics that has both infuriated and fascinated foreign observers. But now, he argued, France was stepping into line, and it was this 'banalisation' of French politics that the essays all aimed to describe (*ibid*: 11).

The end of the 'French exception'? Is God still French?

The timing of this publication was significant: it was the year of the re-election of François Mitterrand as President on a campaign for '*ouverture*', the loosening up of the Left-Right party divisions and an apparent attempt to move towards the centre ground. It was also the year before France was to celebrate the bicentenary of the Revolution of 1789, founding moment of the French exception. Furet's claims that the 'Revolution was over' (Furet 1978) were not of course new, and the journal *Le Débat* had, in September 1983, launched a discussion, which continued in subsequent issues, as to the relevance of the Revolution in the context of the forthcoming bicentenary celebrations: 'to what extent did the divisions of 89 continue to pervade the national consciousness? With the Republic now definitively in place, what remained of the great antagonisms of two centuries of social and political struggles? ... What was left, if anything, of the fundamental divisions and irreconcilable sensibilities?' (Ozouf 1983; Furet 1983; Duhamel *et al* 1984). Whilst acknowledging a certain loss of identity as an inevitable consequence of the political transformations experienced, due to the blurring of the traditional reference points of French political culture, the main conclusion was that a turning point had been reached in the history of the French Left, which made it possible to break out of the political tradition derived from the Revolution, and this, for them, was a cause for celebration and a certain optimism (Julliard 1988). They therefore saw the bicentenary of 1789 as 'the shroud of a tradition' (Furet *et al*: 10) and portrayed this 200th anniversary as an opportunity to bury it. There was a clear conceptual link here with the discernible new mood of political consensus underpinned by Mitterrand's attempt, albeit short-lived, at an *'ouverture'* to the centre under the first government of Michel Rocard, which was a significant aspect of the 'banalisation' of politics that the essays welcomed.

This process had already been masterfully described by Serge July in 1986; July's book retraced what he called the very paradoxical history of the 'normalisation' of France under Mitterrand, 'whose soul was sufficiently baroque to do France the extraordinary favour of turning it at last into an ordinary democracy' (July 1986: back cover). He saw the turning-point of March 1983 as a necessary crisis that brought about a *'rupture'* which made normalisation possible. But the 1983 crisis had only taken place as a result of the Socialists' policies, which brought about a collective *'prise de conscience'* of the crisis and the constraints it imposed. France needed to go through this experience, he claimed, and thus Mitterrand's greatness was to have contributed to 'making us ordinary'. Roger Fauroux, former chief executive of St Gobain who became director of the Ecole Nationale d'Administration in 1986, echoed these feelings when he said in the same year that the experience of having the Left in power at least had the virtue of having brought about a change in people's mentalities and dispelled a certain number of myths as to the origin of the crisis of capitalism, which could now be seen as a global phenomenon rather than a national one (Fauroux 1986). In this sense the beginning of the end of the French exception can in fact be situated in the context of the Socialist experience in power (Kesselman 1991), starting with the election of the first Socialist president of the Fifth Republic in 1981 and the acceptance by the Socialist Party of these Gaullist institutions, despite earlier opposition, notably by Mitterrand himself (Mitterrand 1964). Contrary to common expectations and despite 23 years of opposition for the Left, political *'alternance'* had shown itself to be possible after all. Together with the decline in influence of the Communist Party, these developments were seen by July and Fauroux as a positive move towards France's becoming more like other nations.

However, whereas Furet and his colleagues and Serge July accepted the alleged end of the exception with some optimism, others writing at about the same time emphasised the sense of malaise and the crisis of national identity that France seemed to be experiencing during this period as people lost their political bearings.[3] The failure of the Socialist experiment had led to a sense of gloom and doom for the many '*déçus du socialisme*' who found it hard to accept that there was apparently no alternative to the policies of economic austerity and the espousal of a more liberal model (Espaces 89 1985; Schmitt 1986; Gauchet 1985; Lipovetsky 1983; Finkielkraut 1987; Barret-Kriegel 1989; Bruckner 1990; Duhamel 1985 and 1989; Duverger 1988; Le Roy Ladurie 1990). This identity crisis tended to be set within the framework of the dialectic between the decline of the nation-state and the process of European integration which was beginning to erode certain traditional practices and customs (Formesyn 1984; Hayward 1988; Kramer 1994). The implicit, if gradual, abandonment of national sovereignty and loss of status in the world seemed to be hitting France harder than her neighbours. The distinctiveness of the French model meant that the process of reform was particularly problematic and provoked strong resistance in a number of different policy areas. Was it possible or even desirable for the French model to survive in face of increasing Europeanisation? Internal and external causes of the malaise became increasingly entwined as the integration process moved inexorably forward. Yet the signing of the Single European Act in 1986, which was to lead to the completion of the internal market by 1992, thus irreversibly opening up the French economy, was agreed upon by both Left and Right, and did not cause nearly as much opposition and debate as would the Maastricht Treaty in the early 1990s.

Thus by the mid-1980s, it was clear that an unprecedented but broad political consensus had been reached by the mainstream parties over economic policy and the need to pursue the process of European integration, rather than sticking to the pursuit of 'socialism in one country' that some Socialist Party members (and a number of government ministers) had still believed was possible before March 1983. This did not of course mean that there was total convergence between the main parties; indeed, the period of '*cohabitation*' between a president of the Left and a prime minister of the Right from 1986–8 was largely conflictual, with both sides at pains to emphasise their political differences. Yet these differences were becoming more blurred, even if the accompanying rhetoric sought to hide this fact for reasons of electoral expediency. However, the re-election of François Mitterrand in 1988, on the famous '*ni ni*' campaign promise not to pursue either national-isations or privatisations, was a clear indication of the general trend towards policy convergence and the at least partial acceptance of the idea of consensus that certain observers had been identifying and encouraging for some time (Duhamel *et al* 1984; Ferenczi 1989).

Yet consensus was still a controversial issue, and many decried what they saw as the '*consensus mou*' ('soft consensus'), a sort of compla-cent 'opting out' or resignation that was often negatively (and in fact incorrectly) identified with those who welcomed the end of the French exception as an opportunity to convert the *dirigiste* model of the state into a more liberal, free-market economy more akin to the 'Anglo-Saxon' model (Debray 1989: 95–111, 210–13). The publication of *La République du centre* thus came at a time when underlying trends sug-gested both change and continuity, convergence and divergence of ideas as to the way in which French politics was being conducted. Furet and his colleagues clearly saw the recognition of the end of the French exception as the first step towards 'opening the discussion as to the political future of France' (Furet *et al*: 12). In this, they were certainly successful, since the book provoked an intense controversy and numerous reviews, some of which were reproduced under the heading 'Critiques et commentaires' in a second edition published later the same year.

Reactions to the book showed that there was in fact considerable con-fusion about what the authors were actually saying, and many reviewers even picked up on what they saw as contradictions between the three essays. As Rosanvallon admitted: 'What has been little understood is what is fundamental to our venture: the simultaneous critique of the illu-sions and the dangers of a "soft consensus" and the archaism of a tradi-tional socialist vision' (Furet *et al*: 183). Moreover, as Julliard pointed out, although the 'end of the exception' meant that old political habits had been broken, that politicians now had a better grasp of reality, and that this would hopefully lead to better government, nothing was guaranteed for the future, and fundamental change was still really at the embryonic stage: 'For the moment I don't see any great democratic ambition in this country' (*ibid*). Finally, the three authors expressed the shared hope that 'the pacification of minds', which they welcomed, should not give way to 'a complacency which would hide the resignation of politicians and the indifference of citizens' (*ibid*: 12).

The debate initiated by *La République du centre* was in fact far from passive or consensual, even if during the initial phase – what Jill Lovecy has called the 'first wave' (Lovecy 1999) – the tone of optimism seemed to be winning the day. Claude Imbert's article in *Foreign Affairs* in

1989, expounding and espousing Furet's thesis, boldly announced to the 'Anglo-Saxon' world that France no longer considered that its model was unique; it had brought to an end the ideological battles between Left and Right, accepted new concepts of sovereignty and asserted that a strong majority consensus had now formed around the principles of a market economy and a political system similar to those of other major Western democracies. Yet very soon, the journal *Esprit* was wondering whether Furet had not been too quick to assume the end of the French exception (Roman *et al* 1990). Similarly, James Hollifield (1991: 292) concluded from his 'Searching for the New France' that given all the changes of the 1980s, 'one might be tempted to jump to the conclusion that some type of non-ideological, classless pluralism [was] just around the corner. Such a conclusion not only would be premature but would be wrong'. Throughout the 1990s the debate continued, as commentators argued about whether or not, and to what extent, France could still justify its claim to exceptionalism.

There was also more than a whiff of nostalgia in the air, expressed, for example, by Raymond Soubie when discussing the theme of 'banalisation': 'So do we not have any regrets for the past? Will we not have to repent for having exchanged the banalisation of France for simple material satisfaction? To abandon these old relics and to lose a part of our soul in the process, was this really the price to pay in order to be able to exist and to succeed in the great economic game? And are we prepared to continue in this direction? (Soubie 1991: 14) ... In finally acquiring a sense of economics, have we fallen into line, after our loss of power, of our illusions, and a part of our soul? Are we condemned to be a middle-size nation like any other? Is God still French?' (*ibid*: 17).[4] For Soubie the central issue was clear: 'The country must make a choice. Either to accept or to refuse the "end of the French exception", either genuinely to espouse the European cause or to maintain her haughty tradition ... of national independence, resign herself definitively to the market economy or pursue her dream of a path which is different to that of other Western democracies' (*ibid*: 155). This question should be the central theme of public debate in France, he argued, in order for people to become aware of its importance. 'Europe is the reconciliation of tradition with what is new, it is the only great collective ambition left open to us. God, if he is no longer French, will certainly be European' (*ibid*: 281).

The question of France's role in Europe had become all the more pressing as a result of the unexpected events of 1989 that led to the collapse of the Soviet bloc and the reunification of Germany, which France had always feared. These events had a significant impact on the end of exception debate for three reasons; first, because the redefining of borders in the new geo-political map of Europe meant that France's world role, as defined by De Gaulle in the 1960s and based on a policy of claimed independence *vis-à-vis* the Cold War power blocs, was no longer tenable. In revising its international position, the relevance of the French exception was called into question. Secondly, insofar as they represented the ideological triumph of liberal thought over communist ideology, it was hard to see how it could be possible for France to resist the new wave of liberalism. Finally, because they led, more or less directly, to the signing of the Maastricht Treaty, which was a way for France to ensure that the new Germany did not decide to turn eastwards and neglect her commitment to European integration. It was in the context of the debates leading up to the signing of this treaty that the French exception once again started to appear in political rhetoric. Predictably, it was the opponents of the treaty who used the notion to defend French sovereignty, and most notable in this respect was Philippe Séguin: 'I am against Maastricht because I believe in the French exception' (Séguin 1992b: 49 and 1993). The extreme right also took this line, fuelling the fears expressed by many that the principal beneficiary of this debate was in fact the Front National. The main thrust of political argument however was to toe the European line, even if this was sometimes presented as being not the end of, but more modestly the 'modernisation of the French exception' that would enable the French model, which was out of step with the new international environment, to evolve (Saint-Etienne 1992a and b).

'Exception culturelle' and *'pensée unique'*

This international environment had a significant impact on the way France viewed its role in Europe from the early 1990s onwards, and this was articulated quite clearly through the 'end of exception' polemic as it evolved over the decade. The two main strands of the debate can be usefully referred to under the headings *'exception culturelle'*[5] and *'pensée unique'*, and the origins of both can be located in the context of the Uruguay Round of multilateral trade negotiations that took place within the GATT framework from 1987–93. For this round, new issues were added to the list of negotiable products, including cultural goods, because the US felt that the EU was too protective towards its cinema and television production. However, France felt strongly that cultural goods were not like other products, and that they should be excluded from (or more precisely, not included in) the negotiations. This argument became known as the *'exception culturelle'*, because culture was seen as being different. France's EU partners did not all feel the same however and intense lobbying was necessary on the part of the French government to persuade them that this approach was for the general good of all non-anglophone cultures, and not simply an attempt to promote or defend French culture. Realising the need for allies in this battle, France started to emphasise the notion of cultural diversity (decried for so long within the boundaries of the Hexagon in the interests of the 'one and indivisible Republic'), which would embrace all European languages and cultures, as well as other francophone cultures (Védrine and Moïsi 2000). French success in winning over some reluctant member-states, and in then going on to win the battle to preserve the cultural exception in 1993, then again at Seattle in 1999 under the WTO, demonstrated the importance of the European dimension of national policy-making, and served as a reminder that it could no longer play an independent world role, thus reinforcing the sense in which the nation's future lay deep at the heart of Europe.

While the *'exception culturelle'* is not the subject of this chapter (see contribution by Dauncey in this volume), it is nevertheless relevant here to note in passing the relationship between the two notions, of the 'French exception' and the 'cultural exception', since the latter would appear to have been conceived in the conceptual framework of the former. There is a certain paradox to be noted in the fact that what originated as a defence of the French exception in the cultural domain (especially cinema, but in fact, French culture more generally) should end up being successfully defended not at the national but at the European level. This battle over the cultural exception, perceived widely as being between France and the US, even if the European Commission was in fact the negotiator, was to take the end of exception debate into the international arena, and would make the *'exception culturelle'* one of its most tangible manifestations.

Indeed, during the rest of the 1990s and on into the 21st century a battle was fought out, essentially in the French and American press, although supported in no mean measure by *The Economist* (Pedder 1999), over cultural issues, which could be seen as a struggle for cultural supremacy in its broadest sense (Gordon and Meunier 2001; Kuisel 2001). The French accused the US of cultural imperialism, while the US accused France of living in the past by refusing to accept globalisation, and justifying this position by evoking the 'French exception'. The hostility of the American press towards France was grounded in an understanding of the French exception as not just difference or uniqueness, but as a claim to superiority (Frank 1998). Moreover, the initial focus on cultural issues such as television and cinema soon widened to include lifestyle and eating habits, as José Bové took up the battle against '*la malbouffe*', so that before long Franco-American relations seemed to be totally dominated by this extension of the 'exception' debate, as acknowledged by Baudrillard: 'The old Franco-American antagonism, the almost genetic rivalry, has been aggravated... The idea of a French exception, a French difference, is absurd, but a certain American triumphalism and our own relative decline has turned the idea into an obsession' (quoted in Cohen 1997).

The second strand of the end of exception debate (around the *pensée unique*) was more of a continuation of the nation-state versus European integration dialectic that was rekindled by the Maastricht debate. The most striking textual example of this position was the report commissioned by Prime Minister Edouard Balladur from the Commissariat général du Plan in 1994, under the presidency of Alain Minc (Minc 1994). Moving on from the acknowledgement that France had reached the end of an era, he argued that it needed to develop a new project (because France, being what it is, cannot thrive without an ongoing project), and that this project should be its integration within the new Europe. 'France can only have a powerful world role if it is part of a European plan. ... We do not have any alternative to our European choice' (*ibid*: 10). He claimed that France had benefited from the opening of the economy and the imperatives of productivity, and that it would be less buffeted by the forces of the open market if it were well entrenched within the European entity. France needed to find a compromise between the imperatives of productivity and the desire for social cohesion to create a society based on solidarity, efficiency and equity (rather than equality). Economic and Monetary Union would be fundamental to achieving this aim, and would serve as an instrument for the necessary transformation of French society, notably in the fields of social spending, fiscal policy, and the organisation of the state and public services.

The message conveyed in this report was also being echoed in numerous different publications and press articles, to the extent that it soon appeared to some to have become oppressive and inescapable. Jean-François Kahn was the first to write about this in his news magazine *L'Événement du jeudi* in the early 1990s (see also Kahn 1995); then in 1995, *Le Monde Diplomatique* published an article by Ignacio Ramonet which was a violent diatribe against this 'new doctrine' whose key words were: market, competition, globalisation, strong currency, privatisation and liberalisation. He identified the European Commission and the Bank of France as institutions which were champions of the new dogma: 'The constant repetition, in all the media, of this catechism, by nearly all politicians, gives it such a power of intimidation that it stifles any attempt at independent thinking, and makes it very difficult to resist this new obscurantism' (Ramonet 1995: 1). The reference to the Minc report as the best example of this discourse was explicit. The two main causes for objection seemed to be both the 'blind' commitment to the euro and the sense that there was 'no alternative'. Strength of resistance to the *'pensée unique'* was such that in 1997–8 two different groups of opponents organised themselves into foundations in order to articulate a *'pensée critique'*: The Fondation Marc Bloch brought together a motley collection of mainly gaullists and *chevènementistes* such as Régis Debray, Serge Halimi, Didier Motchane, Emmanuel Todd, Pierre-André Taguieff and Jean-François Kahn, whereas the Fondation Copernic was founded by the communist historian Jacques Kergoat in order to 'put an end to the hegemony of the liberal Left "in the field of new ideas"' (Kergoat 1999a). Despite these ventures of resistance, the successful launch of the euro and the increasing liberalisation of the French economy, under both Left and Right, reinforced the dominance of the social-liberal discourse that grew out of the end of exception debate.

Given the significance of this outcome, and pertinence of the end of exception debate to it, the reader may be forgiven at this point for feeling somewhat unsure as to how to situate in political terms the aspirations of Furet and his colleagues when they published *La République du centre*: was this the sort of transformation they had been hoping for? How can the publication of one small book have achieved such a great impact on political and economic life in France? A clue to answering these questions lies in the foreword to the book, where the astute reader will notice that these three essays were commissioned by the Fondation Saint-Simon (hereafter referred to as the FSS), in order to 'foster an initial awareness and to launch the discussion as to our political future' (Furet *et al*: 12) What then was this Foundation, and what role did it play in the instigation and dissemination of the debate over the end of the French exception?

The Fondation Saint Simon: the rise and demise of the French exception

The Fondation Saint-Simon was founded in 1982 by a small group of men whose proclaimed objective was to provide a forum for developing analysis of the contemporary world. Significantly, the founding fathers were François Furet (historian of the French Revolution), Pierre Rosan-vallon (professor and leading researcher in the field of political and social ideas, attached to both the EHESS and the IEP in Paris), Alain Minc (leading economist), Emmanuel Le Roy-Ladurie (a social historian), Pierre Nora (founder of the journal *Le Débat*), his brother Simon Nora (top civil servant), and Roger Fauroux (director of ENA and future Minister for Industry in Michel Rocard's government). Somewhere between the model of the British or US think-tank and its more hexagonal version of the 'club', the originality of the FSS was to aim to bring together in fruitful discussion representatives from two worlds which hitherto had refused any type of dialogue: businessmen and intellectuals.

There were two main ideas underlying this project: the first was that greater communication between intellectuals and business people would actually be beneficial to both communities. Fauroux himself was the first to admit for example that he had made errors in his business decisions due to a failure to consult specialists regarding social and political conditions which affected his investments, and other leading entrepreneurs also began to recognise the value of seeking advice from 'experts' outside the business world. At the same time, many intellectuals and university researchers began to see the opportunity to increase their meagre salaries by engaging in studies financed by business and taking on consultancies that would previously have been politically unthinkable. This was made possible by the changing political and economic climate soon after the Socialist victory in 1981: the deteriorating economic context meant that the first steps towards a reconciliation between the Left and the business world became not only possible or desirable but essential, as even hard-liners were increasingly forced to accept the imperatives of the market place, although this could not yet be admitted publicly.

The traditional antipathy between these two communities of business people and intellectuals originated of course in the long history of political cleavage established at the time of the Revolution, which placed them quite clearly on opposing sides of the Left-Right divide. The persistent intensity and rigidity of this divide, exacerbated by the bipolarising institutional arrangements of the Fifth Republic, was seen by many leading decision-makers as being detrimental to the nation because it prevented any real debate between the two sides. This absence of informed, constructive, 'apolitical' discussion (such as that which characterised the 'Butskellite' era in British politics) meant that problems were always approached from within a highly partisan agenda and any solutions proposed would inevitably be contested by the opposition, if only to make a political point. However, the election of a Socialist president in 1981, which made the idea of *'alternance'* a reality, paradoxically also paved the way for a fresh approach to the problem; indeed, the idea that it might be possible to move beyond this rigid Right-Left divide was the second big idea (albeit less explicit) behind the founding of the FSS in 1982.

The FSS was set up officially not in fact as a *'fondation'* but as an *'association loi 1901'*, financed by a combination of private subscriptions from members (500 francs in 1997) and business donations (120,000 francs per year) from companies such as la Caisse des Dépôts, Suez, Publicis, Saint-Gobain, BSN Gervais-Danone and MK2 Productions. Activities of the FFS centred around a monthly lunch with a guest speaker and the organisation of various *'groupes de réflexion'*, whose analyses of economic, social or international issues led to publications of various kinds. Pierre Rosanvallon was particularly active in organising and supervising these research projects from his professional positions at the Institut d'Etudes Politiques and the Ecole de Hautes Etudes en Sciences Sociales in Paris. During the 1990s, these publications became almost monthly issues and certain studies were diffused more widely through for example *Le Nouvel observateur, Le Débat, Politique internationale, Commentaire* and *Esprit,* with which the FSS had close links through its members.

What the subscribers to the FSS mainly had in common was a commitment to the idea of modernisation, a programme which had its origins under the Fourth Republic when an attempt was made to reconcile the market with state intervention in preference to the pre-war system of *'laissez-faire* combined with protectionism' (Laurent 1998). Pierre Mendès-France had been the main political representative of this movement, supported by top civil servants such as François Bloch-Lainé and Simon Nora. In the early 1980s Michel Rocard was seen as the logical spokesman of the 'modernisers', opposed to the 'archaism' still strongly represented within certain *tendances* of the PS. So roughly speaking they could be classified as the 'second left' (*'deuxième gauche'*).[6]

The way the FSS worked in practice was to build a system of networks or concentric circles around the central nucleus formed by the founding fathers, who used the idea of 'bridging personalities' (such as Roger Fauroux, Simon and Pierre Nora, Jacques Julliard) to establish and develop the links between the different components: civil servants, trade unionists, industrialists, intellectuals, the press and publishing. So, despite the apparent diversity of its members, the existence of a shared overarching intellectual project facilitated the bringing together of a wide range of approaches to a common cause. By deciding what issues it wanted to highlight at any given moment, it could orchestrate the dissemination of a particular line of argument through the publication of these views in different media. In addition, its members were frequently invited to participate in official commissions and working parties which gave them an ideal platform for informing discussion. A good example of this is the Minc report discussed earlier: one third of the commission members were also members of the FSS or '*saint-simoniens*'. Thus it was possible for the FSS to have a large measure of influence over the agenda of national debate without this being easily discernible to the outside world. Furthermore, the fact that many key members such as Roger Fauroux had connections in all of these different worlds, facilitated 'the circulation of discourses, ways of thinking, themes and issues that converged to produce common approaches' (Laurent 1998). Over time, the FSS came to represent what Alain Minc called 'the circle of reason', advocating a new pragmatic approach to solving the problems of contemporary society, and defending an 'appeased vision of social relations' outside the pernicious ideological battles of the world of party politics.

However, as Vincent Laurent pointed out in a critical article published in *Le Monde Diplomatique,* this 'end of ideology' approach could also be seen as 'nothing other than an ideology that does not declare its name. ... It aims to create the conditions for the implementation of a conservative project that is presented as inevitable. This is how the "narrow road" [for which read "*pensée unique*"] followed by France's political leaders over the last 15 years has emerged. In this way the democracy of the market appears as "the end of history" and social-liberalism as the only viable political project for our societies' (Laurent 1998). Thus, the FSS was seen by its critics as 'the melting-pot in which a specific political project has been developed' (Kergoat 1999b) or 'the cooking pot that produced the famous and woolly-minded '*pensée unique*', that represents the deadening consensus of the last twenty years' (Musso 1999). Indeed, by the mid-1990s, the quiet success of the FSS had almost become counter-productive because the sense and strength of '*la pensée unique*' with which it became associated meant that there seemed to be no possibility of an alternative to the new liberalism. For some, this represented a grave threat to democracy, by undermining pluralism (Chardon and Lensel 1998), and led to the creation of the 'counter-foundations' described above.

Perhaps rather paradoxically, it was the apparent success of the FSS's political project that led to its demise when, in 1999, a decision was taken to cease all activities. As Pierre Rosanvallon explained in an article in

Le Monde, the FSS was 'a completed project' (23 June 1999): the Left had been converted to social-liberalism; 'transversality' had been created between people from different *milieux*, 70 public seminars had been held, 40 books published (most of them in the 'Liberté d'esprit' collection with Calmann-Lévy), together with 110 study documents and other shorter notes, some of which had achieved great notoriety (for example Patrick Weil's paper on immigration or Emmanuel Todd's on the political malaise in France). But he felt there was 'a risk of slipping into a routine', and after the death of Furet in 1997, the spirit of the whole venture was no longer quite the same.

From end of exceptionalism to '*déclinisme*'

Ten years after the demise of the FSS, the term 'French exception' continues to be widely used in discussion about France, both in general contexts, as any Google search will testify (road safety, gynaecology, the teaching of mathematics and philosophy, the *grandes écoles*, and so on), as well as in academic analysis (Picq 2002; Mathy 2008; Maus 2005; Bainbrigge 2001; Gorrillot 2008; Bozo 2008; Ramsay 2008; Brouard *et al* 2008, Teysseire 2006). But as France moved into the 21st century, public debate about the French exception became much less prominent. Like most buzzwords, it seemed in some way to have come to the end of its shelf life, and as Jacques Julliard conceded: 'we became tired of it' ['on s'en est fatigué'] (personal communication, 15 June 2008). But the issues it had raised were still pertinent, and indeed Pierre Rosanvallon, despite his earlier claims of success in completing the aims of the FSS, went on to found another think-tank in 2001 called 'La République des Idées' (see www.repid.com), with the expressed intent of bringing about 'the necessary intellectual rebirth of a reformist Left' (*Le Monde*, 22 November 2002), no doubt at least partly with a view to the upcoming presidential election. A collection of publications with Le Seuil accompanied this initiative, and in many ways it seems to have followed on from where the FSS left off, organising seminars and funding research and working papers using sponsorship from the business world, but with less secrecy than the FSS. Rosanvallon further increased his personal access to the media by becoming an 'associated editorialist' with *Le Monde,* which enabled him to initiate special tribunes in the sections of the paper called 'Rebonds' or 'Débat', the first of which saw a double page spread entitled: '*Le Monde/* La République des idées' (14 April, 2004). At the same time, his appointment to a chair at the Collège de France in 2001 consecrated his authority and influence in the world of academia. So the ongoing intellectual project to change France by reforming the Left simply took on a rather different form, but continued to inspire scorn and derision from the 'left of the left', which saw La République des idées as 'a supermarket selling ideas … this group of wind-bags is redefining a "left" that embraces the euro with gusto' (Plan B 2008).

At the same time, the discourse of the 'end of exception' debate and its underlying concepts would soon be 'recycled' and subsumed in a new debate over the alleged decline of France, spearheaded by the '*déclinistes*' or '*déclinologues*' (Bacqué 2006). The ongoing French obsession with its own decline was given a new lease of life after the publication of a report by the European Commission in 2002 which claimed that France had fallen from third to tenth place in terms of purchasing power over ten years (Allemand 2004). Although these figures were later shown to be misleading, it nevertheless fuelled the debate over the decline of the French economy, and in the Summer of 2003 the young economic historian, Nicolas Bavarez, penned an article called 'Le déclin de la France?', published in *Commentaire* (Bavarez 2003a), developed into a book published shortly afterwards, called *La France qui tombe,* and which very soon became a best-seller (Bavarez 2003b). Many of the ideas expressed in the 'end of exception' context were echoed in Bavarez's sweeping critique of France's inability to come to terms with the realities of globalisation, in which he argued that radical reforms ('shock therapy') were needed in the name of modernisation. His accusations against the political class on both Left and Right were seen by many as being an open invitation to his friend Nicolas Sarkozy to take the lead in advocating a more 'libéral' set of policies to lead France out of its inexorable decline. There followed a stream of books and articles in a similar vein (including another volume by Bavarez himself in 2006), and the famous bookshop Gibert Jeune in Paris even set up a dedicated section called 'La France va mal'. All the weekly news magazines did a cover feature on some aspect of 'the French decline', while *Le Monde* devoted an issue of its *Dossiers et Documents* to 'Le déclin de la France en débat' ['Debating France's decline']. But the alleged decline was not only economic, it was also cultural and intellectual, and the Marxist sociologist Perry Anderson wrote two major articles in 2004 lamenting this decline, in which he criticised the various attempts by Nora, Furet and Rosanvallon to create what he called 'an *union sucrée* in which the divisions and discords of French society would melt away in the fond rituals of postmodern remembrance' (Anderson 2004b). The articles provoked much debate on both sides of the Atlantic, and were then published in French as a book under the title *La pensée tiède. Un regard critique sur la culture française,* which included a response from Pierre Nora called *La pensée rechauffée* (Anderson 2005).

As we saw above, French anxieties about national decline had always been closely associated with the twin processes of Europeanisation and globalisation, and underlying concerns about France's weakening position in Europe, exacerbated by the prospect of EU enlargement, were set out at some length in a report to the National Assembly in 2004 (Floch 2004). The report documented the loss of French influence politically, linguistically and institutionally, and concluded that France had to take its European commitments more seriously in order to strengthen its position. But in the event, all the fears of dilution of French power and identity, which had already dominated the Maastricht referendum under the 'end of exception' debate, came together to underpin the referendum campaign which resulted in France's rejection of the EU Constitutional Treaty (ECT) in 2005. During this campaign, much of the nostalgia that had accompanied the end of exception debates found expression in what became essentially a debate about how best to ensure the survival of the 'French model' in the post-ECT Europe, in face of the widely perceived threat from the 'Anglo-Saxon model' advocated by Blair's Britain (Collard 2006). The central question turned around how best to protect it: by voting 'yes' or 'no'. As the campaign developed, the choice was increasingly presented as being between *'une Europe "à l'anglaise" ou "à la française"'* (Le Boucher 2005). The former was seen as 'legislating as little as possible, celebrating diversity, competition and flexibility, a polygamous Europe in which each country would choose its partners according to its interests and needs, a club with flexible rules which would impose a minimum of constraints and solidarities, a vast free trade zone devoid of political ambition' (Langellier 2005). The latter, would be 'an interventionist Europe, an ambitious Europe, a Europe that is determined to become an international power and in which a social model that is different from the American one takes root' (Duhamel 2005). Interestingly, the spectre of rampant 'Anglo-Saxon' neo-liberalism overwhelming the 'French model' within a post-ECT EU was invoked in the debate by both proponents and opponents of the treaty. For the 'yes' lobby, a vote in favour provided the best bulwark against the triumph of a Europe *'à l'anglaise'*, on the grounds that, if the 'no' vote were successful, this would represent the triumph, by default, of 'a liberal Europe, all ready to become the pole of a transatlantic zone, part of the great Anglo-Saxon grouping' (Duhamel 2005). Proponents of a 'no' vote, on the other hand, used the same threat of the triumph of 'a liberal Europe' to construct a case for the opposite argument: they claimed that the terms of the constitutional treaty as presented would simply consolidate what they saw as the very 'liberal' objectives and values written into the document, which they perceived as 'the Trojan Horse of globalisation' (Martucci 2005). Their argument was that, if France voted 'no', this would provoke a 'salutary crisis' within Europe, which would then lead to a renegotiation of the treaty on terms more favourable to the French social model and less open to future 'liberalisation'. On each side of the argument, concern about the survival of the 'French model' was all the greater when juxtaposed with the apparent success of the Blairite, liberal, 'Anglo-Saxon' model. Thus the campaign provided an interesting example not only of the pertinence and durability of the notion of the 'French exception' in French public debate, but also of the way in which the notion can be mobilised in defence of opposing political positions.

Conclusion

The conclusions to be drawn from this analysis of the 'French exception' debate seem quite clear: the launching of the 'end of French exception' debate as a result of the publication in 1988 of *La République du Centre* must be understood as an important instrument used in the pursuit of an ambitious political project conceived by members of the *deuxième gauche,* which aimed to encourage the 'normalisation' of French political life in its broadest sense, and more specifically, to convert the French left to social-democracy. The weight of the FSS behind this project was critical to its success. It is impossible to know of course how political life would have developed had the book not been published and had the FSS not existed: to what extent would the force of events alone have coerced the French Left into some sort of compromise with the market economy? Yet the answer to this question is almost irrelevant to our initial line of enquiry into the origin and nature of the discourse of French exceptionalism, since what is more important is the demonstration of how the debate about the 'French exception' and its proclaimed demise came to permeate public discourse in France in the 1990s in a way that was not reproduced anywhere else. The ultimate paradox is that this debate, although intended to consecrate the end of the French exception, in fact constituted a striking example of its survival. Indeed, as shown above, the developments over the past decade have confirmed the continuing French attachment to the notion of exceptionalism (and to a lesser extent its discourse), and the 2008–9 financial crisis, widely presented in France as a crisis of the 'Anglo-Saxon' capitalist model, has re-energised defenders of the 'French model' (Fressoz 2009) and breathed new life into the debate about the 'French exception'.

Notes

* An earlier version of this chapter, entitled 'The Elusive French Exception', was published in E. Godin and T. Chafer (eds) 2005. *The French Exception*, pp. 30–44 (Oxford: Berghahn).

1 See for example Cole 1998; Hewlett 1998 and the colloquium at the Bordeaux Institut d'Etudes Politiques in October 1998, 'A la recherche de l'exception française'.

2 Jacques Julliard confirmed that he and François Furet had 'invented' the expression specifically for the book, in an interview with the author, 15 June 2008.

3 If the concept of a national identity crisis is not meaningful for some, it should be remembered that in France it was the State that created the nation, and inculcated a sense of national identity, which no doubt explains why it continues to have significance for a large number of well-known authors and commentators and indicates that it was (and arguably still is) a common preoccupation among French elites, if not for the ordinary citizen.

4 A reference to the book written by the German writer Friedrich Sieburg in 1930, 'Is God French?' and reprinted in 1991 by Grasset & Fasquelle. The question 'Is God French?' was also taken as the central theme of the debates at the Festival de Radio-France organised by *Le Monde* and France-Culture in the Jardin de Petrarque at Montpellier in July 1995.

5 Jack Lang is said to have invented this expression in the 1980s (Farchy 1999: 7).

6 *La Deuxième gauche* was the title of a book by Hervé Hamon and Patrick Rotman (1982).

Section I
The French State

2
Reviving the French Exception? Sarkozy, Authoritarian Populism and the Bonapartist Tradition

Nick Hewlett

The modern governmental history of France is peppered with heads of state whose rule may aptly be described as personalised, authoritarian and populist. The latest such example, President Nicolas Sarkozy, has thus been likened to Charles de Gaulle, Philippe Pétain, Napoleon III and Napoleon I. A list of other leaders who stand out from the more run-of-the mill (but without the same degree of personalised, authoritarian or populist characteristics as those mentioned above), might include François Mitterrand, Pierre Mendès France and Léon Blum. Beyond France, any roll call of heads of state with both populist and autocratic tendencies should include the Anglo-American examples of Margaret Thatcher, Tony Blair and John F. Kennedy, to mention only some of the more obvious. Elsewhere, notable populist autocrats include Vladimir Putin in Russia, Silvio Berlusconi in Italy and a host of strong leaders associated with either right or left in Latin and Central America, including Hugo Chavez in Venezuela, Fidel Castro in Cuba and Juan Perón in Argentina, to take a classic example from the past.

By presenting this rather random amalgam of political leaders who arguably stand out as strong autocrats, I am indeed suggesting from the start that the study of the cult of the leader in politics is somewhat of a minefield, but I am also suggesting that it is a more common phenomenon than we might be inclined to believe. The nature of out-of-the-ordinary leadership is often treated entertainingly and sometimes insightfully in biography, in other words in a narrative form, perhaps with implied or more overt reference to psychoanalysis. Meanwhile, some comparative academic studies of political leadership are highly descriptive. Many recent treatments of the subject emphasise the role of the mass media in the construction of strong, charismatic leaders, suggesting that there is a sort of vicious (or virtuous, depending on one's standpoint) circle, whereby the media concentrates in a highly personalised way on the maverick, ambitious individual in order to attract readers, viewers and listeners, and for their part the leader and their public relations team encourage media coverage because it tends to make success more likely. There is, of course, some truth in this latter perspective, as I shall argue below, but I shall also suggest that it is only part of the story.

In what follows, I contend that in order to understand the Sarkozy phenomenon, one must include a broader analysis of the socio-economic and political context of both France and elsewhere. The classic Marxist perspective on authoritarian, populist heads of state takes as its starting point Marx's *The Eighteenth Brumaire of Louis Bonaparte* (Marx 1968), where he suggests that Napoleon III ruled by concentrating power in the executive wing of the state, which he controlled, and by weakening the legislative wing, particularly after the *coup d'état* of 2 December 1851. The authors of a number of recent publications agree that there are strong Bonapartist characteristics in both the style and substance of Sarkozy's rule, which include: a highly personalised and autocratic approach to government of the country; a mix of ideo-logical references whilst all the time speaking in terms of national salva-tion; a populist approach to relations with the French people, attempting to appeal directly to ordinary people; intense use of the media to achieve his aims; and talk of a clean break with what went before (e.g. Duhamel 2009; Hewlett 2007; Musso 2008; Rozès 2007).

In this chapter I offer an argument which accepts the main lines of the Bonapartist case, but which goes on to put a greater emphasis than many of those who apply it on more general characteristics of the politics of liberal democracy in late capitalism. In particular, I argue that the depoliticised nature of many liberal democracies encourages the celebrity or quasi-celebrity status of many political leaders and this, combined with other developments that encourage passivity in the electorate, means that Bonapartist characteristics are in fact far more widespread than one might imagine. Moreover, the Sarkozy project as originally conceived by the presidential hopeful and his collaborators was in large part about the introduction of more solidly neo-liberal conditions for the operation of business in France, with a view to bringing the country more in line with many other advanced capitalist countries. The Sarkozy phenomenon, then, whilst it is a clear example of Bonapartism, nevertheless does not constitute as strong a break as one might at first think with many other regimes in the liberal-democratic world, or for that matter with what went before in France.

Bonapartism and French political history

Both Marxist and non-Marxist analysts have suggested that there is in French politics a long history of Bonapartism, dating back to Napoleon I, but perhaps more particularly to Napoleon III. For both Marx and Engels (who also found Bonapartist elements in Bismarck's rule in Germany), Bonapartism is an exceptional form of political rule which results from an unstable situation where neither the ruling class nor the working class is able to assert sufficient authority, and where an authoritarian leader steps in and claims to speak for all classes. From a non-Marxist perspective, René Rémond suggests in his classic *Les Droites en France* that there are three main currents on the right in France, namely the liberal-conservative Orleanist, the extreme-right counter-revolutionary and the Bonapartist current. He argues that Gaullism is – or at least was – strongly imbued with elements of Bonapartism, which were, notably: a personalised cult of authority; a strong state; a claim to rally the French people as a whole, from whom its authority is derived via universal suffrage; a strong modernizing impulse; national independence and grandeur, especially with regard to foreign policy; and an association of capital and labour (Rémond 1982: 322–3).

In highly schematic and oversimplified fashion, we can thus summarise the main elements of Bonapartism in the following way. An authoritarian but charismatic leader is able to rule with an unusual degree of popularity for a relatively short period of time within the framework of a strong state and with claims to being above party politics. He or she is populist, with electoral appeal across classes, a situation made possible in part by disarray amongst other political forces. The discourse of Bonapartism tends to be of nationalism and national unity, of modernisation and progress whilst conserving all that is seen as valuable in the past, and with nods in the direction of equality. The circumstances which bring a Bonapartist leader to power and allow them to rule are exceptional, or characterised by crisis, and the threat of return to crisis or instability if the leader departs. This was the case with the first two actual Bonapartes and with de Gaulle; Napoleon I came to power in the 18 Brumaire of 1799 in the midst of military, financial and political crisis, Napoleon III came to power in the wake of the revolution of 1848. De Gaulle, meanwhile, came to power in the midst of political and military crisis over Algeria. He ruled with an authoritarian yet populist approach, notably warning of mayhem if his reforms put forward by referendum were rejected, which would, he warned, prompt his immediate departure (this finally happened after the No vote in a referendum in 1969).

A brief look at the constitution of the Fifth Republic will remind us that the formal context within which parliamentary and presidential politics have been operating since 1958 is one which has a strong Bonapartist orientation and that the constitution provides a suitable framework for the construction and consolidation of personalised power. Olivier Duhamel (1993: 181) comments that de Gaulle's most important idea about the Constitution was that 'it goes without saying that government should not stem from Parliament'. According to de Gaulle, it was indeed the supposed excessive power of the lower house over the composition and programme of government under the Fourth Republic that was the main cause of instability. Therefore, effective government should rely on a Constitution which gave government and the President far more autonomy from and power over the legislature. The Fifth Republic does indeed allow for a great deal of executive (presidential and governmental) power and relatively little parliamentary power. The President is elected by universal suffrage (this was an amendment to the constitution introduced – by referendum – in 1962) and is responsible for the choice of Prime Minister and his or her dismissal, and he (never yet she) nominates the rest of the cabinet in consultation with the Prime Minister. The President may submit proposed changes in legislation to the French people in the form of a referendum and may dissolve the *Assemblé nationale*, thus provoking an election.

The most controversial presidential power of all is described in Article 16, which allows the head of state 'exceptional powers' (defined very generally as being those 'required by the circumstances') for a certain period during a time of crisis. This provision has been used only once since 1958, by de Gaulle, between 23 April and 30 September 1961 after a *putsch* by four generals in Algeria, during which period de Gaulle ruled by decree. But it is a highly significant provision in that it is a symbol of the power of the President and is always there, to be used if necessary. Although the constitution gives substantial powers to the President there is nevertheless a degree of ambiguity which allows room for interpretation. Although the President chairs cabinet meetings, the government 'determines and conducts the policy of the nation' (Article 20) and 'directs the action of government' (Article 21), and although the President is military leader (Article 15), the government 'is in charge of the administration of the armed forces' (Article 20) and the Prime Minister is 'responsible for the defense of the nation' (Article 21). In the text, then, it is nowhere clearly laid out who actually governs, but in practice it has been the Presidents of the Republic who have dominated the legislature, the government, the civil service, the judiciary, the army, foreign policy and defence. This dominance prompted Maurice Duverger (1974) to call the Fifth Republic a 'republican monarchy'. (Also Choisel 1987; Volpi 1979).

In practice, one of the main ways by which parliamentary power has been curtailed by the executive is by recourse to a provision which allows governments to force through legislation where normal procedures might not produce a parliamentary majority in favour; Article 49-3 of the Constitution allows the government to make a bill a 'question of confidence' in the National Assembly, meaning that to defeat the bill there must be a motion of censure against the government, tabled within 24 hours and supported by an absolute majority of members. Since 1958, no motion of censure has ever brought down a government, despite article 49-3 being used over 80 times up to 2009. (Incidentally, recourse to this article has been curtailed under constitutional revisions in 2008.)

The Constitution itself, then, has strong Bonapartist leanings, which Mitterrand described in his book published in 1962, entitled *Le Coup d'état permanent*, although when Mitterrand became President of the Republic in 1981 he made no attempt at radical reform of the constitution. But it also contains more liberal democratic elements, in a blend which closely reflects de Gaulle's own politics.

Sarkozy: personalised, authoritarian populism

During the 2007 election campaign, it became clear that Sarkozy was making the election more plebiscitary in nature than any others had been since de Gaulle, a contest that if he won he would interpret as a mandate to rule in highly autocratic fashion. At every rally, in every television appearance, every interview and press release, Sarkozy built the image of himself as personal bearer of the formula necessary to bring France out of the political lethargy and economic crisis into which he said it had been allowed to sink, and it was his idiosyncratic mix of ideological references with a strong neo-liberal flavour that would bring salvation. His manic and at times irascible approach served to underline his singe-minded determination, an approach summed up in the first line of his best-selling book *Témoignage*, where he told the French people that he had always, as long as he could remember, been a man of action: '[J']ai toujours voulu agir' (Sarkozy 2006: 1). In his first speech after the presidential election results became known on 6 May 2007, he declared:

> The French people has spoken. It has chosen to break with the ideas, the habits and the behaviour of the past. I will therefore rehabilitate work, authority, morale and respect. I will ensure that the nation and

> national identity is honoured once again and I will give back to the
> French the pride of being French, and will finish with repentance
> which is a form of self hatred and multiple memories which feed
> the hatred of others. The French people has chosen change. I will
> implement this change because this is what I am asked to do by the
> people and because France is in need of it. (Sarkozy 2007d: 4)

Once in power, Sarkozy did indeed set about ruling the country as an
autocrat, involving himself personally in as many areas as he possibly
could, in a constant flurry of all-seeing, all-knowing, relentless activism
that earned him one of the kinder nicknames, *l'hyperprésident* (Maigret
2008). At times this manic omni-presence seemed to bring on delusions
of omnipotence, with comments such as '[w]hether growth is at 1.9 or
2.3 per cent doesn't change much in the end. What I want is three per
cent.' (in Hauser 2008: 29), and when the economy began to deterio-
rate seriously in late 2007, he lapsed into exaggerated paternalism:

> 'Times will be difficult, but I will help you in the work that needs to
> be done. Be courageous. I will protect you.' (in Hauser 2008: 29)

This style of government has meant that the President does indeed
appear as supreme ruler, with both Prime Minister François Fillon
and parliament becoming almost incidental to the governing process.
Jean-Pierre Dubois, President of the Ligue des droits de l'homme, suggests that in the first year of Sarkozy's presidency, democracy was
'asphyxiated by a *président-soleil* who runs the state like a personal
undertaking in a jet-set atmosphere which is free of any complex or
scruple'. He goes on to argue that the role of government has been
reduced to that of a few 'collaborators' (Dubois 2008: 6) and Hervé
Algalarrondo (2008) argues that, thanks to careful placing of close
friends and collaborators as ministers and special advisors, 'Sarkozy is
not only the real Prime Minister, he is single-handedly the entire government.' The perception of Sarkozy as leader seeking to incarnate
the will of the people is at times expressed in more positive terms by
close colleagues, and perhaps most clearly by Rachida Dati, at the time
Minister for Justice, when she explained that 'supreme legitimacy is held
by the French people who elected Nicolas Sarkozy in order to restore
authority...and magistrates carry out justice in the name of this supreme
legitimacy' (in Dubois 2008: 6).

Although for many French people the first period of his presidency
was dominated by momentous developments in his private life, Sarkozy's

hyperactive and commanding approach meant that there was an unprecedented number of reforms put forward during his first 18 months in office, many of them inspired by a desire to follow the Anglo-American neo-liberal economic model. These included reform of the 35-hour week, the attempted introduction of Sunday shopping (so great a departure that it was defeated by his own majority), substantial changes to established pension schemes for train and underground train drivers, devolution of budgets in higher education and changes to the school curriculum accompanied by job cuts in schools. Other proposals were often informed by the high-profile law and order agenda, including tighter laws on immigration (including DNA tests) and expulsion of a greater number of illegal immigrants (*sans papiers*), facilitated by the newly-created Ministry for Immigration and National Identity. Sarkozy also sought easier recourse to imprisonment, the stepping up of surveillance procedures, and a general overhaul of the legal system. Many proposals met with strong opposition from people most directly concerned, and many were abandoned or drastically altered. Proposals for constitutional reform drew opposition in particular to plans to allow the President to address both houses of parliament in a speech which would be akin to the annual state of the union speech in the US and which, according to its opponents, would formalise the *de facto* eclipsing of the Prime Minister.

With this personalization of power goes the authoritarianism and aggression which are other hallmarks of the presidency, and in this respect the influence of the extreme right is clear. As Minister of the Interior, Sarkozy had become closely associated with a repressive approach towards unrest in Parisian suburbs, saying in June 2005 that the Courneuve suburb should be cleaned out with a *Kärcher* (high-pressure industrial cleaning equipment), and calling aberrant suburban youth *racaille*, which is usually translated as 'scum'. Thus he was already seen as an exceptionally tough and determined defender of law and order, which remained a key part of his image throughout the election campaigns, with little time for those who attempted to understand deviance or perceived deviance by reference to social deprivation. His praise of hard work and personal achievement and determination to combat what he perceives as weak political correctness prompts such comments as: 'We must dispense with this culture of permanent excuses which consists of explaining everything and then excusing it' (in Leclerc 2008: 29). Sarkozy's aggressive style was revealed on television (and then seen by many thousands of viewers of YouTube) when in response to a man in a crowd who refused to shake his hand, he responded: 'casse-toi, pauv'con!', which translates politely as 'sod off, loser!'.

The mixture of arrogance, autocracy and authoritarianism which plays on the anxieties of ordinary people has come to epitomize what has indeed been described as Sarkozy's 'government by fear' (Dakhi *et al* 2007). It is part of the style, image and conduct which has led various analysts to suggest that he has many of the hallmarks of the archetypal populist leader. This certainly goes to the heart of the relative success of the Sarkozy phenomenon and it is perhaps worth dwelling for a moment on the notion of populism. Although the populist label was originally a name given to political groups in late 19th-century Russia, in its more extreme forms it has become associated in particular with regimes in Latin America, most notably in Brazil under Getúlio Vargas and in Argentina under Juan Perón, but in many other countries as well in less extreme form. From these examples of populist rule is derived the broader notion which emphasizes the importance of the leader's rhetoric, which is intended to encourage support from some of the least progressive (and often underprivileged) sectors of society, a rhetoric which is moralistic, anti-intellectual and lacking in programmatic detail, and which is designed to manipulate and divide. The role of the state (but not parliament) is particularly important, as is loyalty to the leader who becomes a quasi-embodiment of the state, and both voice and protector of the mass of ordinary people. (Gellner and Ionescu 1969). These characteristics would certainly seem to apply to Sarkozy's approach. An example of his manipulative approach is the way he talks directly to the French people as individuals (for example using first names on television and radio), but at the same time divides the alleged majority from the minority by suggesting that there are clear 'good' and 'bad' individuals: those who work hard as opposed to those who do not; those who depend on their own resources and those who constantly expect the state to help them; those who are responsible young people as opposed to *racaille*. It is of course the good ones who are invited to be part of the Sarkozy project and this is highly reminiscent of Le Pen's populist approach to the mass of ordinary French people, where a relatively small number of individuals are to blame for the ills of society as a whole.

It would be quite correct to argue that much of the personalised, authoritarian populism I have described above also characterised the Thatcher era in Britain, and to some extent the Blair era as well. This suggests that, whilst the Sarkozy phenomenon is in some respects peculiarly French, many of its characteristics are also found in other countries.

Depoliticisation, presidentialism and the media

In the discussion so far, I have emphasized what might be described as the extraordinary, or exceptional characteristics of Sarkozy's rise to power and his subsequent rule. But I will now point out how in many other advanced capitalist countries with liberal democratic systems of government there are also tendencies – albeit often less pronounced – in similar directions. As Domenico Losurdo has argued, Bonapartism (at least in its milder forms which he describes as *soft* Bonapartism) should be viewed as being more prevalent than it is usually seen as being (Losurdo 2007). Such an approach, I argue, allows us convincingly to go beyond the idea that a leader such as Sarkozy is somehow entirely at odds with the 'normal' politics of other liberal democracies (or with what preceded it in France, for that matter), and rather that he and his rule are on the same continuum – if at times extreme and sometimes caricatural examples – of trends in the nature of political leadership more generally.

Perhaps the first point to make is that, as I have argued at greater length elsewhere (Hewlett 2003), stable and successful capitalism requires a certain depoliticisation of the people and that although this was slow to arrive in France, it was certainly in evidence by the mid-1980s. This is a depoliticization which, internationally, has been crucial to the neo-liberal era and which has characterized the capitalist system on a global level for several decades. In many liberal democracies indicators such as levels of abstention in elections and levels of party membership have been pointing very firmly in this direction, and France has on the whole been part of this trend. Despite the high level of participation in the Presidential elections of 2007, the general participatory direction in France has been has firmly downwards (Hewlett 2007; Subileau 2001) and in the parliamentary elections of 2007 there was an all-time low turnout. Thus the Sarkozy phenomenon, relying as it does in part on a certain portion of the electorate who will be drawn in by simplistic slogan-led responses (*rupture*, 'work more to earn more', and so on) to what are in fact highly complex problems is drawing on a low level of political engagement.

With this increasingly passive and depoliticised electorate and dumbing down of the way in which the political agendas are presented goes the rise of the political leader as celebrity, not unlike the film or rock star. Sarkozy, again in an exaggerated way compared with many other political leaders, seems to be emulating such stars with his *bling* fashion accessories, his lavish and ostentatious holidays, rich friends and his whirlwind romance followed by marriage to the singer Carla Bruni. But the relative normality of the Sarkozy presidency compared with other advanced capitalist societies is highlighted by more sober examination of what is sometimes termed presidentialism or presidentialisation, a phenomenon that has been increasingly prevalent for some years. Poguntke and Webb, for example, suggest in their 14-country study that 'democratic political systems are coming to operate according to an essentially presidential logic, irrespective of their formal constitutional make-up' and that presidentialisation is evident in increased autonomy and power for leaders in both governmental structures and political parties, not to mention election campaigns. This process, they argue, is explained in part by the internationalisation of political decision-making, the erosion of traditional political cleavages and the changing structure of mass communications (Poguntke and Webb 2005: 1). Taking the US as the most obvious example of this sort of arrangement, they conclude that 'modern democracies are moving towards a fusion of elitist and plebiscitary models of democracy, which offer a highly imperfect form of democratic accountability' (p. 142).

Of course the media plays an important role in this generalized trend, as indeed it did in the development of Sarkozy's career. With decreasing interest in politics on the part of ordinary people goes trivialization of the question of politics as expressed in the media. Preoccupation with politicians' personal lives becomes ever-more dominant and this in turn tends to reduce politics to a series of game-like contests between leaders, rather than a process for deciding how power is distributed in a more profound way (e.g. King 2002). In almost all advanced capitalist societies, then, the image of political leaders in the media is crucial, and teams specialising in marketing and public relations ever more important to the success or failure of a leader; the logic of this is to establish a direct bond between leader and electorate with a reduced need for the traditional intermediary of the political party, and a tendency to marginalize other intermediary elements, including parliament. Artufel and Duroux (2006) describe how the Sarkozy machine carefully controlled relations with the media, feeding almost endless sound bites and eye-catching headlines, creating photo-opportunities (such as Sarkozy in running shorts, on holiday and with his children) and generally courting sympathetic journalists. This could, of course, also be said of political contests in Britain, Italy, the US and many other countries, as it could be said of the Ségolène Royal campaign in 2007. (See also Vedel 2007).

Moreover, despite what I have been arguing regarding the Bonapartist characteristics of Nicolas Sarkozy, it is important to point out that in some important ways he is a textbook conservative career politician, and certainly far more so than were de Gaulle, Pétain, Napoléon III or Napoléon I. At the age of 28, in 1983, Sarkozy became mayor of one of the most wealthy areas in France, the Parisian suburban town Neuilly-sur-Seine, where he remained mayor until 2002. He served two stints as Minister of the Interior in governments presided over by Jacques Chirac (2002–04 and 2005–07) and in the mean time had a brief spell as Minister of Finance. He became leader of the Union pour un Mouvement Populaire in 2004 and oversaw its transformation into a party with a greatly increased membership and more activist orientation. Notwithstanding his promises of *rupture* if elected in 2007, and constant assertions that the French needed to move beyond the mixture of lethargy and crisis that characterized the Chirac era, he was himself very much part of that era and many changes during that period bore his imprint.

As we have seen, some of Sarkozy's major policy objectives as President have been designed to bring France – in particular the French economy and labour relations – in line with other countries which have more market-oriented economies. This mix of conventional conservative politician, Bonapartist populist and far-right-leaning strong man has prompted some analysts to argue that Sarkozy has managed to unite the three right-wing currents in France identified by René Rémond (1982), namely Bonapartist (mainly Gaullist), Orleanist (centre-right) and counter-revolutionary (extreme right), which had for many years been acting fairly separately (e.g. Dupin 2007; Rozès 2007). I believe there is some truth in this, given what I have said above, but his orientation is in fact more influenced by the Bonapartist tradition than by either of the other currents, and there is certainly still opposition to Sarkozy's politics from within the parliamentary right.

Ironically, given what I have discussed above in relation to depoliticisation, a key to the election success was to set about a certain 'modernization' and reassertion of the values of the right, or a reassertion of the importance of politics as opposed to managerial pragmatism. Sarkozy has spoken of the need for a 'droite décomplexée', meaning an unapologetically right-wing right. Part of this was his declared aim to rid France of its caution and 'political correctness' and its obsession (according to him) with the values born of May 1968. There was certainly a certain amount of vacuousness in all this, but beneath the rhetoric lay a determination to learn from the other modernizers in Western Europe, in particular Margaret Thatcher but also Tony Blair. So as far as economic policy is concerned, although Sarkozy's economic policy is still to some extent one of leading by example from the public sector, especially since the onset of the global financial crisis, he has gone out of his way to argue for the right of the private sector to make money and to encourage it to do so. Again, this approach reflects Sarkozy's own career and personal inclinations, which include an unashamed desire to enrich himself and move in monied circles. For example, he celebrated his election victory at the exclusive Parisian restaurant Fouquet's before setting off for a few days' holiday aboard billionaire friend Vincent Bolloré's yacht. Neither should we forget that Sarkozy's connections with people in high places include media moguls, in keeping with the Bonapartist tradition of strong influence over the views expressed by the mass media. Although the proposed media reforms largely failed, their intentions were certainly to increase governmental control over the media. (See Farbiaz and Mamère 2009)

Certainly, Sarkozy's emphasis on a new 'droite décomplexée' and all that went with it helped attract a large number of former Front national voters to his camp. Pierre Musso analyses the aggressive right-wing agenda and image of the French President in his book *Le Sarkoberlusconisme*, where he contends that there are many similarities between Sarkozy and the Italian Prime Minister Silvio Berlusconi, including the heroic new-man image, the promise to put the country back on its feet via a highly business-oriented economic programme and a political programme which confronts many supposed enemies, including the foreigner, communism and an over-powerful state (Musso 2008: 26). Sarkozy and the UMP were attempting to do – albeit far more rapidly – to the FN what Mitterrand had done to the PCF. Just as in the early 1970s Mitterrand stated publically that in his view out of five million Communist voters three million should be voting Socialist, in 2007 and before the elections Sarkozy declared:

> Yes, I want to attract Le Pen voters. Who could blame me for bringing these people back into the republican fold? I will even go and find them one by one – I don't mind that at all. The Front national made progress and that means we on the right did not do our job properly. (Fourquet 2007: 1)

In a highly revealing article by Jérôme Fourquet, we see that in the areas where Le Pen was strong in 2002, Sarkozy made real gains in 2007 over candidates of the mainstream right in 2002. The increases were particularly large in the Mediterranean departments and Sarkozy's highest score anywhere in France was in the Alpes-Maritimes, with 43.6% of votes. In a large-scale survey, Fourquet found that Sarkozy's tough reaction to clashes between youths and police at the Gare du Nord in Paris in March 2007 encouraged former Le Pen voters to vote Sarkozy instead of Le Pen, as did Sarkozy's more general positions on what might broadly be termed delinquency. Given the choice between various different aspects of his policies, they were particularly impressed by the President in waiting's views on law and order: Fourquet notes that a quarter of what he describes as the most faithful, 'hard core' FN supporters had even more faith in Sarkozy's views on the key theme of *sécurité* than in Le Pen's (Fourquet 2007: 5). To Marine Le Pen, it seemed that Sarkozy was indeed Le Pen-lite; as Sarkozy's victory was being announced on television, she commented: 'It's a victory for the ideas of Jean-Marie Le Pen', adding that the French 'preferred appearance of change to actual change' (in Forcari 2007). Certainly, Le Pen's age and uncertainty over who will take over as leader after him played a role in his and the FN's relative misfortunes, but there is little doubt that Sarkozy's part in Le Pen's fall was crucial.

Alain Badiou, a philosopher with an approach that is influenced by Maoism, has gone as far as suggesting in a highly controversial and provocative work that the key to understanding Sarkozy is to compare with Philippe Pétain and that the movement that brought Sarkozy to power has its unconscious roots in Pétainism, which is located between Bonapartism and fascism (Badiou 2008). In some respects Badiou's thesis is convincing, such as the way he reminds us that there are strong elements of Pétain's rallying cry of 'travail, famille, patrie' in Sarkozy's words and deeds, and Badiou suggests the theme of *rupture* is familiar as well, as is the highly police-oriented approach to governing, together with the notion of overcoming moral decline and scape-goating particular sections of the population. Pétainism should be understood, Badiou argues, as a phenomenon which pre-dates Pétain himself by many years and which in fact began with the restoration of the monarchy in 1815; in this current the role of negative propaganda as simplification of history and the need for simplistic response is always particularly important: negative propaganda for the restoration concentrated on the decapitation of the King, Pétain's propaganda on the Popular Front government of 1936 and Sarkozy's in 1968. Although Badiou's analysis is useful in the way in which it identifies certain similarities with the Pétainist right which are rarely pointed out, it underestimates the degree of defeat and/or capitulation for the labour movement and for the mainstream (socialist and communist) left that

Pétain's regime reflected. Whereas under Pétain these forces were either driven underground or capitulated, there is now a very active resistance to the Sarkozy reform movement. To an extent, then, it is a case of degree, but degree becomes particularly important in this comparison, and others have pointed out that full cooperation with the deportation of tens of thousands of Jews to Germany is, to say the least, a crucial difference between Pétain's regime and Sarkozy's. Moreover, Badiou's argument tends to under-emphasise the characteristics which Sarkozysm has in comment with other mainstream politics around the world.

The reassertion of the political during and after the election campaign was particularly effective because of the weakened state of the major left-wing parties in France. The Communist Party has of course been reduced to less than a shadow of its former self, particularly in national elections. The Parti socialiste's presidential candidate, Ségolène Royal certainly broke the PS mould to the extent that she was not an entrenched and long-running participant in the major power struggles within the party, or at least not as much as other key figures. Her views were eclectic and sometimes idiosyncratic, rather than rehearsing well-worn themes. She had quickly won a great deal of support for her nomination within the party, easily beating the other two contenders for presidential candidate nomination, Dominique Strauss-Kahn and Laurent Fabius. In terms of campaigning and policies, Royal's emphasis on the experience of ordinary people was on the whole popular and she spoke often of family values, discipline, authority and the protection of children. But her programme was perceived by many as being vague and short on detail, with far less talk or in-depth knowledge of international relations or economic policy than might be expected from a presidential candidate.

The PS has now had three defeats in a row in presidential elections, which has provoked further battles over ideological orientation, leadership and strategy. For example, should the party make a concerted attempt in the immediate future to open up to the centre? Should it, on the contrary, return to being a more militant, campaigning organisation with a stronger orientation towards the labour movement? Should the party firstly look to other forces with whom to ally, or get its own house in order before doing so? In short, the major opposition party is in disarray and this is of great benefit to Sarkozy.

Conclusions

I would suggest that the political situation in France is both volatile and complex and that the Sarkozy phenomenon is a somewhat bizarre manifestation of this. Sarkozy is in the Bonapartist tradition of auto-cratic, controlling and centralising populism, a phenomenon which reflects a certain crisis of democracy and is in part a reaction against the 'phony' political situation since the election of 2002, when the unpopular Jacques Chirac was elected against the deeply unpopular Jean-Marie Le Pen in the second round of the presidential elections. This Bonapartism has been a (only partially-successful) vehicle for the introduction of neo-liberal economic measures combined with an emphasis on law and order, facilitated by a crisis of democracy which is indeed international and not in the least unique to France. Sarkozy became deeply unpopular with the electorate some months after his election and was able to regain some popularity largely due to his actions on the international stage, as well as toning down some of the more farcical aspects of his private life. He also dropped some of the most bewildering proposals, including the highly controversial and almost certainly unworkable idea that every primary school child should 'adopt' a Jewish French child who had died in a German concentration camp during the Second World War.

I have argued, however, that both the style and detail of Sarkozy's election campaign and presidency to some extent reflect developments in many other advanced capitalist countries. Most fundamentally, there has been a decline in interest in politics in many countries and disillusionment with mainstream parties which increasingly resemble one another, reflected in part in decreasing participation in elections. This partially explains the way in which Sarkozy was able to capture the political high ground via superficial sloganising and celebrity-style campaigning. This itself was in harmony with the way in which other countries were witnessing an increasing personalization of politics where even in non-presidential systems elections are more and more conducted like contests between individuals and where the candidates enjoy celebrity status.

Another, paradoxical ingredient of Sarkozy's success is the conservative legitimacy he enjoys as a result of being a central part of the old order as presided by Chirac, paradoxical because of his insistence on the impor-tance of *rupture* with the past. He has, though, been able to operate a partial unification of what are often seen as the three different strands of the right, namely Bonapartist, **orleanism** and extreme right; although I have argued that the dominant influence on Sarkozy's politics is Bona-partism, his insistence on questions of law and order and tough attitudes towards immigration and illegal immigrants (*sans papiers*) – and in parti-cular the linking of the issues of law and order on the one hand and immi-gration on the other – have drawn many votes from former Front national voters. Next, the mainstream left opposition to Sarkozy, in the form of the Parti socialiste, is in a state of disarray into which it has been descending at least since the end of the Mitterrand era and arguably well before, given that the politics of left-oriented pragmatism conducted by the PS began in the early to mid-1980s. The Communist Party, meanwhile, is of course hugely weakened compared with even ten years ago. The reassertion of aggressive politics in this otherwise rather dull landscape, then, in the form of an unapologetically right-wing (and in some ways extreme right) platform and as a vehicle for many neo-liberal reforms, certainly contrasted strikingly with the lack-lustre politics of the PS and open squabbling between its factions, all of whose politics were variations on the theme of increasingly pragmatic and centre-oriented positions.

The global economic crisis has presented an additional layer of complexity in this already complex situation, particularly as many of Sarkozy's reforms were designed to deregulate aspects of the economy which were seen by much of the right as barriers to free enterprise. Given that unfettered free enterprise, particularly in the US and Britain (the general models of which Sarkozy is following), is now widely identified as a crucial part of the problem, Sarkozy is somewhat wrong-footed and, together with the lack of unity amongst the Socialists, this has given additional impetus to the already growing grass-roots movement against Sarkozy, in which the far left is playing an important part.

3
Social Policy and France's 'Exceptional' Social Model

Susan Milner

Introduction

Although France has many features in common with the continental welfare regime cluster to which it is held to belong, French academics in particular contest this positioning and tend to insist on the specificities of the 'French social model'. France stands out in European comparison as having relatively high levels of social expenditure and consequently a high tax take (taxes plus social contributions), as many countries have shifted away from social contributions as a means of financing welfare. France has maintained its high social contributions which are held by many to deter businesses from creating employment, although it has attempted to shift towards tax-funded benefits, especially family benefits. A further specificity is the horizontal redistribution on which the social protection system rests, with benefits and tax exemptions directed towards families with children rather than towards the childless poor. Finally, France is one of only a few European countries to have retained a pay-as-you-go pension system, in the name of intergenerational solidarity.

Under pressure (not least from the European Union) to reduce budget deficits, and in the context of concerns about an ever narrower band of wage-earners (therefore tax- and contribution-payers), recent governments have attempted to cut costs and shift sources of funding without fundamentally altering systemic features. However, successive reforms have eroded the social protection system. Hence, although in European comparison France may appear to represent the archetypal 'stalled society', reforms have taken place, albeit in a path-dependent way which limits the impact: reform at the margins. The 2007 election campaign saw more fundamental debates about the long-term sustainability of the system and the need for systemic reform, in particular with the introduction of new debates around welfare dependency.

The chapter begins by identifying and analysing these distinctive features of the French social model within a European comparative context. It goes on to discuss recent changes, focusing on two case studies: health policy and policy on pensions. In health policy, the Right has attempted to introduce a new discourse of making the patient responsible for expenditure, which could well entail systemic change as the reforms unfold. There have also been reforms to the pension system in order to relieve the pressure on the state budget, with a similar emphasis on individual contributions and actuarial principles, but the reforms have been presented as cost-containment measures rather than systemic change, accompanied by a discourse which stresses the need to reform in order to retain the basic principles of the pension system.

Basic features of the 'French social model'

The basis of the French social model was constructed in the immediate after-war period, then subsequently modified in phases (see e.g. Palier 2008). The four branches of the social security system were established in 1967. In the early 1970s, government sought to bring social partners (trade unions and the employers' associations) together in joint administration of parts of the system. A further phase, beginning in the 1980s, was characterised by attempts both to contain costs and to alleviate gaps in coverage as concerns over new forms of poverty emerged. It is based on the key value of solidarity but is not a universalistic system; the key solidarities are those between generations (the pay-as-you-go pension system) and between non-parents and parents (pro-natalist family policy) rather than between income groups.

With reference to Gøsta Esping-Andersen's (1990) classic welfare state typology, France falls squarely in the 'continental' or 'conservative' model. It relies on full-time work and on social insurance contributions rather than general taxation; benefits tend to be relatively generous, although conditional on labour market position; the French social model tends to penalise labour market outsiders (labour market entrants, notably the young, and the unemployed) and its labour market is therefore relatively rigid. It has a rather idiosyncratic system, developed over several decades, of management of its social insurance funds, involving complex forms of bargaining between social partners but where, crucially, the state remains the key actor. Despite its complexities and idiosyncrasies, the model is nevertheless broadly consistent with the continental model.

However there are some notable exceptions to the model: in particular, France mobilises women in the labour market to a much greater extent than the classic conservative model; it is arguably characterised by the 'social wage', that is, social insurance not only covers social risk of contributing groups but has wider redistributive features in line with the ideal of solidarity (Friot 2004). This feature makes the system more solidaristic than the continental model's social insurance principles, which are based on a relationship between individual contributions and individual entitlement. Moreover the French model is complemented by newer additions since the late 1980s which introduced minimum income elements: principally the *Revenu Minimum d'Insertion*, which later became *Revenu Minimum d'Activité* in order to reinforce the work requirements. The introduction of minimum income guarantees reduced the number of holes in the social safety net, although some still remain, in particular for younger unemployed, since the RMA is available only to those aged 25 or over.

Many French scholars reject the Esping-Andersen classification and prefer to see France's welfare model as exceptional, having developed in specific historical-political circumstances and to respond to specific socio-demographic and political concerns. They argue that Esping-Andersen's clustering of welfare states does not adequately capture the rather different relationships between market and state that the continental model (the most diverse and catch-all of the three) covers. Rather than outputs, these scholars tend to emphasise the broad principles and discourses underpinning the system.

As Bruno Palier and Laura Petrescu (2007: 61–2) argue, the French version of welfare exceptionalism is based on the conviction that the French model does not fit the Bismarckian/conservative ideal type, but rather represents a unique version of universalism based on solidarity, despite the obvious gaps in provision. The gap between the French ideal of solidarity and the reality of an insider-outsider labour market means that debates are clouded in ambiguity and that veto players tend to resist any reform. Defensiveness is a key feature of attitudes to reform which is perceived as coming from the outside and threatening the integrity of the French system of social protection, resulting on 'social model anxiety' (Ross 2006).

As welfare reform has become a key variable of macroeconomic performance for policy-makers, the continental model is seen as particularly in need of reform because it appears most at odds with the activation model which has become the dominant paradigm. The activation model sees participation in the labour market as the primary means of alleviating poverty and reducing social exclusion; it therefore seeks to incentivise work and to penalise non-participation in the labour market. But at the same time the continental model is particularly difficult to reform because it has developed as a response to certain social groups which have vested interests and will therefore resist reform. Systemic reform is in any case difficult because the societal consensus which underpinned the original development of welfare states may still prevail, and even if it has broken down there is no guarantee that it can be replaced by an alternative societal consensus. These broad observations apply to France as well as to other continental welfare states. Whether France retains its exceptional features depends ultimately on domestic political circumstances and the mobilisation capacity of domestic actors.

France and the European policy environment

Social and employment policy is the 'Cinderella' of EU policy-making: a deliberately hybrid policy area with weak legitimacy, subordinate to broader macroeconomic policy. In its most recent form – the Lisbon strategy aimed at making European economies employment-rich and knowledge-rich – it is strongly normative, promoting the activation model, but it lacks the legislative instruments to make its recommendations binding. Through the Open Method of Coordination (OMC), targets are set and then applied across member states; performance is monitored and recommendations are issued to individual member states. But the OMC is not binding in the sense of legislative instruments (directives or regulations).

Countries which do not fit the model are regularly held up as examples of bad behaviour (especially contrasted with models of good practice elsewhere); indeed, from a European perspective, France came in the first half of the 2000s to be singled out as a 'laggard' or a prime example of a 'blocked society' in which the insider labour market locks out the possibility of reform (Giddens 2007: 34–7). In recent years, it has improved its performance: for example, in the annual scorecard published by the Brussels-based think-tank the Center for European Reform, which measures member states' progress on the Lisbon targets, France has moved from being a 'laggard' to a more respectable ninth place in 2008 (up from eleventh place in 2006). However, it still fails to meet the Lisbon targets on the main employment indicators (see Tables 3.1–3.4).

However, the EU cannot enforce its recommendations. Pressure comes from the annual reporting process and benchmarking against commonly-

Table 3.1 Employment rate (% aged 15–64 years) (EU target = 70%)

	1996	1998	2000	2002	2004	2006
France	59.5	60.2	62.1	63.0	63.1	63.0
EU15	60.3	61.4	63.4	64.2	64.7	66.0

Source: EU 2007: tables p. 4, p. 14 (Eurostat data).

Table 3.2 Youth employment rate (% aged 15–24)

	1996	1998	2000	2002	2004	2006
France	28.1	28.4	31.9	33.6	34.0	33.3
EU15	36.9	38.2	40.5	40.6	40.0	40.1

Source: EU 2007: tables p. 4, p. 14 (Eurostat data).

Table 3.3 Older workers' employment rate (% aged 55–64) (EU target = 50%)

	1996	1998	2000	2002	2004	2006
France	29.4	28.3	29.9	34.7	37.3	37.6
EU15	36.3	36.6	37.8	40.2	42.5	45.3

Source: EU 2007: tables p. 4, p. 14 (Eurostat data).

Table 3.4 Female employment rate (% aged 15–64) (EU target = 60%)

	1996	1998	2000	2002	2004	2006
France	52.2	53.1	55.2	56.7	57.4	57.7
EU15	50.2	51.6	54.1	55.6	56.8	58.4

Source: EU 2007: tables p. 4, p. 14 (Eurostat data).

agreed targets and against identified national 'best practice', as well as scorecards and recommendations. Europeanisation is thus normative and ideational rather than directive in its impact on policy design and practice. Comparisons between member states indicate that national governments tend to treat European policy as an 'à la carte' menu, selecting and highlighting those aspects which most closely fit their own policy priorities (Büchs 2007; Kvist and Saari 2007).

On the other hand, the European policy environment can act as a resource for those within the French policy-making system who want to see reform. The main protagonists for reform are the big business lobby (whether directly and openly in the Mouvement des Entreprises de France, the main employers' association, in their consultative role in parliamentary committees and reports or behind the scenes in more informal relations with politicians) and politicians and policy-makers. Consequently, European social and particularly employment policy provide a 'leverage effect' (Erhel *et al* 2005). The ideational convergence encouraged by the EU gives domestic actors powerful resources which contribute to new analyses of the French welfare state (Palier 2006). In addition, of course, the European policy environment provides a space for mutual learning and more informal policy transfer.

Pressures for reform also come indirectly but strongly from macro-economic policy which since the Treaty on European Union has acted as a powerful curb on welfare spending (Milner 2005; Palier 2006), coupled with internal pressures to cut costs (increased health costs due to increased longevity and treatment of new or hitherto untreatable diseases; rising expectations in healthcare; worries about territorial and socio-economic inequalities in healthcare; demographic change and fears about dependency ratios; employers' refusal to countenance increased social contributions and arguments about the employment disincentives created by dependence on payroll taxes).

In these latter two respects, 'Europeanisation' pressures on policy-making resemble 'globalisation' pressures in the sense that globalisation creates a normative and ideational framework for productivist rather than welfarist social policies. On the first point, there is no international policy framework to match the EU's, but the OECD's normative pressures through the publication of reports and organisation of international policy conferences not only mirror but influence the EU's ideational output. The EU's normative framework appears stronger than the OECD's according to international comparisons (see Armingeon 2006), due to the specific mechanisms of the OMC, even if the convergence pressures are strongly mitigated by national path dependency.

In such a policy environment, it is difficult for countries to remain 'exceptional'. Whether they do or not depends on two key factors: first, the 'stickiness' of existing institutions (how entrenched are they either in other sets of institutions or in societal values?); second, the strength of veto actors and their resources within the domestic political system, which is also contingent on electoral and other political circumstances. Where both factors apply (institutions are sticky and veto actors strong), reform (erosion of exceptionalism) is dependent on exceptional circumstances, notably external economic shocks or possibly internal political factors such as charismatic leadership.

Instead, in the French context, it will be argued here that France has sought to reform or adapt in a controlled way using the external (particularly European) environment as a motive for reform. At times of course this strategy has backfired (e.g. in 1997 or in 2005), especially as it increases the perceived gap between policy and rhetoric, between France's self-image and its external reputation. Overall, this means that France has aligned itself more closely with its European neighbours and begun to be seen as less 'exceptional'.

As a result, change is not systemic but path-dependent. It may also be segmented, as reforming governments attempt to take on potential veto actors one by one rather than all at the same time. On the other hand, it does not mean that change is simply cosmetic or tinkering at the margins. On the contrary, it is possible to observe a slow erosion of the basis of the French social model over time, with effects which may be beneficial in the short term (reduction of budget deficits) but could be detrimental in the longer term (increased social inequalities, stronger polarisation of social values and social outcomes).

Hence, most commentators writing about the direction of social and employment policy in France emphasise significant change within boundaries set by existing institutions, actor preferences and cultural values, in line with institutionalist frameworks and particularly work on 'the new politics of welfare' (Pierson, 2001) and with empirical analyses (Starke *et al*, 2008) which confirm the idea of very limited, bounded convergence (Vail, 2008). Reforms are negotiated with the social partners, and based on a *quid pro quo* whereby government and social partners negotiate a shift from social contributions to general taxation in funding (see Table 3.5), and a shift away from social partners to the state (government, parliament, and decentralised authorities and agencies). In this process, the basic logic of social insurance is maintained even as its funding role becomes less important in relation to other private and particularly public sources of finance; and the social partners retain a role and stake in the system (Palier 2006). Reform can thus be paradigmatic without necessarily being systemic. These points will now be illustrated with reference to healthcare, pensions and family policy.

Health policy

France has arguably one of the best healthcare system in the world. Since the introduction in 2000 of Universal Healthcare Coverage (*Couverture Maladie Universelle* or CMU), which extended cover to the remaining

1 per cent of the population uninsured and brought in a supplementary scheme for the lowest income group, it is universal. It was ranked top in the world by a World Health Organisation (WHO) report in 2002, and remains high in international rankings. Benchmarked against the best-performing European countries,[1] France spent the third highest amount on health as a proportion of gross domestic product (GDP) in 2002 (after Germany and Switzerland) and the third highest amount of public expenditure, after Greece and Switzerland (WHO 2006: 31; see also the OECD comparisons in Table 3.5). In an ideal Europe, Anthony Giddens (2007: 28) argues, we would have French levels of healthcare.

Citizens' satisfaction levels are high, especially as patients retain an exceptionally high degree of choice over their healthcare provider. There is little or no sense in public opinion that healthcare is 'rationed', particularly as recent reforms have limited reimbursement for short-term illnesses whilst retaining a high level of coverage of expenses for more serious, long-term illnesses and conditions. In contrast, the US healthcare system is more expensive but has much less egalitarian outcomes and – along with the other English-speaking countries, that is Australia, New Zealand, Canada and the United Kingdom (see Blendon *et al* 2002) – registers much lower levels of public satisfaction (Rodwin 2003).

The main problem is that this rather enviable exceptionalism is, of course, very costly to maintain, and France finds itself under continued pressure from the EU to curb its spending appetite (it regularly exceeds its budget deficit and debt limits under the Stability and Growth Pact). The healthcare deficit currently stands at an estimated 4.1 billion, following record deficits in 2003 and 2003 (largely in excess of ten billion euros) which prompted the government to introduce two successive cost-cutting plans. The opportunity for increasing revenue is limited by the impact of raising payroll contributions (only a very partial and

Table 3.5 **Taxation and social insurance contributions as a percentage of GDP**

Year	Social contributions (% GDP)		Total taxation (% GDP)		Social contributions as % of total taxation	
	France	OECD mean	France	OECD mean	France	OECD mean
1980	17.2	8.0	40.2	33.3	42.8	24.6
2004	16.1	9.4	43.4	37.3	37.1	25.2

Source: Starke *et al* 2008: pp. 989–90 (OECD data).

temporary solution at best) and by the state's ability to pay out of general taxation. With a series of right-wing governments committed to tax cuts, increasing revenue is effectively ruled out.

France's health system is based on a national social insurance scheme covering the employed, self-employed and farmers and their families, which is flanked by employment-based supplementary insurance schemes controlled by the social partners (MEDEF and the main trade union confederations) and to a lesser extent by private voluntary supplementary pension schemes. In recent years, as we will see, the state has attempted through its reforms to gain more control over funding, allocation and management. The system's institutional complexity means there is a lack of coherence and leads to tensions between the state, the health insurance funds managed by social partners, and medical services providers (Sandier *et al* 2004; WHO 2005). Moreover, the existence of several rival trade unions encourages conflictual rather than consensual behaviour, particularly as these unions compete for employee votes in workplace elections, as well as for members, and therefore have incentives to differentiate their positions in relation to employers (Hassenteufel and Palier 2005). Cost-containment is constrained by the government's relationship with the medical establishment and pharmaceutical companies. Previous attempts by governments of both the Right and the Left to encourage doctors to prescribe less or to prescribe cheaper drugs had little success, establishing a path-dependent effect discouraging governments from confrontation with this powerful veto group.

Moreover, healthcare is a universally sensitive issue in public opinion, even more so at a time when individual purchasing power (and therefore sensitivity to increased individual contribution and state retreat) dominates public attitudes and government responses. High levels of satisfaction with existing provision mean public resistance to change; hence, reform proposals need to be legitimated with reference to systemic and societal values (notably the central value of solidarity, and also equality between socio-economic groups), over and above concerns with efficiency and sustainability.

This leaves a choice between a strategy of systemic change (wholesale recommodification of healthcare, that is, a shift from state to market provision) or of a compromise between cost-containment and cost-cutting with partial or segmented recommodification as the most likely outcome. Reform is piecemeal and there is a gap between policy discourse and resultant policies; discourse is purposive and seeks to legitimate reform and to increase the room for manoeuvre, by highlighting a sense of crisis and urgency.

The current proposals on healthcare illustrate these points rather neatly. The overall thrust of the report and proposals announced on 24 June 2008 is to contain costs, but the implementation of the proposals is left to the social partners. The government sought to push the social partners into increasing the input of complementary insurance funds (a form of recommodification, but a very particular kind, since the funds are still collectively managed) by threatening more wholesale state retreat. It also aimed to obtain some limited cost containment by urging medical practitioners and drug companies to address the risks involved in failure to manage costs (such as systemic breakdown, medical risks due to individual inability to pay, etc.), although with little hope of major change in this area. Again, reform is justified by the argument that it is necessary to preserve the system, and the objective of a reduction of social inequalities is also deployed in policy discourse to legitimate change. The process itself was remarkably rapid, in order to minimise exposure to veto actors. But the impact of reform is likely to be limited by the lack of penalty for non-compliance by practitioners, and its implementation will crucially depend on the determination of the employers' lobby to cut costs.

A similar logic may be seen in health minister Roselyne Bachelot's proposals for hospital reform, announced in 2008 following her well-publicised suggestions that the management of the entire system should be overhauled. Public hospitals account for half of the health budget and the majority of hospitals are in deficit. The 2008 proposals strengthen budgetary control indirectly rather than directly, by grouping hospitals together at regional level (thus allowing for some rationalisation of provision in the longer term, although the plans are implicit at this stage) and by increasing hospital managers' control of expenditure and making them more accountable for deficits. The reforms immediately encountered resistance by hospital professionals, with strikes and protests in many hospitals, and petitions and media lobbying by top surgeons.

When considered overall, the thrust of reforms has been to encourage a dualisation of the healthcare system (Palier 2006, 2008), with three main innovations which erode the social insurance principles of health policy. First, the universalisation of healthcare, whilst contributing to rising costs, may also be seen as part of a broader shift, more visible in labour market policy, away from passive to active policies aimed at integrating the unemployed into paid employment. In this context, the introduction of the CMU in 2000 must also be viewed alongside the introduction (by the centre-left coalition) then strengthening (by the centre-right) of labour market integration measures in the (*Revenu Minimum d'Insertion*, renamed *Revenu Minimum d'Activité*); by the introduction under centre-left governments of a tax measure to incentivise low-paid work by topping up benefits (*Prime pour l'Emploi*, PPE) and of job-search requirements (*Plan d'Action de Retour à l'Emploi*, PARE, or Action Plan for Return to Employment) for recipients of unemployment benefit, previously seen as an insurance right drawn from earlier contributions.

Second, and more importantly, the General Social Contribution (*Cotisation Sociale Généralisée*, CSG) marks a new mode of funding based on general taxation rather than social insurance. A flat-rate tax introduced by the left at a rate of 1.1% of all income (including investment income), it was raised by the centre-right government in 1993 and in 1995. In 1998, under the centre-left, the rate was increased again, to 7.5% of all incomes, replacing the bulk of employee health insurance contributions, and now provides around 35% of all healthcare resources (Palier 2006: 122). It is now the biggest direct tax in France (where income tax or *l'impôt sur le revenu* represents a relatively small share of taxation) and contributes around 18% of social protection revenue. A smaller, similar tax (*Contribution de remboursement de la dette sociale*, at a rate of 0.5% of incomes) was introduced as part of prime minister Alain Juppé's healthcare plan in 1996; initially a temporary measure to help cover the healthcare budget deficit, it was programmed to last until 2014 but will continue to be levied as long as the healthcare branch of social security remains in deficit.

Third, power has been redistributed from the social partners to the state. Juppé's 1996 health plan was highly significant in this respect, accompanied as it was by a constitutional amendment obliging parliament to approve the social security budget as part of the annual budget round. By concentrating on bargaining on unemployment and complementary pensions, the MEDEF not only freed up space for the state to focus on health, statutory pensions and family benefits (Palier 2006), but also helped the state to draw the line between social insurance and general taxation, in favour of the latter.

In addition, governments since the 1990s, particularly those on the right, have sought to make the system more coherent by introducing wholesale reforms or healthcare 'reform plans' (WHO 2005). In this they have undoubtedly benefited from their closeness to the employers lobby, which at the end of the 1990s adopted an unambiguous and coherent strategy of welfare state reform and used both bargaining with trade unions at national level and its place within the management of the social protection system in order to further its objectives of cost-cutting and encouraging a shift away from social contributions to general taxation and to private provision. This overlapping of political agendas may be seen as giving right-wing governments confidence to intervene more boldly than the incrementalism of the past. Alain Juppé's 1996 healthcare plan brought about a 'profound reorganization' of the healthcare system (Sandier *et al* 2004: 121), its mode of adoption – by ordinances rather than by law – indicating strong political will. More recently, the March 2003 healthcare law set out a comprehensive framework for policy, based on a strategic plan for the various sectors of provision, together with objectives and targets (WHO 2005). It was followed by the 2004 plan which raised employer healthcare contributions, but also sought to tackle systemic inefficiencies by discouraging multiple visits and 'shopping around' (through the introduction of a charge of one euro per visit to physicians and the improvement of computerised patient records) and reducing waste of pharmaceuticals, notably by reducing reimbursement and encouraging physicians to prescribe more parsimoniously.

Moreover in this process of reform, governments have strenuously sought to reform in a directive fashion rather than working through negotiations with social partners and particularly the health unions, in line with the institutional logic of the Juppé plan. In this they have learned from the lessons of past reform based on negotiation. Although the direction and nature of reform mean that France has moved away from the social insurance logic of the continental model, reform does not therefore simply mean convergence with a broader European or 'Anglo-Saxon' (liberal) model; if anything, it reinforces France's exceptionalism in strengthening the role of the technocratic elite within the state (Hassenteufel and Palier 2005) and the role of the central state (government and civil service) as an agent of both policy delivery and policy reform.

Pension policy

As with healthcare, the pension system established in 1945 was clearly based on the logic of social insurance, rooted in work and financed by contributions from employers and employees. It comprises a general regime which provides for the basic statutory pension based on defined benefits (up to 50 per cent of a reference wage) and a second tier of complementary pensions according to occupational sector based on defined contributions. The social partners administer the complementary pensions schemes independently of the state, and also co-manage the statutory pensions funds at national level (Mandin and Palier 2005).

Pension reform is an area where France is deemed by its EU counterparts to have acted rather slowly, but to have caught up to some extent, particularly since 2003. From the 1980s, governments identified long-term financial sustainability as a major concern. Along with other mature welfare states, France faces the funding consequences of an ageing population: the number of people aged 65 or older is expected to grow from around 16 per cent of the population in 2003 to 24 per cent in 2030 (OECD 2005). Thanks partly to its excellent healthcare, France enjoys high life expectancy, even in relation to its wealthy European neighbours; but this in turn places greater pressures on the healthcare system which needs to shift towards (expensive) geriatric care, management of chronic diseases and long-term care (Sandier *et al* 2004). Although the trend towards an ageing population is offset to some extent by France's exceptionalism in increasing its birthrate (whereas the birthrate of its European neighbours is stable or declining), the worsening age dependency ratio puts strain on funding of pensions, particularly as France has a mature pay-as-you-go system. In terms of expenditure, France's pattern mirrors that for healthcare, spending less as a proportion of GDP (10.48 per cent) than Germany (11.29 per cent), but significantly more than the US (5.47 per cent) or the UK (5.47 per cent) (OECD 2008a).

In pay-as-you-go (PAYGO) systems, pensions are paid out of current tax or contributions revenues rather than accumulated funds. Mature welfare states are seen as severely constrained by existing institutions and reform tends therefore to be piecemeal and incremental (Pierson 2001). In line with this analysis, mature continental welfare states display a remarkable degree of consistency and continuity in the recent period despite internal reforms (Tepe 2006). France conforms broadly to this pattern. However, it deviated from the pattern in 1995, suggesting both broad path dependence and the possibility of decisive change at particular moments due to political will.

Reforms have been adopted which may be considered systemic in the sense that they undermine fundamental principles of the existing system and the key Mitterrand reform of the right to retirement at age 60. The broader principles of social solidarity have been undermined by an emphasis on actuarial principles, that is, the idea that benefits must be based on the amount of money collected rather than an absolute entitlement, and they must be linked to individuals' contributions record. Replacement rates have decreased and, whereas they exceeded the OECD mean in 1980, by 2002 they stood below it (Starke *et al* 2008). Reformers were able to overcome veto points in order to carry out these reforms, largely because of active attempts by governments of both right and left to influence public opinion, notably in a series of official reports which presented the demographic challenge in terms of urgency (Mandin and Palier 2005).

On the other hand, the reforms fall short of systemic change in that they retain the institutional features of the old system, they have barely addressed let alone managed the shift to private provision (hence increasing social risk for the most vulnerable groups). The overall impact is limited by cohort-specific implementation. Moreover, the process of reform is dependent on the action of 'social partners' (employers' organisations and trade unions) to reach agreement on the reform of other parts of the system, such as complementary insurance scheme. This gives an opportunity for trade unions and other actors to delay, thwart or change the direction of reform, particularly if they can mobilise support through protest actions or other means (for example, media interventions) of influencing public opinion. For these reasons, recent reforms have been described as 'half-baked' and having more symbolic than effective value (Hassenteufel 2008: 242). Rather than breaking the link between contributions and benefits, reforms have sought to reinforce the idea that benefits need to be linked more closely to individual contributions. The discourse of reform is presented as a means of saving the PAYGO system rather than replacing it (Milner 2005).

The 1993 Balladur reform, capitalising on the reports which had prepared public opinion for change, represented a key milestone in the reform process (see Levy 2001). It introduced a new formula for calculating pension benefits, applicable to private-sector workers, based on 25 rather than the ten best years of salary, and to qualify for the full pension employees need to have contributed for 40 rather than 37.3 years; pensions were linked to prices rather than wages. By increasing the length of the qualifying period, the reform discouraged early retirement, which had become a feature of the French labour market from the 1980s as successive governments sought to reduce youth unemployment by incentivising early labour market exit. By extending the period for calculation of benefits, the government decreased the replacement rate. The 2003 Fillon reform applied the changes to public sector workers, as Alain Juppé had tried unsuccessfully to do in 1995. Followed shortly afterwards by proposals to restrict early retirement and to incentivise work for the over-50s (see Milner 2007), the changes introduced in 2003 represented a 'decisive step' in pension reform (OECD 2005).

In 1995, the unions were able to mobilise mass protests against an unpopular prime minister whose reforms were dressed in a discourse of austerity and sacrifice; but by 2003 the path to reform had been paved by further reports warning of a demographic crisis (notably the Charpin and Teulade reports of 1999, commissioned by Lionel Jospin). In 2003, the asymmetric membership of trade unions (heavily skewed towards the public sector, with 'deserts' in the private sector) allowed the government to divide private versus public sector workers. When it came to tackling the powerful public sector unions, the new right-wing government was able to turn public sympathy against them: not only did the government focus attention on the impact of strikes on public service users (hence the importance of the 'minimum service' requirements which became the first reform of the Sarkozy presidency) but it also highlighted inequality of treatment between public and private sector workers and thus fed a long-standing public debate about the 'privileges' of public sector workers.

Crucially, trade union division played a part in both the 1993 and 2003 reforms. The CFDT (Confédération Française Démocratique du Travail, which went on to support the Juppé healthcare reforms in 1996, causing a bitter internal split) was persuaded in 1993 to accept the change in the calculations formula and took part in negotiations to set up the new national pensions fund (Fonds National de Vieillesse). In 2003, the last-minute change of heart by the CFDT's leadership allowed the government to announce its reform proposals, jeopardising the cautious moves which had meanwhile been made by other parts of the leadership towards a united union front, including with the other major confederation the Confédération Générale du Travail (CGT). The CGT then refused to take part in the pensions negotiations and tried to organise protests against the reforms, but its failure to build a mass movement against the reforms led to grassroots disillusionment which dissipated only with the campaign against proposals for a new youth employment contract in 2006, orchestrated not by the unions but by students' organisations. Pension reform therefore needs to be seen in the light of the MEDEF's campaign since 1999 to 'refound' all aspects of the relationship between state, business and trade unions (see Milner 2007).

The dualisation identified by Bruno Palier for healthcare policy also applies to pension reform. Whilst private pension funds remain relatively marginal in France, private savings have been encouraged by incentives introduced by governments of both the right and left, and by concerted attempts to influence public opinion by lobbying about the need to protect French business against predatory foreign pension funds, especially by the insurance groups which are influential in the employers' association MEDEF and in policy circles.

Conclusion

France presents a particularly interesting case in the debate between proponents of convergence and exceptionalism. Due to a series of far-reaching reforms which change the relationship between work and welfare, France is losing much of its exceptionalism and appears to be moving closer to a broadly defined European model. The European policy process offers a policy menu from which France has been able to draw in order to legitimate its own reforms; as a result, alignment is apparent at least at the level of ideas and broad policy direction, and although France still presents marked differences in terms of the EU's own performance-related measures (such as employment rates) it has moved closer both to actual European averages and to reform targets. On the other hand, several important aspects of the reform process and its outcomes suggest the persistence of elements of exceptionalism. In terms of social expenditure and configurations of expenditure, France continues to stand out as possessing a distinctive pattern of spending and redistribution, along with other continental welfare states. At the very least, the reform process itself is path-dependent in that it depends on mediating institutions which are rooted in the domestic social contract and cultural values which help to determine the strength of potential resistance and veto points.

The central state – and in particular government – has been the key actor in the reform process. In the case of healthcare, and more generally in the shift away from social insurance to general taxation in the funding of social expenditure, the state has significantly increased its powers in relation to non-state actors (employers' organisations and trade unions or other employment-based actors). In this sense, as we have seen, France appears not to follow the 'governance' template which characterises European-style convergence. However, due to entrenched institutions and the potential strength of veto players, social dialogue with institutionalised interests remains important both as a tool and a constraint in the policy process (Milner 2005, 2007; Vail 2008). French exceptionalism is in this respect highly ambiguous.

The reform process is thus complex, path-dependent and sometimes pragmatically responds to opportunities which arise domestically and externally. Moreover, discourses of change and reform are polysemic and subject to use for political ends (Milner 2005; Palier 2006). The European policy level has allowed political leaders to develop a 'double discourse of protection and reform' which is particularly evident in social and employment policy (Milner 2005: 107), whereby reform is explicitly presented as necessary in order to protect the existing system based on institutional specificities which are the product of historical settlements. The idea that preservation necessitates change is widely used in social policy in France, but is most visible in policy discourses around pension reform. As a result, assessing the real extent of change is sometimes a matter of perspective: positional (external or internal), chronological and ideological.

Rather than viewing France as an example of a stalled or blocked society, it is possible to interpret French exceptionalism more positively. Seen in this light, France may well appear to be finding its way towards its own version of social solidarities today, whether by accident or design. For example, the highly influential economic organisation the OECD in a series of reports has highlighted the societal choices which appear to characterise France: it works shorter hours than other western nations averaged out over the year and over the lifecourse; it is relatively egalitarian in its values and outcomes, and in 2008 is the western nation which has done the most to stem the rise of social inequality (OECD 2008b). Specific policy measures have helped to reduce working time (most recently, the Aubry laws on the 35-hour week) and social inequality (most notably, France's minimum wage, which is regularly raised in relation to prices and which is also periodically increased for political reasons, as well as extensive welfare benefits for the unemployed and those on very low incomes). However, social outcomes may be due more to unintended outcomes of the reform process than to the design of specific policies. Incrementalism in reform – encouraged by institutional complexity – can help to preserve the most socially acceptable and culturally rooted elements of the existing system by widening debate and by allowing veto players to build public support and tactical alliances.

Note

1 The WHO benchmarks countries against a selected group of states with similar outcomes on indicators such as general mortality rates and child mortality rates. In this case France sits in the best-performing group for Europe (EURA).

4
'L'exception culturelle'

Hugh Dauncey

Introduction

In what ways can France be considered 'different' in terms of its approach to 'culture'? Apart from the pervasive and – to the French at least, attractive – idea that French culture is somehow inherently 'superior', perceptions within France have traditionally been – at least during the Fifth Republic – that French culture is different to that of, say 'Anglo-Saxon' countries, by virtue of its privileged relationship with a voluntarist and culturally interventionist State, which promotes and encourages culture. The reverse view, from more 'liberal' countries, is that French culture is 'protected', 'subsidised' and manipulated by government. In terms of 'popular music' for example, the perception amongst French commentators has generally been that whereas creativity in France is both encouraged and constrained by public cultural policies, in the UK, the 'Britpop' phenomenon is a pure product of the free-market, although recent comparative research on music in France and the UK (Dauncey and Le Guern 2008) suggests that as British governments have recently become increasingly interested in the earning power of the 'cultural industries', the interventionist/protectionist versus free-market/laissez-faire framework for understanding France's 'difference' in approach to culture is being undermined by developments outside France, as much as by any changes in French policies.

During what might be described as the heyday of France's contemporary relationship with its culture and cultural policies – the early Fifth Republic until the early 1980s – the 'French exception' in culture was indeed defined by its central features of a strong Jacobin, centralist state, a society divided between left and right in which resolution of conflicts was difficult, but within which the Republican model recognised individuals rather than communities or other groupings, and a political, cultural and social tradition inherited from the Enlightenment and the French Revolution which gave France a belief in its 'universalist' message for the world. These features coalesced during the 1960s under successive Gaullist governments to produce 'cultural policy' which stressed democratisation of 'high' culture to the masses and celebration of French cultural achievements in high culture as part of the 'rayonnement' of French values (Cabanne 1981; Caron 1989; Fumaroli 1991). The cultural policy of de Gaulle and Malraux was inflected somewhat during the 1970s, when the aftermath of May '68 and new social and cultural aspirations came to the fore, loosening the definition of 'culture' to include varieties of 'popular' culture as well as traditional forms, and after the election of François Mitterrand in 1981, significant developments occurred as the new Ministry of Culture under Jack Lang worked to interpret 'French culture' in the widest sense, and thus to find cultural strengths and successes to celebrate in domains as wide-ranging as cuisine, circus arts and popular music (Rigby 1991). Increasingly, concepts of 'le tout-culturel' linked culture and commerce in the general defence of France's 'exceptional' role to play in the international system and in the protection of the French language and of French 'cultural industries' whose survival was increasingly threatened by global English and by the Americanisation (or globalisation) of culture.

The ideas of the 'French exception' and of 'l'exception culturelle' are of course closely related, as in many ways, the notion of a special approach to and treatment of 'culture' is based on and within the traditional framework of thinking on how France differs from other Western European democracies. Increasingly, in terms of French culture, France's 'difference' is perceived with apprehension, with fears that French civilisation is under attack, besieged linguistically by global English and culturally by worldwide free trade in cultural products and services. The need for French culture to be protected by an exceptional status in commerce came to the fore during the Uruguay Round of multilateral trade negotiations between 1987 and 1993, as France battled for exemptions for cinema and audiovisual industries, and in 1994, in a well-known example of 'protectionism', the French state legislated to protect French and the French music industry by imposing a quota of French-language songs on radio play-lists (Hare 2003).

This short consideration of these themes focuses on four 'case-studies' – diverse but complementary – of France's approach to the encouragement and government of culture. Firstly, we examine the key concept of 'diversité culturelle', as it has evolved over recent years since the Uruguay

Round. Secondly, we consider the debate triggered by Jean-Marie Messier, when, as head of Vivendi-Universal in 2001, he declared the death of France's 'exception culturelle'. Thirdly, we study how the French state has recently moved to support the national videogames industry. Lastly, we will discuss the problems which arose during the mid-2000s around the 'special' position of culture embodied in the peculiar – and specific to France – employment status of 'les intermittents du spectacle'.

Cultural 'exception' or cultural 'diversity'?

Official discourses and academic studies of French cultural policy have, since the 1990s and particularly in the new millennium, become interested in the semantic differences between 'exception' and 'diversity' (Creton *et al* 2005; Mattelart 2007). The original terms in which French mistrust of free trade in cultural goods and services was couched during the Uruguay Round and afterwards – which implied a desire in France and Europe almost to be 'excused' from normal rules – soon came to be seen as disserving wider cultural and political ambitions of policy. It was thus that the more semantically neutral vocabulary of 'diversité culturelle' began to be employed. Under Chirac, and also, so far, under Sarkozy, France has continued to espouse the rhetoric of a 'different' approach to culture.

Whereas the traditional contemporary discourses of 'exception culturelle' which had evolved during the late 1980s and early 1990s emphasised – negatively – the need and desire of French culture to 'protect' itself from Americanising and globalising forces of international trade, 'diversité culturelle' arguably refocuses the debate towards a more positive interpretation of the role of cultural policy. Official statements on cultural policy now explicitly state that its objectives are to protect France's national cultural heritage and to democratise access to it, and, within the encouragement of artistic creativity, to foster cultural diversity. Although the idea of 'cultural diversity' was the subject of debate during previous decades at Unesco, it was during the late 1990s, that, with active French support, the concept was developed. Notably, in June 1999, the Unesco conference organised in collaboration with the French and Canadian governments on 'La culture: une marchandise pas comme les autres?' prepared the way for what became, in November 2001, the *Unesco Universal Declaration on Cultural Diversity* (Unesco 2001). This stated clearly that cultural goods and services should be treated differently, that nation-states should have the right to define and implement specific cultural policies, that international cooperation and solidarity were essential for the establishment of viable cultural industries, and that cultural policies should be based on partnerships between government, private sector and civil society. In early 2003, the French Foreign Affairs Ministry organised a series of interministerial discussions which led to the proposal, by France, of a Unesco 'Convention'. Drawn up during 2004 despite significant US opposition, the *Convention on the Protection and Promotion of the Diversity of Cultural Expression* was adopted in October 2005 and ratified by France in July 2006.

Given the traditional bases of the French 'Republican model', in which linguistic and cultural minorities have generally entertained problematic relationships with the state, the new-found enthusiasm of French governments for cultural pluralism – internationally and within France – in the late 1990s might seem surprising. However, support from the state for new and varied forms of artistic creativity which accompanied the 2005 Unesco Convention built on existing thinking in a Ministry of Culture that was keen both to widen definitions of 'culture' and to facilitate the greatest possible levels of cultural creativity. Jack Lang's 'Ministry of Fun' (Looseley 1995) during the 1980s had attempted to graft more inclusive and pluralist interpretations of creativity onto the more monolithic doctrines inherited – albeit via the cultural upheavals of the late 1960s and 1970s – from De Gaulle and Malraux. Whereas in the 1980s, the redefinition of 'culture' responded significantly to an agenda aiming to rehabilitate 'popular' arts and practices – considered to have been oppressed by dominant 'élite' cultural forms – within the context of 'cultural exception' in GATT and 'cultural diversity' for Unesco, cultural pluralism in the 2000s reflects more an instrumentalist and commercial understanding of the importance of the cultural industries, to the extent that discourses and policies are negotiated in a creative tension between the fostering and defence of French 'culture' and cultural industries and the promotion – worldwide – of all cultures in an attempt to resist American globalisation. Policy discourse(s) and policy content(s) are always complex and sometimes confused and even contradictory, in appearance or reality: the fact that one of the few elements of the aid budget that has been protected from cuts in recent years is for 'cultural cooperation' demonstrates how a traditionally 'voluntarist' mechanism of French external cultural policy continues to serve France's interests by supporting Francophonie and French-language cultural products and services.

In practice, the application of 'cultural diversity' by the French state has meant that what is encouraged by cultural policy is now more varied, more heterogenous, more innovative, and arguably, more popular. Realising that supportive interventionism in the past has often stifled creativity at the same time as allowing certain forms of production – those which are best understood by Ministry officials, or which respond best to centralised support – to flourish, 'cultural diversity' aims to foster all kinds of activities, in an environment which provides more flexible state support, as well as allowing a greater freedom from regulation and oversight, intended to inject new commercial dynamism into France's cultural industries. A key feature of the encouragement of cultural diversity within France – and beyond, as wished for by Unesco – is that importance is attached to international collaborations in all fields of artistic creation. Thus in terms of the application of 'cultural diversity' in music, the Ministry of Culture has supported 'musiques du monde' in the domestic music sector, through organisations such *as Zone Franche* and music festivals. Conversely, the commercial dimension of 'diversity' is strongly represented in the work of the *Bureau Export de la Musique Française* and of *Francophonie Diffusion*, which promote French and francophone musics abroad. The contribution of 'diversité culturelle' to 'exception culturelle' in music represents a refocusing of existing policies and discourses, many of which date from the early 1990s and beyond, but as we shall see in discussion of the more recent rise in importance of the videogames industry during the 2000s, the French state maintains its voluntarist approach, albeit within a context of avowed 'pluralism' rather than cultural and linguistic 'nationalism'.

Vivendi-Universal: State 'exception' or commercial 'diversity'?

The flamboyant captain of industry Jean-Marie Messier was an iconoclastic contributor to the ongoing debate over 'exception culturelle' and 'diversité culturelle' during the early 2000s. Most visibly, in 2001 he proclaimed the death of 'l'exception culturelle' and espoused the notion of cultural diversity, whilst simultaneously championing the free-market and globalised business. At the time, Messier was CEO of the French-owned international media-music-film conglomerate Vivendi-Universal, which was aggressively expanding worldwide operations, after having grown from the diversified Compagnie Générale des Eaux and subsequent merger with Seagram-Universal.

Messier's views enraged many in France, but they stemmed from a modern and 'liberal' reaction to the typically negative French interpretation of the dangers of cultural globalisation and the consequent need to preserve national cultural traditions and practices. Writing in April 2001 to present his understanding of 'diversité culturelle', Messier explained that Vivendi-Universal's objective was not solely 'to construct a "global" company' but 'to build a *universal* grouping – as its name suggests – in the cultural industries' (Messier 2001). For Messier, such a grouping would take 'local' cultural products and distribute them worldwide, thereby strengthening the diversity of cultural production: 'if "global" means standardized products that are imposed on all, "universal" means individual works, born somewhere, which then go around the world'. In a swipe against the cultural 'protectionism' of which France is often accused, Messier also explained how his view of 'cultural diversity' rather than 'exception' is superior: 'Defending cultural diversity means allowing everyone to enjoy their own culture and to access the culture of others. Cultural diversity is not the juxtaposition of hermetically-sealed claims to identity which are essentially nationalistic, but reflects the vitality of societies which are increasingly interbred, of cultural legacies revisited and creativity with many roots'. These views were guaranteed to upset the French cultural establishment by their defence of globalised 'Anglo-saxon' capitalism in asserting that global companies in the culture industries (film and music in particular) do not necessarily mean Americanisation/McDonaldisation of French culture.

Where Messier's interpretation of 'cultural diversity' differed from that of the French state – and of the *Unesco Convention* – was in the means through which it was to be fostered and delivered. Whereas the encouragement and protection of cultural diversity is for the French Ministry of Culture essentially to be guaranteed through regulation and intervention, and ultimately 'protection', Vivendi-Universal's approach was that of a highly liberalised strategy of niche-marketing for cultural products and services. When Messier again declared the death of 'l'exception culturelle' in a speech in New York in December 2001, politicians, artists and those working in the cultural industries of all political persuasions joined to express disagreement. In a climate of discourse heightened by the preparation of the upcoming presidential election, left and right – with the notable exception of the ultra-liberal Alain Madelin – rallied to the defence of France's traditional positions on French culture in a world threatened by globalisation, and interpreted Messier's conceptualisation of 'cultural diversity' as a self-serving instrument of Vivendi-Universal's strategy to mimic US cultural conglomerates' success in Hollywood cinema and 'world music'. The left-wing Republican Jean-Pierre Chevènement proposed that far from being dead, *'exception culturelle'* was in fact a universalist value, to be adopted by nations and cultures all over the world, and Bruno Mégret of the extreme-right Front National accused Messier of treason to his country, suggesting that although other right-wing parties might congratulate Vivendi-Universal for flying the flag for French business internationally, in fact, once companies reached a certain scale, they cease to serve the interests of their home nations (Bezat and Chombeau 2001).

The furore that arose around Messier and Vivendi-Universal in the early 2000s and their apparent 'hijacking' of the concept of 'diversité culturelle' as well as their undermining of 'exception culturelle' was exemplary both of the French cultural establishment's enduring attachment to the exception of cultural goods and services and to a strong role for the state in managing culture. The notion of 'cultural diversity', while on the one hand being advantageously neutral, was also considerably 'weaker' in terms of the political position it demands of government. Although 'l'exception culturelle' has always been legally ambiguous and controversial as a concept, it has, at least, the advantage of imposing political will – a key feature of the traditionally voluntarist Fifth Republic – at the centre of its discourses and practice. Messier's interpretation of cultural diversity and the role of private enterprise in delivering it was essentially to say that what was good for Vivendi-Universal was good for France (and also for other national cultures lucky enough to figure in the Vivendi-Universal catalogue), thus obviating any need for either an exception to a rule (the free market in goods and services) or an 'exceptional' attitude on the part of government towards culture. As Messier concluded in his long statement of faith of April 2001: 'Future generations will see neither the hyper-domination of the United States nor cultural exception *à la française*. Their horizon will be the accepted and respected difference of cultures. There is no place for cultural exception because exception excludes, and exclusion is incompatible with culture. There is similarly no place for cultural domination, as culture rejects wearing uniform and being regimented. For Vivendi-Universal, our success will be gauged by the simple measure of whether in the years to come, we are known as the conglomerate which above all others embodies the idea of cultural diversity, born in Europe and aspired to by the whole world' (Messier 2001). In sum, the Vivendi-Universal 'affair' of the early 2000s demonstrated to the French State and cultural establishment some of the conceptual and indeed practical difficulties – as the private-sector claimed its stakeholding in the idea and its commercial exploitation – of replacing 'exception' with 'diversity'.

The videogames industry: old habits die hard?

Vivendi-Universal's principal interests were music and cinema (particularly through its ownership of Canal Plus). These fields of artistic creation have been longstanding preoccupations of the French state, and public policies to favour them – either as 'exception' or 'diversity' – have been the subject of multiple studies over the years. During the period in which discourses and policies around 'exception' were increasingly integrating the notion of 'diversity', however, a relatively new area of cultural activity with a significant commercial and industrial importance came to prominence in the form of the videogames industry. To take 2004 as representative, the industry of *'loisirs interactifs'* exceeded €1 billion in consumer purchases, selling more than 33 million items of software to French households. The industry supporting these sales employed directly or indirectly over 12,000 people in France, more than for the famed *'septième art'* [cinema], and the most popular *'produit culturel'* of the year was not a book (*The Da Vinci Code* sold only 800,000 copies) but the million-selling videogame *GT San Andreas*. Videogames and videogaming are in many ways something of a sector of comparative advantage for France. The industry that has grown up in France serving the strong French national demand for videogaming and providing the international market is a prime example of France punching above its weight in world competition in *'produits culturels'* as only four countries worldwide cover all aspects of the videogames industry: far in front are the US and Japan, but the UK and France in particular also compete strongly.

In the earlier 2000s a number of official inquiries into the videogame industry concluded that the sector was indeed of special relevance and importance, and it was in 2002 that the beginnings of a real *'reconnaissance politique'* of videogames was observed. The model of this *'reconnaissance politique'* is, in essence, to present videogames as, after films and then later popular music, as cultural artefacts and practices worthy of and eligible for state aid. It was the Le Diberder Report of July 2002 which drew attention to two principal difficulties of the French videogames industry: the lack of a solid and well-tried funding structure and the absence of an appropriate legal framework for the creation of videogames as *'produits culturels'* (Le Diberder and Le Diberder 2002). It is these problematic aspects of France's comparative advantage in videogaming that the French state has attempted to address within the new environment of 'cultural diversity', by supporting the industry financially, and negotiating compromises over the intellectual property rights of game creators.

In addition to the general difficulty of getting the cultural establishment to accept videogames as legitimate cultural practice and artefacts, there are other problems with the redefinition of videogames as 'art': firstly, in the heyday of videogaming, when French producers were surfing on the crest of the gaming/internet wave, publishers such as Infogrames were wary of any reform of the legal and artistic status of the industry, since recognising creators and software developers as 'authors' of *'oeuvres culturelles'* raises the vexed question of intellectual property rights and royalties. Secondly: if the inventors of videogames are 'authors' and 'artists' following the terms of French law, then a redefinition of the whole status of the profession is theoretically required, in order to bring employment contracts into line with other artistic professions. It is legal complexities like this which have thus far prevented any satisfactory overall resolution of the status of videogames: their latest legal definition is that they are neither *'oeuvres audiovisuelles'* nor computer software, but *'oeuvres multimédia de collaboration'*.

It is specifically the difficulties of *'création'* that have held the attention of successive governments, starting with the Fries Report of June 2004 (Fries 2004). Whereas the major French publishers and distributors of videogames such as Infogrames and Ubisoft (which often have in-house creative studios) have regularly undergone troubled periods, they have essentially always managed to survive, but smaller creative studios have however suffered much from competition from the US, Canada, the new economies of the Pacific Rim, India, Russia and the Czech Republic. And it is *'création'* around which crystallise debates over the intrinsic nature of videogames as 'art' or mass entertainment, as 'culture' or computing. One of the measures taken as part of the Raffarin government's new support for videogames was precisely the creation of an Ecole nationale du jeu des médias interactifs numériques in Angoulême. A financial measure that was also taken by Raffarin was authorising the creation of videogames to be supported in the same way as cinema: *the* Centre national de la cinématographie (CNC) is now in charge of the budget of the Fonds d'aide à la production des jeux vidéo FAJV (FAJV) which works on the principle of *'avances sur recettes'*, originally devised to support the film industry. Since 2004, the FAJV has actively funded videogame projects, and in 2005 and 2006 Culture minister Donnedieu de Vabres and Prime minister Villepin both called for additional financial aid in order to protect French video from being overwhelmed by competition. President Sarkozy also declared his support for state aid to the video industry and, after much negotiation in Brussels, the proposed tax-credit system was approved by the European Commission in December 2007.

The still-unfolding story of how the French state is coming to terms with the commercial importance and cultural significance of the new popular cultural products, services and practices of videogaming tends to suggest that old habits of *dirigisme*, interventionism and 'exception' are dying hard. Many of the mechanisms being employed by the state to foster the video industry are similar to those already used in previous decades in favour of cinema and music – such as the CNC-FAJV – and, as well as creating renewed irritation amongst countries not sharing France's views on exception and diversity, are open to the same potential dysfunction.

The *'intermittents du spectacle'*: resistances to change

One of the major dossiers of French governments in the field of culture during the 2000s has been the vexed issue of the *'intermittents du spectacle'* and how the (un)employment, tax and pensions status of these contributors to French cultural life can be brought into line both with the straitened finances of the public purse and with equitable treatment of all citizens. Various studies have focused on differing economic, sociological and legal dimensions of the problem (Corsani and Lazzarato 2008; Creton *et al* 2005; Menger 2005). Although some pre-existing mechanisms of this special employment regime date from the 1930s, the current system was essentially a creation of Gaullist cultural policies piloted by André Malraux in the 1960s: since 1969 *'artistes-interprètes'* as well as technicians working discontinuously in live theatre or cultural productions have been subject to rules of taxation and unemployment benefit which compensate them for the 'intermittent' nature of their work. In much simplified terms, this has allowed actors, theatre or cinema technicians or other artistic professions to enjoy up to a maximum of 12 months unemployment benefit on condition of having been in paid work for at least 507 hours in the year preceding their period out of work. During the 1970s, 1980s and for the most part of the 1990s, this idiosyncratic vestige of the 'heroic' period of French cultural policy attracted relatively little attention, despite its important function of subsidising cultural activities 'through the back door' of national social security transfers, rather than directly *via* the Ministry of Culture (*via* taxation of the general public) or through citizens' consumer choices to pay for theatre tickets or other performances.

This system of supporting national cultural activities is largely held to be a proper French 'exception': few other countries would arguably even consider such a tortuous procedure, still less perpetuate it over a period of 40 years, although within the EU, Spain, Italy, Germany and Belgium do have some recognition of 'seasonal' work. Only France, though specifically supports culture through this kind of mechanism. According to the 2007 report of the Cour des Comptes which considered some of the problems of the compromise regime agreed by sectoral trades unions and government in June 2003, the special financing of *'l'intermittence du spectacle'* was indeed a cornerstone of employment in French cultural activities (Cour des Comptes 2007). According to Cour des Comptes calculations, in 2005, *'intermittents'* numbered some 100,000, within total employment of 430,000 in the cultural sector overall, and this figure was constantly increasing, having risen from a mere 9,000 in 1984 in the early years of Jack Lang's tenure at the Culture Ministry. Although little attention had seemingly been paid to its remarks, the Cour des Comptes had repeatedly – in 1982, 1993 and 2002 – criticised the existence and operation of the special regime for *'intermittents'*, and its evaluation of the system in 2007 recapitulated concerns about its lack of transparency, its financial inefficiency, its openness to abuse and mismanagement, and the deficit of the Unedic finances which underwrote it.

The initial agreement of June 2003 between government and *'intermittents'* followed months of high-profile protest, demonstrations and threats to summer festivals, some of which – such as that at Avignon – were cancelled. The corporatist backlash against ambitions to reform the system surprised some, but was an essentially foreseeable reaction from a sector in which workers are mainly low-paid, and who see the advantageous aspects of their unemployment regime as just compensation for poor wages, irregular hours and unpredictable working periods. Moreover, just as outrage amongst *'intermittents'* was also partly based on their resentment that their contribution to culture should be under-valued, the movement of support which grew around them mobilised the cultural establishment in general in support of generous state subvention of cultural activities.

Despite the state's desire to modernise certain aspects of the traditional French social model and particularly to restore financial order to retirement and unemployment rights, the compromise agreement of June 2003 which instituted a 'transitional fund' intended to smooth the transfer from the old regime to a new, *slightly* less favourable one essentially reflected an inability or unwillingness to make radical changes to the system. Pressure from taxpayers' associations and other outcry at what was seen as the wasteful use of money paid by other citizens to the *'régime général'* of social security seemed less helpful in support of the right-wing government's agenda of financial balance than the critical pressure applied by the mobilisation of the '*intermittents*' and their varied and vocal supporters. The official Guillot Report of November 2004 commissioned to investigate the difficulties of work in the fields of live theatre, audiovisual productions and technical professions linked to the arts was also broadly in favour of protecting and encouraging special measures for employment in these areas (Guillot 2004). Following continued unrest and protest over the minor changes to the system, in December 2006 a new agreement between trades unions and the government was reached, the new regime coming into application on 1 April 2007. Since 2007, the new system has apparently functioned much as before, and the new government has tried to conciliate protesters and allow time for reflection.

The long-running problem of the '*intermittents du spectacle*' is an interesting example of the difficulties the French state encounters in attempts to reform the deeply-entrenched practices and mind-sets of traditional cultural policy. Against a backdrop of increasing budgetary constraint and concern over the viability of the French social model, governments have been keen to reduce the wastefulness of the special regime which has so benefitted the '*intermittents*', but at the same time they have been mindful that the cultural industries are increasingly important to the French economy and therefore that employment in them has to be nurtured, even by special means. And even where the state is whole-heartedly committed to reform, the direct-action and weight of lobbying of corporatist interests such as the '*intermittents*' and their supporters makes change from the 'exceptional' practices of the past a difficult process.

Conclusion: from '*culture unique*' to '*culture bigarrée*'?

In March 2008 a demonstration swelled by hundreds of '*intermittents*' not far from the Ministry of Culture in Paris protested against what was seen as the French state's 'disengagement' from culture. Around Ariane Mnouchkine – founder of the famous Théâtre du Soleil – and actors of the venerable Comédie Française, and in an ambiance of disquiet and anxiety, those working in 'culture' expressed concerns about perceived failing support for the sector and – one of the banners called for '*Culture bigarrée et pas culture Bigard*' – voiced their faith in cultural diversity and variety ('*culture bigarrée*') rather than old-fashioned and reactionary conceptualisations ('*culture Bigard*') of cultural value (Silber 2008). Suggesting that cultural policy was redolent of the reactionary comedian Jean-Marie Bigard was perhaps a little unfair, but Prime Minister Fillon's uncompromising and accountant-like response was essentially to remind the demonstrators that the world of culture had to contribute – as all areas of public policy – to the reduction of the national debt. Although there are those – such as right-wing taxpayers' associations – who complain that the French state's contributions to encouraging culture are too expensive, there still seems to remain general consensus that cultural activities and industries are a public good which needs to be supported. It is not only those such as the '*intermittents*' who support generous public funding: an LH2 poll in March 2007 for radio RMC demonstrated that 78 per cent of those questioned favoured an increase in the budget of the Culture Ministry (RMC Sondage sur la culture 2007).

The French state is indeed attempting to negotiate a modernisation of France's traditional approaches towards culture which simultaneously satisfies the demands of its own citizens for a generous, inclusive, pluralist and diverse cultural policy and responds to the requirements of EU integration and fair international trade. Such a modernisation requires policy to develop a rhetoric of 'diversity' which supplements and supports the more traditional and complex concept of 'exception', to integrate the new concept of diversity into a continued role for a strong but increasingly impecunious state, to develop new mechanisms of light intervention in developing sectors of cultural activity such as videogaming, and finally, to address the needs of vested interests such as the '*intermittents*'. At the same time as the French state is adapting its traditionally interventionist – and essentially 'exceptional' – approach to culture in a dialogue between the *dirigisme* of the past and its newer neo-liberal convictions, the rising commercial importance of the cultural industries worldwide is making other governments such as that of the UK pay greater attention to the active role they should play in supporting their own cultures of film, music, video and television. The French exception in culture, if it ever existed as a true strong national specificity, is evolving from both within and without France in a complex and fascinating tension of discourse and practice played out in a dialogue between the past and France's future place in the world.

Section II
Conflicts and Polarisation

5
The French Extreme Left and the Persistence of a Revolutionary Myth

David Bell

French exceptionalism has many aspects, but one is the persistence of the extreme left on the political party spectrum and the size of the extreme left within the left as a whole also needs to be noticed. In particular this party system exceptionalism is evidenced by the Communist Party and the small Trotskyite parties, electorally significant, but on the margins of mainstream politics with an influence that is both direct and indirect. There are Marxist inspired parties in other European countries, and there are other varieties of Trotskyite and anarchist movement as well as social upheavals and riots in deprived urban areas, but the French extreme left has unusual features.

French culture gives a privileged place to the revolutionary tradition. On the left the big parties have maintained a commitment to a revolutionary outlook that has ensured a vigorous growth of minor sects and philosophies. Over a century and more these traditions have been maintained and nourished as a central part of the ideology of the left. Smaller groups, like rivers on a limestone plateau, disappear and merge or split and then reappear with vigour in unexpected places. In the late 20th century it could have been anticipated that the extreme left would disappear but it has re-emerged as a powerful, if marginal and fragmented, force (Moreau 2003).

The revolutionary tradition in French politics

Importantly, the French extreme left activity reaches back to the Revolutionary myth and to the rejection of incremental change that was characteristic of most continental socialist movements at their origins. Socialist parties had a relationship with parliamentary politics and universal suffrage that was ambiguous (to put it no more strongly) or even hostile. However, whereas the mainstream parties in Europe dropped the revolutionary reference and embraced the parliamentary route, the tradition of revolution persisted strongly in France. This mutation was consolidated in the Second International with the rejection of Russian Communism after the First World War. In the aftermath of the Russian Revolution socialist parties, although nominally Marxist, consolidated their belief in peaceful and parliamentary change. 'Revolution', of course, did not immediately disappear from the socialist lexicon but changed meaning and Marxism ceased to be the reference point for the social democratic left.

However, France, was different. After the Russian Revolution most socialist parties faced a Communist attack from the left but in most cases this was small. In France the old socialist party, SFIO, was split and although the party's parliamentary force stayed loyal and the main body of activists and resources (including the newspaper *l'Humanité*) went to the newly founded pro-Moscow party. Léon Blum, the SFIO's then leader, chose to maintain the socialist commitment to Marxism and to 'revolution' the better to contest the threat from the Communist party. This revolutionary outlook, at least at a rhetorical level, was retained long after the mainstream socialist parties had dropped it and was still a feature of François Mitterrand's party in the 1980s.

Marxism was a very powerful ideological force and, given the cultural socialisation on the French left, it is unsurprising that it has lingered on into the 21st century. With the collapse of the Soviet Union, however, the 'model' of socialist development that was implicit in the Marxist perspective ceased to be credible. This Soviet utopia still has adherents on the left, and is still attractive to some, but it is a diminishing part of the French exception. What remains is the conviction that unless everything changes, nothing changes: that the incremental and piecemeal reforms characteristic of western societies are a mirage or a diversion from the task of the movement which is to ensure total change to the entire system. Pragmatic politics, the bargaining and give and take, is thus rejected by the extreme left. This, rather than the impressive electoral advances, is what marks out the French left as exceptional.

Hence, this electorally visible section is not the limit to the French extreme left; there are other tiny '*groupuscules*', including anarchists, of the Confédération nationale du travail (3,000 or so members) and the Fédération anarchiste (800 or so members). Some Maoists turned to violence but there remain the Parti communiste de France (Maoist) and the Organisation Communiste (Marxist-Leninist), although the Parti du travail de Belgique maintains a shadowy international of parties in European nations circulating around the remaining totalitarian states. (Particular attention is paid to Cuba and some to North Korea with visits, meetings and fund-raising). Hence this exceptional feature in France appears to be a prolongation of the Communist and Marxist outlook on politics beyond the disappearance of the world communist system and of the perception of working class solidarity. However, before discussing the anatomy of the French extreme left, it might be useful to establish the European comparator.

The two other aspects of the French extreme left are its electoral presence and its union force. There are small extreme left movements elsewhere in Europe (and some have had electoral successes). Denmark's Socialistk Folkeparti has had a parliamentary representation since 1960 and an MEP since 1979 but it has invested in themes like anti-Europeanism and anti-NATO on the left of the Danish political spectrum. In the Netherlands the Socialistische Partij (SP), more radical than Second International counterparts and with Trotskyite and post-maoist factions, has been a presence since 1960 (it has 11 MPs). In other countries there are small Trotskyite movements that play a part in heterogeneous coalitions of the left and in the UK there are the remnants of Militant (in non-entryist forms) and the SWP. In Portugal the extreme left, that struggled under the shadow of the PCP, has been significant within the Bloco de Esquerda, a Marxist coalition, and managed to get eight deputies elected in 2005. In Italy and Spain the extreme left is present in the post-communist coalitions (RC and IU). Even allowing for the different elections and the different circumstances, these are small relative to France (Delwitt 2004: 82).

As a component of the French left, the revolutionary tradition has implications for the mainstream Socialists and for French politics in general. (Even the right in France does not proclaim its free market credentials). Socialist leaders have to garner the full complement of votes from the left as well as votes from the centre in order to win national elections. Yet the persistent pressure from the left has a radicalising effect on the Parti socialiste in opposition and through its potential partners, mainly the Communist Party, in government and in local office. This pressure can be seen in an increasing factional problem for the Socialist Party as well as increasing its difficulties in moving to the centre 'floating voter', where the elections are traditionally won. These pressures are capable of bursting the fragile coalition inside the Parti socialiste, as they did over the European Constitutional Treaty, when senior figures opposed the Party's established line, or to outright splits (as when J.-L. Melenchon's supporters left the PS). So far no leader on the left has overcome or mastered these divisions.

Exceptional communism

In Italy, Greece, Portugal, Cyprus and France (and to a lesser extent in Spain) the Cold War Communist Parties had large memberships, ran unions and were supported by a large core professional party apparatus. Mass communism, has often been categorised as a 'Southern European' phenomenon, although this does not take into account the big communist party of Finland or the smaller, but influential communist parties elsewhere, including Sweden and – for a time – Germany. These parties were able, through their organisational power, to exploit dictatorships or occupation regimes to impose themselves as the hegemonic party (or a dominant party) on the left. Communist resources, professionalism, including a dedicated activism, multiplied their influence through leverage on society and the deployment of ideological Marxism. Thus one plausible view is that the decline of Communism created a space for the extreme left and bequeathed an activist force that could be mobilised around issues that the Communists had once espoused.

There are also post-Communist Parties in most countries and, although it is difficult to generalise in electoral terms, they can be influential in unions and pressure groups. Some, like the Swedish SKP and the German *Die Linke,* that brought together the PDS, and activist groups under Oscar Lafontaine, are significant presences in parliamentary politics to the left of the Socialists. Others, like the Italian Rifondazione, have been squeezed to the margins of the party systems and look barely viable as electoral forces. However, in Europe the parties to the left of the spectrum are significant only in a few of the smaller states and in these they are a less important part of the left than in France. These include Portugal, Sweden, Finland and the Netherlands and perhaps Italy and Spain. Hence even if Trotskyites are present in these parties, they have neither the appeal nor the dominance that they do in France.

Communism itself remains a distinctive aspect of French exceptionalism. For much of the post-war period the French Communist Party was the biggest in the western world (until overtaken by the Italians in the 1970s) but it was a subordinate member of the world system. There was a Communist system, a 'counter society', built around the strong professional central apparatus, which ran publications (newspapers and journals), unions and it had satellites of 'peace movements' and pressure groups. French Communist leaders never came to terms with the rise of the Socialist Party under Mitterrand in the 1970s and its response to finding itself the minor partner on the left was inconsistent.

But the Party had other problems as well. It had endured the ending of the Socialist régimes and of the USSR itself by ignoring this world-shaping event. It at first sought allies in the remnants of the Communist world (Cuba, North Korea and surprisingly, given their previous hostility, China) but it was isolated internationally and in France itself. Adaptation to the post-Communist world would have to be made and would be painful. Today's Communism finds it difficult to both remain faithful to the past (with important factions still committed to the Soviet systems) and repudiate the record of the Communist bloc. For the Party opposition to 'globalisation', the US and (frequently) Europe has replaced its commitment to state Socialism. It is still campaigning against the free market and the domination of the financial markets while promoting a vision of a grim future in a world at the whim of market demands but the exact shape of the 'alternative' is now unclear.

French Communism remains partially incorporated into the system and partly outside of it. Its alliance with the Socialists (without which it would win very little) mean state finance and that in turn is important for the maintenance of its large apparatus. While, on the one hand if it is a coalition partner with the Socialists in many institutions from local government to the Cabinet, it has on the other been keen to profit from outside and extra-parliamentary protest. It has not abandoned the hope of reviving its position through the medium of protest movements and anti-capitalist actions (occupations, for example) and it has tried to build bridges to the diverse social movements. In this enterprise, supporting libertarian issues, the PCF is at risk of finding itself going counter to the conservative instincts of its voters on these matters and where this has been tried, notably in the European elections, it has been a singular failure (Grunberg *et al*: 203–37). At the same time the Party itself has changed in power structure with authority passing from the old apparatus to personalities (sometimes referred to as 'barons'), such as Patrick Braouzec, who are major figures in the parliamentary party. Party leaders have had to navigate a line between these positions and to compromise to maintain a unity of sorts. But the leadership in place has tended to attribute its current low position to its period in government (1997–2002), although its leader Marie-George Buffet was a Minister at that time. In 2005 it supported, and more-or-less organised, the anti-European campaign for the referendum which put it at serious odds with its Socialist partner.

At the core of the Party is still the paid 'professional revolutionary' who is devoted full time to party work and who is dominant – and amenable – on Party organs. Communists still run a daily newspaper (*L'Humanité*) which, although in trouble financially and with a tiny circulation (53,000) and 20 per cent owned by companies, is a constant mouthpiece for the Party's views. Its 'transmission belt' into the masses, the biggest of French union federations, the CGT, is no longer under its control but it remains the most effective of the small parties of the left at local level (even though this municipal base was steadily declining as old mayors stood down) and in this it is far ahead of its nearest rivals even though the Trotskyite parties have won some council seats (Reynié 2007) There is also a small Assembly group but one which might be 'pivotal' – necessary – to any left-wing government in the Assembly. Several possibilities were therefore open to the Communist Party even in its debilitated condition.

In 2002, after a devastating electoral failure, Robert Hue was replaced as leader by Marie-George Buffet. Buffet is from a Communist family and one of the 'prodigious mediocrities' who rise through the Party apparatus to the top of the Communist system. However, one of the consequences of the decline of the Communist Party was the ending of Party discipline, even if it remains a disciplined formation relative to other parties. As a result the old infiltration of organisations and institutions is no longer possible and local government (where individual positions are dug in) has led to a differentiation of the Party so that it resembles, as has been noted, an archipelago of loosely connected strongholds. Party 'barons' control big federations and cannot be disciplined by the centre, which has been correspondingly weakened. But another consequence is the emergence of 'factions' in the Party, a development that would have been unthinkable to the disciplined Communists in the Cold War years.

Communist cells, which in 1999 numbered 12,000, as with political activism elsewhere, have atrophied, and as few as a quarter vote in some of the Party's internal consultation processes (on the *quinquennat* [five-year presidential term] only 21,567 voted). But, once capable of organising enthusiastic activists, Communism is an ageing cause. Party membership is ageing fast and the numbers are declining. A membership of 800,000 was claimed in 1978 (in reality it may have been half a million (Courtois and Lazar 1995: 423) and 134,000 in 2007 but for Buffet's nomination as candidate in 2007 there were under

100,000 voters in the internal primary (*Le Parisien* 24 March 2007). Whereas in 1978 the Communist claim to be the *'jeunesse du monde' had* some substance, in 2000 almost a quarter of the Party members were over 60 years of age (24.4 per cent), only 10.5 per cent were under 30 and most members (61 per cent) had joined before the 1990s (Platone and Ranger 2000). In 1979 45.5 per cent of Party members claimed to be 'workers' but in 2000 they represented 31.3 per cent although white collar workers (32.9 per cent), middle managers (19.8 per cent) and professionals (11.3 per cent) had increased in proportion. This change in membership may have compromised the PCF's position in the working class to the benefit of its Trotskyite rivals.

There were broadly three points of view in the Party. On the one side there are the so-called 'refounders', who look to rebuild the party on a new basis, and on the other there are the unreconstructed Communist 'stalinists', who remain nostalgic for the old Soviet Union, and in between was the leadership maintaining a balance between competing factions. Buffet's Party is more suspicious of the Socialists than was Robert Hue's and is keen to win back ground from the Trotskyites by radicalising its message, for example, toughening its line on European integration. They hope to rebuild a radical anti-capitalist and anti-globalisation alliance with groups on the far left. These so-called 'sans' (*sans-terre, sans-emplois, sans-papiers* etc) include ATTAC, some Trotskyites, the unions and others to build a new radicalism which would (probably) be dominated by the Communist Party. Various incidents, from the strikes in 1996 and 2006 to the anti-globalisation movement around José Bové, the rejection of the European Constitution and the anti-globalisation movements, are adduced to show that a popular surge of support for a radical party can be tapped.

Also problematic, for the left, are the remnants of the pro-Soviet idealists who once ran the Party and who, at the 2003 Congress, had as much as a third of the activists' support but who were distributed in several groups. These people do not repudiate the Soviet bloc, the USSR or their many homologues and they maintain ties with many former leaders and still strive for a non-market Socialism on the Leninist model. There is a belief, though less credible as time passes, that the Party can make progress through their influence in the unions and the strike movements in the authentic working class and that should remain the focus of activist efforts.

Yet the Communist Party has had to change and it has shed its once corseting Marxist outlook and now only refers indirectly to the working class (preferring to talk of 'people' rather than 'workers') and trying to turn a page on the USSR (a 'failure') insofar as the old guard will allow it. This is not very far. A sense of Party and of heritage remains intact and the Communist community does still exist. Thus the Party has tried to write the USSR out of the history of Communism, tracing it back to More and the Christian divines of the Middle Ages, presenting communism as a humanitarian ideal rather than a power structure, or disavowing the 'Real Existing Socialism' of the East. With a new leadership in the 1995 elections and a weakened Socialist Party this was enough to give the impression of renewal and advanced the Party to the position of potential governing partner. At the same time the leadership was willing to use opportunities to exploit protest issues but this also had its limits as the leadership was not willing to contemplate the dissolution of the Party that would have been required by the 'renovators' (or possible partners) in their strategy. Party structures and party autonomy thus remained intact but at the price of compromises. Moreover, and this is the major constraint on movement towards either of these two factions, the force of the Party's elected members depends on local alliances with the Socialists. Communism itself, however, faces rivals on the left and has not relinquished its claim to represent the 'revolution'.

A brusque change of direction would cause a split with the Socialist Party but its main resource – local councillors – means that the Party remains dependent on Socialist goodwill and 36 per cent of the PCF's budget comes from elected officials (*Le Parisien* 24 March 2007). However, the Buffet leadership chose to muddle along implying that there was an alternative and that the Party still represented a left wing project. This was a continuation of the old line attempting to balance factions by sometimes siding with the Socialists and sometimes dissolving into the radical protest movements, which resulted in an incoherent message veering from leftism to modest reform. Buffet's platform for the 2007 elections, 'Changer vraiment la vie' (the 1970s programme was 'Changer la vie') was intended to be debated at the grassroots but it did not rally the party. Faced as it was by the rising tide of Trotskyites in LCR and LO, it failed to catch the mood on the left.

Under Buffet the Party joined the Party of European Lefts (headed by the Italian Rifondazione leader Fausto Bertinotti and including the PDS, IU, Synaspismos and others) after a poll of activists on its European strategy. Internal Party consultations have become common but are a sign of the PCF's failing confidence and a search for legitimacy rather than of a new-found strength through party democracy. Communist leaders have also tried to associate themselves with the left's more libertarian struggles and have even co-opted personalities from the 'alternative' movements in the action for '*sans-papiers*', against sexism, racism, anti-semitism and homophobia.

As leader Buffet, however, faced the same problems of how to modernise the Party without destroying it and how to manage a relationship with the dominant Socialists. In other words this was a continuation of the ride on the Socialist's coat-tails, but with a more determined effort not to allow the Trotskyite left to adopt the issues long regarded as Communist. It also refrained from breaking with the Socialists on major issues. This was evident in its strategic impasse in the 2007 elections. It could have supported an independent candidate of the alternative left or run its own candidate. In the event Buffet's lone campaign failed to rally either its traditional support or gain new voters, she came below Besancenot in some of its former strongholds (Allier, Haute-Vienne, Nord etc) and polled a humiliating 1.93 per cent. In the general elections the PCF withstood the 'blue wave' better than anticipated, taking 4.2 per cent of the vote on the first ballot (as against 4.82 per cent in 2002) and, despite further losses, it remained, with 15 seats, a parliamentary presence. Buffet, was able to ride out the subsequent storm of criticism of the poor election result by postponing the discussion.

However, it was Communist municipal strength that enabled it to survive. In the 2008 local elections: it kept most of its City Halls and won some. It had some success in the Paris region and elsewhere and it won back Dieppe (Seine-Maritime), French Communism remains a force because of its local implantation (something the Trotskyites have yet to rival). For this it needs the Socialist Party's support but then it is unable to bring the leftists into the parliamentary left because its attraction to the marginal groups is limited. It should be noted that the Socialists, by the same token, need the Communists to ally with at local level and are in this way attached to the continuing 'revolutionary tradition'.

France unions are amongst the smallest (relative to the working population) in the western world and have a distinctive relationship with the parties. This has, unlike 'northern Europe', not followed a social democratic model. One paradox is that highly politicised unions derived their principles from the Amiens Charter of 1906 that formalised the mistrust of parties and the independence of the unions. However, in complete contradiction with these precepts, the main union confederation, the CGT, was run by the Communist Party as its fiefdom from 1947. There has been a strong tradition of revolutionary union activity linked to party activity or dominated by party strategy – unlike 'northern Europe'. For the Communist Party the CGT was a source of support and of activists, the Party decided on the leadership (CGT Secretary Generals were all Central Committee members) and the unions became an adjunct to Party policy. Communist majorities on the executive have increased but, paradoxically, this has widened the autonomy of the CGT because the splits in the Party have enabled the leadership under its leader Bernard Thibault to set its own course.

Trotskyite minorities, hitherto suppressed, have emerged; the CGT joined the European confederation of unions and they have diverged on key issues (for example on the European Constitution, which the conference and Secretary General supported). More significantly, the CGT has started to take a reformist line in union affairs and has been open to negotiations and compromises, an approach it has derided in the past. It is not possible to say whether these developments have meant an increase in support for the CGT (it seems to have lost members), but the Communists remain firmly implanted at the local and national level.

If the Communist Party *'machine à créer du rêve'* has declined, the space that it once occupied remains open for exploitation (Lazar 2002: 200). These issues include anti-Americanism, anti-racism, anti-Israel, anti-Europeanism, anti-globalisation, anti-capitalism, the priority of the working class and, with the change in the CGT, 'revolutionary' trade union action. Numerous issue groups have sprung up as have radical unions. These pressure groups include the Association pour une taxation des transactions financières pour l'aide aux citoyens (ATTAC), AC! (Agir ensemble contre le chômage), Confédération nationale du travail (CNT), Droit au logement (DAL), Droits devant (DD!!) Motivé-e-s (of Toulouse) and so on. New unions include SUD (Solidaires-unitaires-démocratiques) and the biggest education unions Fédération syndicale unitaire (FSU – with about 180,000 members). All of them are 'socialist' and hostile to 'globalisation' and the free trade movement in the west. However, they are uncoordinated, jealous of their independence and linked to particular issues more than a movement across society as a whole, even though there are attempts to bring them together them from time to time. Trotskyist parties are present in this new phenomenon and sometimes give them organisational backbone (Poulet 1999).

Trotskyism

This contemporary version of left-wing populism, Trotskyism, is by its nature very small and often fleeting, is more difficult to generalise about although the Trotskyites were an opposition both to social democracy and to orthodox Communism on the left of the left. Trotskyite parties have a history going back to the 1930s. Some were the products of entry-ism into the socialist parties but they were prepared to persist after the collapse of the Soviet bloc in 1992 and served – to some extent – as guardians of the socialist orthodoxy when the Communist parties were dissolved or reduced. Thus in one sense the Trotskyite parties maintain, with no need to apologise for the Soviet Union, a readily understood discourse, the Marxist revolutionary tradition and the utopian ideal. But on the other hand they are the beneficiaries of the decline of the major parties, and of their centripetal movements, both in part products of the end of the ideological war with communism.

But in this post-Communist arena, through the high vote for anti-parliamentary extreme left 'Trotskyite' parties, French 'exceptionalism' is evident and has no parallels elsewhere in Europe. France is distinguished by groups on both the right and the left that are contemptuous of normal politics and of the compromises that those entail and which put the bulk of their energy into extra-parliamentary activities, such as union activism, demonstrations and occupations. These processes are designed to force issues onto the agenda and to embarrass the mainstream left. Of course, Trotskyites come from a long tradition of mutual hostility with the Communist Party (for whom they were 'Hitlero-Trotskyites') and the USSR, which they accuse of having perverted the socialist and revolutionary ideal, as well as to social democrats, who they regard as selling out to capitalism. Socialists are dismissed as 'social-liberals' (free marketers) and as incapable of conducting a social change although there were groups in the PS who they were willing to meet (J.-L. Melenchon's in particular). Their candidate in 2007, Ségolène Royal, was dismissed by the Trotskyites and, in any case, looked hopefully to the centre's François Bayrou not to the left of the left.

'Fourth International', or 'Trotskyist parties' are small and secretive but they claim to have their origins in the 1938 'International' proclaimed by Trotsky and refer back to Marx, Engels and Lenin. However, there are several competing 'Fourth Internationals' each calling down anathema on the others in this divided movement that is prone to schisms and chronically unable to unite for common ends. There were flurries of Trotskyite activity in local actions and in strikes in the 1970s and 1980s but the growth of Trotskyism coincides with the mobilisation of the 1990s.

There are many different strands and frequent splits (many bitterly divided) in this sectarian movement which, partially because of its divisions, has not capitalised on its potential. There are three parties of electoral importance: the Ligue communiste révolutionnaire, Lutte ouvrière and the Parti des Travailleurs, but there are outposts of Trotsky-ism in the unions and in the Left wing parties (PCF, Les Verts and PS). What they have in common is an ability to profit from discontents not expressed by the mainstream parties and to channel these. They are shadowy and hierarchical parties whose electoral face is not the real leadership and whose main concern is not parliamentary politics. This, of course, poses problems for a Communist Party utilising a Marxist ideology but willing to play parliamentary politics. European integration, which split the conservative right in the 1990s, has emerged as a divisive factor for the left (in the Pas-de-Calais a Communist motion rejecting the Treaty attempted to split the Socialists).

'*Lutte ouvrière*' is the name of the fortnightly journal of the Union communiste internationaliste, but as LO it is the biggest and best known (as a result of the campaigns of Arlette Laguiller) of the Trotskyite parties. Paradoxically it is highly sectarian and '*ouvrièriste*' [workerist], not tempted by the many spectacular campaigns of popular protest and it is dismissive of electoral politics which it sees not as a means to power but as a recruit-ment method. Its recognition is a testament to the success of its launch-ing of electoral campaigns (from which it expects little other than to recruit and propagandise) that started in 1971 and which became recog-nised with the presidential candidacies of Laguiller. 1995 was a propitious year for LO as the social turbulence and strikes as well as a disillusion with the orthodox left at the end of Mitterrand's double septennate mobilised an electoral clientele and the candidacy gave them a voice. Laguiller, however, was overshadowed in 2007 by Besancenot on the left and has stepped down for another nominee (N. Arthaud).

LO might have had about 7,000 members in 2007 (it claimed 8,200 according to *Libération* 28 May 2007) but its activities are amongst the most secret of the extreme left's groups and very few of its leaders are known to the general public. Its real leader is Robert Barcia, a shadowy figure little known to the public who uses the pseudonym 'Hardy'. Hardy is an industrialist of some consequence despite the LO's commitment to the proletariat and its belief that only the workers matter in politics. LO's activists submit to a severe and austere hier-archical discipline based on 'an apparatus of professional revolution-aries' placed in businesses and works. This devotion makes for a very effective political instrument but few can stand the long-term exclusive commitment or the pace and there is no room for dissent in the ranks, with the result that LO is periodically weakened by splits. In party political terms its ambition is to replace the Communist party as the dominant party of the left and it came close to this during the

2002 presidential campaign although it lost momentum and votes to the other minor parties in 2007 and emerged only slightly stronger than in 1995.

LO, however, maintains its strength in the old working class through its hard-working activists and, in keeping with its unchanged Marxist ideology, expects to see the mobilisation for the revolution in the factories. It does not see any difference between the socialist left and the 'capitalists' and is as critical of the Parti socialiste and the Communists (viewed as 'class traitors') as of the right. For this reason it will have no truck with reformists and refuses alliances with the mainstream parties and has no interest in government (local or national) of the 'bourgeois' system and displays contempt for the orthodox left. Its refusal to back Mitterrand in 1988 went unnoticed but its indifference to Le Pen's appearance on the second ballot in 2002 lost it a great deal of sympathy. Although it has proposed deals with the PCF in the past, there have been conflictual alliances and unceasing polemics with other Trotskysts only occasionally (in 1979, 1999, 1983 and 2003) although they have been electorally advantageous but its rigidity and refusal to compromise make it exceptionally difficult as a partner.

It is possible to make some generalisations about its electoral appeal based on the presidential elections and opinion polls. It is strongest in the north and the east in the former Communist 'red' fiefdoms of the Nord, Pas de Calais, Haute Normandie and Pays de la Loire and the Paris region (unlike the LCR which does best in the Midi-Pyrénées and Alpes de Haute Provence). LO does get a relatively bigger vote from white and blue collar workers and from the less well educated as well as older age groups (46–59 and over 60s) and there is a substantial authoritarian aspect to it, although it is motivated more by anti-free market and social considerations (Reynié 2007: 139). If Laguiller was seen as in touch with ordinary people LO's voters do not form a stable core and few saw their candidate as 'presidential timber', although they thought that Arlette understood their problems. Laguiller's voters were motivated, more than those of other candidates, by the issues of unemployment and poverty although insecurity and pensions also played a part in the decision to support Laguiller. In the local elections of 2008 LO did ally with the PS in 69 cases (it had 117 of its own lists) and had 36 councillors elected (21 on its own lists).

LO and LCR are unusual Trotskyite formations in the attention they give to elections. However, the sectarian Parti communiste internationaliste which runs a front, the Parti ouvrier indépendant (formerly the Parti des travailleurs – PdT), is not electorally oriented. This party may have

1,000 members (it claims 10,071 members according to *Le Monde* 17 June 2008) although it prefers to stay out of the public forum and its influence is above all indirect – infiltration being its preferred mode. This front was intended to bring in a wider support and hence had a vague programme of class struggle, secular schools, union resistance and condemnation of what they see as the Fifth Republic's undemocratic nature. In its view the capitalist world is in crisis and on the verge of revolution but the proletariat, although misled by 'class collaborators', is the emancipating force. This group have an organisation devoted to active entryism into unions and it has been successful in the moderate Force ouvrière (because of its open structure) as well as in other confederations and parties. Its current leader Daniel Glückstein asserted that their party had a right to intervene in the unions to direct its activists as to what stance to take.

In 2007 its candidate Gérard Schivardi polled a meagre 0.5 per cent at the presidential elections but, of course, it is not in votes that its influence is reckoned. The party is not interested in elections or in alliances with other parties and sees industrial struggle in the working class to defend rights as the key to politics. However, it differentiates between the parties of the left and the right (unlike LO) and it is prepared to envisage cooperation with the mainstream for specific purposes or to support the creation of a 'radical pole' on the left of the left. It distributes the journal *Informations ouvrières* and it claims a high membership but its long-term aim is to bring together support from across the left aided by its strategically placed 'moles' and expects to gain from a revolutionary upheaval in which the workers will throw off the hegemony of the old left (*Le Monde* 18–19 January 2004). When André Bergeron stood down as Force ouvrière secretary general in 1989 and Marc Blondel was elected to replace him with PdT help, he substantially changed the orientation of the confederation away from its traditionally reformist and anti-Communist stance to a more confrontational line, which also saw the emergence of Trotskyites into positions of influence. In Blondel's time the FO was very involved in the strikes of 1995 and 2003, but its switch in line lost it members as well as positions on works and labour committees. In 2004 Jean-Claude Mailly was elected FO secretary general with the PdT's support, calling, for example, for a general strike against the '*contrat primière embauche*' in 2006.

Of the three groups, Alain Krivine's LCR (now absorbed into the Nouveau Parti Anticapitaliste) was the most open and is the most flexible having been willing to get involved in and promote social causes at some remove from the traditional working class issues normally espoused by

Trotskyism (and of which LO and PdT are dismissive). It also changed direction in the mid-1980s to take up issues that were more libertarian and 'alternative' (ecology, feminism, *sans-papiers* etc) than the traditional Trotskyists. As a result Krivine's party claimed 4,000 members, is well-represented amongst students and teachers, recruited strongly amongst students and school pupils, but less so in the traditional working class. There was a formal democratic centralism in the LCR until 1981, when its structure was loosened, and it has recognised factions (one called 'Revolution') that compete for power within it and which submit rival resolutions to its congress through its fortnightly newspaper *Rouge*. An electoral strategy is more logical for the LCR, given this outlook, than it is for LO with which it has little in common in the issues it prioritises.

In 2002 it had an unexpected success with the candidacy of the young postal worker Olivier Besancenot who used the presidential campaign as a platform to promote the party. Besancenot polled 4.25 per cent on the first ballot. It was Besancenot who was the first to demand a mobilisation against Le Pen on the second ballot. A letter was sent proposing an electoral alliance that would either join with or support the 'plural left' on the second ballot. This *démarche* was seen as 'reformist' by the leadership of LO and turned down and the LCR accused of incipient 'reformism'. (LCR's pragmatism was one reason why it was rejected as a partner by LO for the local elections of 2000). Krivine followed this with the proposal for a party of the left but without consequences other than to boost its own standing as the most open of the parties of the extreme left. LCR also invokes the possibility of the 'general strike' as a means of advancing (it shares this view with the SUD unions and some factions in FO).

Paradoxically, however, it has been less successful in elections than LO and until 2002 it struggled to make an impact. It has tended to support other candidates (like Juquin in 1988) or to support LO's Laguiller in presidential elections but it is less domineering and envisages a more confederal association of the extreme left than does LO. LCR's support is conspicuously younger than its rivals and polls well amongst students and the 18–25 year cohort. Amongst the LCR's voters there are fewer workers than LO and the farmers and middle managers are slightly better represented than the average. Besancenot did manage to sweep up votes from the disillusioned in the Verts but the former communists are less evident than in LO. In 2002 Besancenot managed to capture the notion of change and that was one of the themes motivating the vote for the LCR candidate, but poverty, unemployment and pensions figured as motivations whilst the environment also featured in the list. In the general elections of 2007 the LCR fielded 495 candidates and took 213,444 votes (66 per cent more than in 2002). Of its candidates 70 got over 3 per cent (only three did in 2002). However, an illustration of the over-centralising nature of the party and its attempt to restrict individuality is the competition it faced from dissidents. For example, ex-LCR 'anti-free market' candidates polled 9.8 per cent in Gap and 6.1 per cent in Toulouse. Although, unlike LO, the LCR refused alliances with the PS, further small advances were made in the local elections of 2008: of the 200 LCR lists 109 took above 5 per cent of the vote and 29 above 10 per cent.

Besancenot's new party, the NPA, has inherited the LCR membership and leadership (having downgraded a troublesome minority in the process) and has an eclectic platform. It is against the Lisbon Treaty, calls for redistribution, a set of nationalisations, an 'alternative' EU and an end to the alliance with the US. As with LCR, and LO, its vocation is to recreate a left-wing party of the workers in the space vacated by the PCF to replace it. Besancenot is the driving force and it has inherited the 'revolutionary' vocation independent of the Parti socialiste.

With the formation of the, mainly public sector, *Solidaires-Unitaires-Démocratiques* (SUD) unions in the late 1980s, Trotskyite union potential increased noticeably. Olivier Besancenot, LCR's candidate in 2007, came from the SUD-PTT unions and this sector, along with teachers, has bolstered the Trotskyite radicalism of the unions. This new confederation (Union Syndicale Solidaires – USS) claims 90,000 members and is a radical formation with a substantial political contribution and present at many of the more spectacular demonstrations.

Conclusion

There have been many comments of the centrality of 'revolution' to French political culture (not just the left). This tradition is available for exploitation by political movements of very different backgrounds and objectives but it is persistent (Gildea 1994). Thus the appeal to 'revolution' is central to the culture of the extreme left and is given an interpretation that is intended to delegitimise its opponents. Troskyism has maintained the flame of Revolution even after the Communist Party has allowed it to dwindle. (In doing so the Communist Party has opened itself to criticisms much as the Socialists had in previous Republics). It is clear that the revolutionary idea in French politics has a long half life.

In its rhetoric the old criticisms of the 'bourgeois' capitalist democracy can still be found as can the perspective of the march of progress but this is more of a disposition or outlook than a sculpted ideology. On the French extreme or alternative left, splits are far from being unusual. Most of the groups claim to be the unique representative of the struggle and most refuse alliances other than for short term and tactical purposes. They are also not oriented to the party system in the way that parties with a governing vocation on the left have been since the acceptance of parliamentary politics. These groups, on the French left, stand outside the parliamentary tradition and are oriented to the union movements (especially) and to the social movements secondarily (or in some cases only intermittently). A premium is placed on political action outside of the parliamentary arena and on a rejection of 'reformist' politics while at the same time proclaiming a better way. If the polls of the Trotskyite formations and the PCF are added up then the total is substantial and a bloc of that size (perhaps 10–15 per cent) could be a considerable force in the political party system, comparable at least to the Swedish Vänsterpartiet. But the vote is recognisably one of the left: it takes votes from the pool and does not (unlike Le Pen on the right) bring in new strata (Reynié 2005: 144).

Where the parties have combined, in the 1999 European and some regional elections the gains in votes to the participating formations have been evident. There have been various examples of this success and these include the issue-based campaigns for immigrant rights, in defence of the employees' rights (November 1995) for the unemployed and against globalisation. However, the most influential has been the campaign against the European Constitution in the referendum of May 2005. This campaign, which resulted in French rejection of the Treaty, saw the Marxist left (along with the dissident right) pitched against the mainstream parties of the centre and conservative right. In fact the strong points of the '*non*' vote had the physiognomy of the Communists in their heyday: the Nord, the west of the Massif Central, the poor farming regions in the centre and the Mediterranean littoral. On the basis of this '*non*' the belief held sway for some time that an agreed joint candidate could be run for the 2007 presidential elections. Public opinion, as far as the polls were able to judge it, seemed to favour this unified appeal and figures like the farmers' activist José Bové seemed to capture the mood.

However, as ever with this political arithmetic, things are not so simple and the divisions between the formations are profound. In the event the various formations could not agree and the Communist domination of the anti-European movement, that had been evident (but restrained) during the referendum campaign, was used to promote Buffet as the presidential figure and the fragile unity split into component parts. Whatever the public on the left thinks of a unified movement, the apparatus of the parties do not want to relinquish authority. There is a mismatch but also a problem because the unity has been forged against globalisation, Europe, government policy and so on. These are 'anti' campaigns, the agreements on the positives are flimsy and, crucially, the spasmodic rallies behind mobilising banners enable the extreme left to evade the questions and compromises that mainstream politics demands.

Where the Communist Parties have survived – as distinct entities – in Western Europe they have adopted one of two strategies. They have, on the one hand, closed in on themselves and espoused a 'Socialism in one country' line, preserving the old order and the trappings of Soviet-style parties. These include the Portuguese and Greek Parties, and some very small remnants, scattered across the continent. Others have adapted to post-Cold War Europe by espousing libertarian radical causes in various combinations: anti-globalisation, environmentalism, feminism, immigrant issues and anti-Europeanism. There are many parties of this type exploiting the move to the right of the social democrats and constituting a sort of social democratic left, a guarantor of the welfare state and of workplace rights. French Communism is distinctive in being a direct continuation of the old Communist Party without a break but in hesitating between these two routes. Both its experiment, under Robert Hue, to pose as the left of the Socialist coalition and its intermittent attempts, under Buffet, to espouse libertarian issues have been failures and have not stemmed its decline.

But, as underlined, these are not simply electoral formations. They are active in the social movements and in the unions. This has ramifications beyond the party system into French political and economic life. They can, when organised, impede changes by the central government to French institutions and to the structure of the market (particularly the labour market). This, despite, the weakness of unions in numbers, makes them an important force. They are alert to, and organised for, protest and resistance movements and must constitute one of the reasons for the divergence of France from the 'Anglo-Saxon' model of society.

6
French Euroscepticism and the Construction of National Exceptionalism

Robert Harmsen

Introduction

The study of 'Euroscepticisms' inevitably engages one in a consideration of national exceptionalisms. Virtually all Euroscepticisms express a view that the project of European integration imperils distinctive and defining features of national political, social, and economic models. The term itself stems from a national exceptionalism, having originally been used in the 1980s as a politico-media label to designate British opponents of European integration or, more precisely, opponents of British participation therein (Harmsen and Spiering 2004: 15–20). The analogous French term *'souverainisme'*, though shared with *québécois indépendantistes*, was also initially evocative of a national exceptionalism, encompassing a specific set of national institutional practices and intellectual traditions seen as standing at odds with core aspects of the European integration project (cf. Lacroix 2002).

Yet, though Euroscepticisms are deeply rooted in national particularisms, there has also, equally clearly, been a more general Eurosceptic trend which has manifested itself to varying degrees in virtually all European Union member and candidate states since at least the Maastricht Treaty debates of the early 1990s. Oppositions have grown to the project of European integration in often similar terms, stressing the democratic shortcomings of its institutional structures, its excessive bureaucratisation, or that which is portrayed as its '(ultra-) liberal' social and economic policy orientations. Correspondingly, a substantial academic literature has grown up around the phenomenon, in its early stages concerned particularly with categorising the diverse range of oppositions to (aspects of) European integration to which the epithet has been applied (Taggart and Szczerbiak 2002; Kopecký and Mudde 2002).

It is against this background that the present chapter seeks to explore the relationship of French Euroscepticisms with ideas of national exceptionalism. It does so with a view to answering essentially two interrelated questions: How have ideas of national exceptionalism figured (or not) in the construction of Eurosceptic discourses in France? Does the French pattern of Euroscepticism appear as empirically exceptional relative to wider European trends in the period since Maastricht?

In responding to these core questions, the chapter initially provides a three part survey of the evolution of French party political Euroscepticism since the early 1990s. The first section underlines the strong presence of a Republican discourse of national exceptionalism in French debates surrounding the Maastricht Treaty. The following two sections then examine the differing ways in which that discourse has been displaced or subsumed on the right and the left respectively in the ensuing 15 years. An extensive concluding section returns to the questions of both discursive exceptionalism and empirical exceptionality on the basis of this survey, further placing French experience in the context of wider European developments and dilemmas.

The defence of the 'modèle républicain' and 'social nationalism'

French 'Euroscepticism' or '*souverainisme*' could traditionally be understood in terms of the discursive construction of a fundamental 'misfit' between the French polity and its European counterpart, in which a distinctive 'Republican model' ['*modèle républicain*'] is portrayed as imperiled by the unchecked development of a European federalism. The clash of the national 'Republican' and European 'federal' models is partly one of templates of governance, the former resting on a strongly unitary conception of political power in opposition to the necessarily more diffuse or pluralistic operation of a multi-level and multi-national system of governance. In this, the French dilemma is that of all 'simple polities', as identified by Vivien Schmidt (2006), in adapting to the demands of the complex realities of EU governance. That clash, however, assumes a deeper resonance in the French case, insofar as the historic construction of the French Republican model is one which may – and often has – been interpreted as demanding that national sovereignty be preserved as a necessary precondition for the maintenance of meaningful democratic deliberation and civic integration. The argument, in this vein, runs that only within the bounds of the nation, linked by a shared language and (civic) culture in a community of destiny, can genuine political dialogue take place and can citizens (in the full sense of the term) participate in a process permitting the expression of their sovereign will.

It is in this respect that the 'Republican model' must be seen as concerning not only a particular set of practices of governance, but also wider (if contested) constructions of political identity. The idea of the Republic is bound up with senses of French exceptionalism and exemplarity – the former pointing to the (non-replicable) distinctiveness of French politico-historical experience, while the latter, somewhat paradoxically, is suggestive of its universal (and generalisable) import (cf. Hayward 2007). To the paradoxical coupling of exceptionalism and exemplarity must further be added that of the 'strong state' and its perceived vulnerabilities. If the national community has been constructed by an act of will – the literal *volontarisme* famously encapsulated in Renan's characterisation of the nation as '*un plébiscite de tous les jours*' [a plebiscite that is renewed daily] – then it may equally be unmade by a failure to sustain that will. Following this logic, forms of Republican discourse correspondingly highlight the dangers of the fragmentation or disintegration of the historically constructed 'state-nation', potentially threatened not only from above by global and European developments, but also from below by territorial decentralisation or the strengthening of '*contre pouvoirs*' in the form of counter-majoritarian judicial or regulatory checks on popular sovereignty.

Such a Republican opposition to the further development of European integration in a putatively federal direction found eloquent expression in Philippe Séguin's campaign against the Maastricht Treaty. Séguin, at the time a rising star in the Gaullist movement, teamed with fellow Gaullist dissident Charles Pasqua to lead the opposition to the ratification of the Treaty in 1992. This opposition was set out in terms of a classically defined Republican model, arguing that the Treaty on European Union (TEU) represented a step too far, as it moved beyond desirable intergovernmental cooperation to an ultimately doomed attempt at artificially creating a European political community. The Maastricht Treaty was, for Séguin, an 'anti-1789', breaking the indissoluble link between national sovereignty and democracy, insofar as 'democracy can only exist where there is a sentiment of belonging to the community which is sufficiently strong to lead the minority to accept the law of the majority' (Séguin 1992a: 36).[1] The general challenge to democratic accountability posed by the Treaty's technocratic thrust was, moreover, made more acute in the French case by the threat which it more specifically posed to the nation's exemplary Republican tradition. As Séguin put it, speaking in the National Assembly:

> There is undoubtedly a 'French exception'. A French exception which translates the extraordinary compromise which the Republic has realised amongst us between the necessity of the state and the liberty of the individual, and which cannot be made to agree with the normalisation, with the banalisation that one wishes to impose on France in the name of the logic of Maëstricht (sic). (Séguin 1992a: 43)

This Republican opposition to the Maastricht Treaty was echoed in broadly similar terms on the left of the political spectrum by Jean-Pierre Chevènement. Having resigned from the government in 1991 over its stance on the first Gulf War, Chevènement followed this in 1992 with a resignation from the Socialist Party over its support for the Treaty on European Union, founding the Mouvement des Citoyens. Chevènement shares with Séguin a core belief that neither democracy nor citizenship could meaningfully be established beyond the confines of the national community – both as a general precept and, more strongly, as regards the particular form which it had taken in the French Republican tradition. As he argued in a book published in early 1992:

> The French conception of the nation has this in particular, in effect, it is founded on values: liberty, equality and fraternity. The French nation is a mediation between the citizen and the Universal. To be French, is to be a citizen of the French Republic....The French nation liberates the individual from ethnic or religious affiliations. It offers him a Republican model of identification. It is by way of the nation that the essential core of social relationships is formed. In this sense, it remains the inescapable framework, probably for a long time yet, of democracy and consequently of the integration of all citizens, immigrant or not, and of our participation in wider solidarities, in Europe and in the world. (Chevènement 1992: 232)

Against this background, Chevènement correspondingly called for a 'reinvention of the French exception', returning to the essential democratic and social vocations of the Republican tradition. In his view, this tradition had been abandoned by the national elite – labelled a 'post-Republican oligarchy' – which had preserved its own place, if not its power, through the submissive acceptance of an American neo-liberal hegemony and its European extension.

Reflecting this common ground between some of the more prominent left and right-wing oppositions to the Maastricht Treaty, Bertrand Benoit (1997), in one of the first major studies of French Euroscepticism, argued that all such resistances to European integration in France might be understood with reference to a shared 'social nationalist' ideology.[2] According to Benoit, this particularly French form of neo-nationalist ideology was defined by a set of interrelated beliefs which stressed the threats posed by the European project to distinctively French identities, institutions, and culture. This position encompasses both a 'national' discourse of political sovereignty and a 'social' discourse concerned to resist the imposition of an 'Anglo-Saxon liberal' model of economic organisation, in this latter respect paying significant attention to the preservation of a *'service public à la française'*. As such, though it is not his central intent, Benoit's work has the merit of painting a clear portrait of the framing of European issues in the French case – drawing out the manner in which both real and perceived 'misfits' between the constitutive properties of national and supranational politico-economic models shape the contours of national discourses of European integration.

Yet, at the same time, Benoit's characterisation of French Euroscepticism as a movement animated by a shared ideology imputes to it an underlying unity, both in political and intellectual terms, which it manifestly does not possess. Intellectually, as Flood (2005: 51) notes, French Eurosceptics hold rather disparate views on the issues highlighted by Benoit – markedly varying as regards the relative attention which they pay to 'social' and 'national' questions, as well as the outcomes which they seek (some such groupings, indeed, not being 'national' at all). Politically, the absence of a cohesive 'social nationalist' pole in French politics was concretely demonstrated by the failure of Jean-Pierre Chevènement's presidential candidacy in 2002. Although briefly emerging as the 'third man' in that year's presidential contest, Chevènement's 'left-wing Gaullism', seeking to build a 'nationalist' coalition across the left-right divide, ultimately did not allow him to escape the status of an also-ran, winning only just over 5 per cent of the vote (cf. Milner 2004: 66–7).

In the decade since Benoit's pioneering study appeared, it might be argued that French Euroscepticism has become a still more disparate entity. Most particularly, the shared Republican reference, centrally invoked by left and right-wing opponents of the Maastricht Treaty, has declined in prominence. Tellingly, while the opposition to the TEU in the 1992 campaign still largely focused on the defence of a traditional national political model of universalist aspirations against the further development of European integration, opponents of the European

Constitutional Treaty (ECT) in the 2005 campaign, where they did not simply seize on fortuitous events, were more concerned to put forward their own designs for an 'alternative Europe'. In this, the two campaigns, moreover, correspond to longer term trends. As detailed below, the language of 'Republican resistance' has given way, on the right, to oppositions centred on the preservation of more particularist national values and, on the left, to an 'alternativist' agenda which seeks to redefine the project of European integration itself.

Developments on the right: From the universal to the particular

Hainsworth, O'Brien and Mitchell (2004) identified the main strands in French right-wing Euroscepticism as those associated with a distinctive (and sometimes dissident) Gaullist vision of the nation, a more traditionalist *souverainisme* most prominently espoused by Philippe de Villiers, and the 'France first' populism of the Front National (FN). These three strands of resistance to the European integration project all continue to occupy a place on the French political landscape, though with a marked shift in their relative political importance. Most strikingly, a strongly nationalist Gaullist discourse, which had long left a defining imprint on both the domestic politics of European integration in France and French policy in Europe, would appear to be at least in abeyance, if not in longer term decline. As a result, French right-wing Euroscepticisms have come increasingly to be marked by 'particularist' defences of national traditions, lacking the breadth – and, arguably, the wider resonance – of earlier oppositions to the European integration project cast principally in terms of the protection of the exemplary virtues of the French Republican model.

The declining place of Gaullist nationalism was very much in evidence during the 2005 referendum campaign. In sharp contrast to the manifold divisions over the Treaty on European Union which had riven the neo-Gaullist Rassemblement pour la République (RPR) 13 years earlier, its successor party, the Union pour un Mouvement Populaire (UMP), remained broadly united in support of the European Constitutional Treaty. This was true at the level of party elites, where the most prominent advocate of a 'No' vote in the UMP, the backbench MP Nicolas Dupont-Aignan,[3] lacked the national stature and audience of the Séguin/Pasqua tandem who had assumed centre stage during the Maastricht debates. It was also true at the level of the party's electorate. While polling data showed that around two-thirds of the RPR electorate voted against the TEU in 1992, this situation was reversed in 2005, with polls consistently reporting that over three-quarters of the UMP electorate voted in favour of the ECT (Hainsworth 2006; Perrineau 2005).

This reversal may, of course, partially be attributed to circumstantial factors. As the left was in power in 1992, while the right itself was in office in 2005, such general 'second order' or 'protest' effects as may shape referendum voting (cf. Taggart 2006) clearly pulled in opposite directions in the two votes. Yet, this weakening of a traditional Gaullist nationalism also appears to correspond to longer term trends. The series of restructurings which have taken place on the French mainstream right since the late 1990s have produced, in the UMP, a dominant party which represents a broad middle ground on European issues relative to the wider right (cf. Sauger 2005). In effect, the UMP has been largely shorn of both the *souverainiste* and the 'federalist' tendencies present on the French centre and right. The *souverainistes* had already significantly broken away from the RPR in the late 1990s, with the formation of the Rassemblement pour la France (RPF). Conversely, at the time of the formation of the UMP in 2002, those of stronger 'Euro-federalist' convictions largely remained in the much reduced Union pour la Démocratie française (UDF), subsequently finding a home in the successor Mouvement Démocratique (MoDem). As a result, the overall profile of the UMP, particularly as further reshaped by the reformist and (relatively) liberalising priorities of the Sarkozy presidency, has come increasingly to resemble that of its comparator parties of the centre-right elsewhere in the EU – muffling, if not definitively abandoning much of its earlier 'Gaullist exceptionalism'.

Following this line of argument, *Le Monde* editor Patrick Jarreau has, in his evocatively titled book *La droite contre l'exception française*, gone so far as to portray Sarkozy's reformist ambitions as systematically seeking a 'normalisation' of France, bringing the country into line with global (Anglo-Saxon) models of social and economic organisation (Jarreau 2008). Jarreau's argument undoubtedly overstates the case, insufficiently appreciating the distinctive 'protectionism' which continues to mark French political discourse across virtually the entire ideological spectrum (see below). It does, nonetheless, underscore the extent of the shifts on the French mainstream right, with the dominant UMP, in contrast to both its own predecessors and the current-day *Parti Socialiste* (PS), having found a pragmatically defined cohesion on European issues.

Turning to the second major stand of Euroscepticism on the French right, Philippe de Villiers was largely able to fill the space left vacant by the absence of a more prominent Gaullist nationalism during the 2005 referendum campaign, emerging as the most prominent right-wing figure in the 'No' camp. De Villiers had long burnished his Eurosceptic credentials, already having refused to toe the UDF party line in 1992 with his strong public opposition to the Maastricht Treaty. Later successes in European Parliament (though not national) elections, both under the banner of his own Mouvement pour la France (MPF) and briefly in tandem with Charles Pasqua in the Rassemblement pour la France, subsequently established de Villiers as the principal representative of a distinctively traditionalist and nationalist right centrally defined by its opposition to the continued development of the European integration project.

Through the years, de Villiers' position on the European Union itself has remained consistent, adopting what Flood (2005: 44) has termed a 'revisionist' stance – i.e. seeking to 'turn back the clock' to an earlier phase of EU development. More specifically, since (at least) the Maastricht Treaty debates, de Villiers has argued that the European project should limit itself to carrying out 'the work of the Treaty of Rome', which he characterises as a restrictively defined 'concertation of national sovereignties' focused on the opening of markets (de Villiers 1992: 25; see also Mouvement pour la France 2007).

Yet, though de Villiers' position on European integration *stricto sensu* has been a consistent one, the broader political background against which this is framed has notably evolved over time. De Villiers' early opposition to the Maastricht Treaty laid particular emphasis on the risks which it posed for entrenching the division of the continent – putatively pursuing the closer integration of its Western half at the expense of focusing on an opening to the newly 'liberated' East. Such a concern with the continent's 'openness' has, however, not been a hallmark of de Villier's positioning in recent years. In particular, opposition to Turkish EU membership has become one of de Villiers' most prominent policy planks. This opposition has, moreover, often been cast in strikingly immoderate terms, with the unmistakable intention of seeking to appeal to the FN electorate. In a rather different vein, de Villiers has also, in recent years, emerged as a strong advocate of the need to maintain France's distinctive 'rural way of life', in an equally clear bid to win over or to maintain those voters who might otherwise be seduced by the 'pro-hunting' Chasse, Pêche, Nature et Traditions (CPNT).[4] To this end, his 2007 presidential programme proposed a refounding of the Common Agricultural Policy as an area of flexible cooperation, bringing together only those member states which 'did not have a consumerist conception of agriculture' (Mouvement pour la France 2007).

The final major strand of French right-wing Euroscepticism, that associated with Jean-Marie Le Pen and the Front National, brings strongly to the fore the mixture of strategic and ideological concerns which may shape the adoption of a Eurosceptic position. It is worth underlining, in this regard, that the FN did not, initially, adopt a particularly strong Eurosceptic line. It tended to temper its more specific criticisms of the 'Brussels bureaucracy' with a more general support for a European project conceived as something of a civilisational rampart (Hainsworth, O'Brien and Mitchell 2004: 25–9). It was only with the Maastricht Treaty debates, and the emergence of a mainstream nationalist opposition to the further development of European integration, that Le Pen shifted to a more hard-line 'anti-European' discourse, (in)famously labelling the Treaty's proponents as '*Maastricheurs*'. This hard-line Euroscepticism, including a Republican referent but more fundamentally defined by an integralist nationalism, has since been consistently maintained. Perhaps most strikingly, Le Pen, virtually alone amongst France's more prominent politicians, has openly evoked the possibility of the nation withdrawing from the EU.[5] Interestingly, polling data shows that such positioning on European issues is of little or no direct salience for FN voters in terms of their self-identified priority policy problems (Mayer 2002: 356). It does, however, appear to be the case that the maintenance of this 'anti-European' stance has become a strategically necessary part of the party's wider profile – both ensuring that it is not outflanked on a nationalist issue and serving to buttress its anti-establishment credentials (cf. Rozenberg 2007: 131–4; Harmsen 2005: 90–1).

The overall portrait of Euroscepticism on the French right, as noted at the outset, is thus one in which a mainstream Gaullist nationalism no longer plays a defining role, leaving the field open, at least by default, to both the more traditionalist *souverainisme* represented by Philippe de Villiers and the Front National's radicalised 'populist' opposition to the European project. The principal terms of right-wing opposition to European integration in France have also correspondingly shifted, losing their earlier universalist aspirations and being cast in essentially particularist terms. Oppositions to the European project are now principally marked by a concern to protect a particular 'way of life' or a particular sense of cultural (or ethnic) community. The universalist qualities of a more broadly based defence of a French Republican model or, indeed, the aspirational lyricism of the Gaullist '*certaine idée de la France*' have thus largely been lost, in a manner which marks a break from the idea of 'French exceptionalism' as usually conceived. In a literal sense, of course, the assertion of a 'particularity' relates to the protection of a national 'exception'. If, however, that 'exceptionalism' is defined not only by the preservation of that which is uniquely national, but also by a strongly articulated belief in the unique and wider value of that national model beyond its own boundaries, then prevailing Eurosceptic discourses on the French right fail the test of providing such wider horizons.

Developments on the left: the Europeanisation of national exceptionalism

The prevailing strains of 'Euroscepticism' on the French left, like those on the right, have shifted away from a preoccupation with defending a traditionally defined 'Republican model'. In contrast to developments on the right, however, the shift on the left has largely taken the form of an intensified critical engagement with the European project itself, making the case for a redefinition of its core terms. In effect, though the term (thankfully for linguistic elegance) is little used, an '*altereuropéisme*' has emerged which both derives from and parallels the wider *altermondialiste* movement. This project for an 'alternative Europe' shares many of the concerns of the 'alternative globalisation' movement, attempting to recast the EU in more social and democratic terms as a rampart against neo-liberal globalisation. It also, discursively, is similarly careful to present itself as an 'alternative', seeking to avoid the potentially negative taint of being perceived as only an oppositional movement. In the present context, this discursive framing may be conceived of as a paradoxical 'Europeanisation of exceptionalism', with proponents of the position seeking to preserve what they regard as defining, and threatened, elements of a national exceptionalism (particularly an idealised national 'social model') by their export to the European level.

The concern to present an agenda for an 'alternative Europe' was very much to the fore in the main left 'No' campaigns in the 2005 referendum on the ratification of the European Constitutional Treaty. The principal left-wing proponents of a 'No' vote were careful to stress that they were not 'anti-European', often indeed deploying both the rhetoric and the symbolism of the wider project of European integration in terms similar to that of the 'Yes' camp (Milner 2006). Rather, the core of the left-wing 'No' campaign defined itself by a more specific opposition to the Constitutional Treaty itself, portrayed as 'constitutionalising a neo-liberal order' (ATTAC 2005). A 'No' vote, following this logic, was thus not a 'No' to 'Europe', but rather would confront national and European elites with a 'salutary crisis', opening the door to the renegotiation of a more favourable text. It was, for example, in this vein that Henri Emmanuelli, one of the leading Socialist 'No' campaigners, made his case for the rejection of the Constitutional Treaty:

> To vote 'No' is not to vote against Europe. On the contrary, it is to preserve the possibility of a federal, democratic and social Europe on the basis of a reduced, voluntary core of countries. It is to demand a new, more simple and readable constitution, which limits itself to defining the [Union's] decision-making processes and to providing a clear demarcation of areas of competence (Non Socialiste 2005).

The focus of the left-wing 'No' campaign on the theme of an 'alternative Europe' may, of course, in part be understood in terms of strategic calculations. In particular, the argument that a 'No' vote was likely to produce a renegotiation was given an inadvertent boost by the remarks of former European Commission President Jacques Delors who had publicly speculated that a 'Plan B' would have to be found in the event of a French rejection of the treaty (*Le Monde*, 13 May 2005).[6] The focus on – and the appeal of – such an alternativist discourse cannot, however, be understood only in terms of strategic or circumstantial factors. As Milner argued in her 2004 survey, French left-wing Euroscepticism in the period since Maastricht had come largely to focus 'on the lack of citizen involvement in decision-making at the EU level and on the subordination of social policy to macroeconomic objectives' (Milner 2004: 76). The 2005 campaign, in effect, built upon and crystallised these sentiments, both impugning an 'elitist' project of European integration for failing to deliver on an anticipated level of social protection (Ivaldi 2006) and making the case that an alternative European order was possible.

This 'alternativist' opposition to the current state of European integration also finds a deeper resonance in national political opinion. Notably, Bélot and Cautrès (2004) have convincingly demonstrated the existence of very different sets of 'fears' as regards European integration on the left and right of the French political spectrum. For self-identified supporters of the (mainstream and extreme) right, the principal threats which European integration is seen to pose are those concerned with the preservation of national identity, coupled with concerns over immigration and France's diminished role on the world stage. By way of contrast, voters on the left show relatively little concern with such questions of national identity and influence, but rather focus on the manner in which European integration may be eroding existing national levels of social protection. A left opposition to European integration, following from this, would thus be unlikely to resonate if cast in narrowly *'souverainiste'* terms – as a defence of sovereignty *per se* appears not to be a strong preoccupation of the target electorate. Rather, the terms of that opposition, consonant with the concerns of the parties' electoral constituencies, must be those which stress the putatively invidious characteristics of the current project of European integration, and make the case for an alternative.

This 'alternativist' discourse continued to find strong expression in the 2007 presidential election campaign. All of the principal candidates to the left of the *Parti Socialiste,* with the exception of the veteran *Lutte ouvrière* candidate Arlette Laguiller, adopted a form of 'Alternative Europe' position consonant with that which had played such a prominent role in the 2005 'No' campaign. Communist candidate Marie-George Buffet, reflecting the party's longer term 'Euroconstructivist' turn (Milner 2004: 67–73), spoke of the need 'to act for a social, democratic, solidarist, feminist, ecological, and pacific Europe' (Parti Communiste Français 2007). Anti-globalisation activist José Bové, in similar terms, called for an act of European 're-constitution', refounding the integration project on the basis of 'common values' with 'those countries sharing the objective of a democratic and social Europe' (Bové 2007). Perhaps the most interesting statement of this 'alternativist' position was, nonetheless, that found in the programme of the Ligue Communiste Révolutionnaire (and its media savvy presidential candidate Olivier Besancenot), which took not inconsiderable pains to distinguish this position from that of a potentially sterile 'anti-Europeanism':

> As it has been constructed since 1957, the European Union has been a liberal Europe, a vector of capitalist globalisation. But we are not, whatever the apologists of the prevailing model of globalisation might claim, any more 'anti-European' than we are 'anti-globalisation'. We simply put forward a European alternative to today's Europe (Ligue Communiste Révolutionnaire 2006).

The extent of the wider intellectual shift represented by this 'alternativist' discursive turn should not be underestimated. By its very nature, it represents a major break with an archetypal 'Republican exceptionalism' or 'Jacobin nationalism', as, for example, (still) espoused by Jean-Pierre Chevènement.[7] As discussed in a previous section, this traditional 'Republican' or 'Jacobin' position held that meaningful democratic deliberation and the bases of legitimation for an extensive social solidarity could exist only within the confines of the national community.

European integration was thus to be 'resisted' as potentially undermining these foundations of both democratic and social order. The 'alternativist' position, by way of contrast, clearly continues to see the 'threats' posed by the European project in similar terms, but now sees the solutions too as situated at the European level. Indeed, in more radical forms of this claim, it might even be argued that meaningful democracy and extensive social protection might find salvation *only* through the further development of European integration, conceived as a bulwark of sufficient size and scope to hold back the tides of globalisation.

If a form of Eurosceptic reconciliation with a European project, the 'alternativist' position nonetheless also throws up new sets of political dynamics and dilemmas surrounding European issues. At the level of party management, it has notably served as an important point of leverage for those within the Socialist Party seeking to challenge the generally more 'moderate' orientations of the party leadership (Crespy 2008). As such, it has created a situation in which the main governmental party of the left is potentially exposed to major fissures over Europe, at a time when its principal competitor on the right has, at least by default, found a reasonable cohesion on such issues. The squaring of the circle represented by a 'Europeanisation of national exceptionalism' further appears, in more general terms, as unlikely to live up to its superficially beguiling promise. In effect, insofar as one may conceive of this as a national strategy for European policy (rather than as a domestic strategy of oppositional politics), it shows little regard for the unavoidably complex dynamics of a multi-level political space in which the policy choices desired must compete with a plethora of differing, and often contradictory, preferences. The risk in this regard is that a sustained effort to translate core elements of a national exceptionalism to a wider stage may largely produce a comparably sustained demonstration of the untranslatability of those exceptionalisms – rendering (more) acute underlying questions surrounding the domestic legitimation of European policy. This core dilemma is further explored in the following section, which places French experience in a wider comparative context.

Conclusion: situating French experience in comparative perspective

In the now more than 15 years since the Maastricht Treaty debates, the terms of French Euroscepticism have clearly come to be framed in markedly less 'exceptionalist' terms. Strikingly, while a Republican referent, as detailed elsewhere in this volume, continues to figure prominently in national political debates about areas such as education, immigration, and civic integration, it has lost this prominence in debates surrounding the process of European integration. As detailed above, while oppositions to the Maastricht Treaty were significantly cast in terms of the defence of an – exceptional and exemplary – 'Republican model', this reference point figured relatively little in debates on the European Constitutional Treaty. The decline (or abeyance) of a traditional Gaullist nationalism on the right has largely left the Eurosceptic field to the traditionalism of Philippe de Villiers and the populism of Jean-Marie Le Pen. The prevailing terms of right-wing opposition to the European project have thus shifted to a more particularist and (culturally) protectionist register than that associated with the universalist aspirations of the Republican model. A discourse of 'national exceptionalism' has also declined in prominence amongst 'Eurosceptics' of the Left, but here largely to be replaced by one of 'Europeanisation' that emphasises the construction of an 'alternative Europe', albeit in terms which often show little regard for the realities and constraints of the European political arena itself.

Less 'exceptionalist' in its discursive construction, French Euroscepticism also does not appear as empirically exceptional relative to trends elsewhere. The broad configuration of the French party system corresponds to Taggart's (1998) now well-established 'touchstone of dissent' hypothesis, whereby he argues that strong Eurosceptic positions will tend to be held by parties otherwise on the margins of national party systems. Stronger Euroscepticisms continue, in this vein, to find voice for the most part in smaller parties on the right and the left who seek, more generally, to challenge the establishment consensus. The exception to this, again in keeping with Taggart's model, is the factionalism more recently exhibited within the Socialist Party, in which the European issue has formed a key part of challenges to the party's dominant leadership group. More generally, the terms of opposition to European integration in the French case – stressing issues of cultural integrity on the right and attacking the excesses of a predatory global capitalism on the left – may also readily be seen to parallel oppositional discourses seen elsewhere.

Neither 'exceptionalist' in its self-presentation nor empirically exceptional relative to wider trends, French Euroscepticism nonetheless remains distinctive. Beyond the trivial sense in which all national manifestations of a wider phenomenon are necessarily unique, this distinctiveness, in the French case as more generally, is crucial for understanding the domestic politics of European integration. In effect, the patterns of 'fit' and 'misfit' between European policies and institutions and their national counterparts will necessarily vary in every national case (cf. Harmsen

2008: 318–20; Harmsen 2007: 70–3). Similarly, the cultural resonance of such frictions as may arise will also necessarily vary, in light of differing senses of the core values of national social, political, and economic order. Different sets of issues will thus be thrown up by the integration process in differing member states – creating distinctive opportunity structures for both those pursuing a Eurosceptic agenda and those seeking to anchor the domestic legitimacy of the European project. In the case of France, that distinctive pattern may be understood, in somewhat inelegant short-hand, as focusing particularly on issues of 'projection' and 'protection'.

'Projection', in this context, refers to a particular concern with the projection or exercise of national influence on the European stage. Clearly, as underlined by intergovernmentalist theorists, the pursuit of national interests via European integration is by no means uniquely French. France, has, however, perhaps more than any other member state, tended to see European integration as a means of exporting its policy choices and amplifying its influence in the wider world. It has also been acutely conscious of its (inevitable) loss of (relative) influence within an enlarging group of member states animated by different preoccupations and centres of interest than the original Six. Much French European debate has correspondingly been preoccupied with, as Helen Drake (2005: 1) has put it, 'seeking to claw back its traditional influence in the EU'. Nicolas Sarkozy's election night pronouncement that '*la France est de retour en Europe*' both captured this underlying anxiety and affirmed his own ambition to rectify the situation.

The leftist project for an 'alternative Europe' discussed above fits easily into this more general pattern of national European discourse. That general pattern is, however, perhaps best illustrated by Statham's (2005) comparative study of the prevailing patterns of political communication about European issues in France and Britain. British politicians tended largely to address 'Europe' as an issue of domestic politics, making 'polit-ical claims' largely only as regards one another. By way of contrast, the 'political claims' made by their French counterparts were largely directed at the European institutions themselves, seeking to secure particular pol-icy outcomes. A clear preoccupation with influence thus emerges in the French case, in marked contrast to a British situation in which 'Europe' has remained something of a contested 'other'.

A focus on the 'projection' of French influence is further coupled with a distinctive 'protectionism'. That protectionism is, in part, of the tradi-tional economic variety – reflecting a distinctive French political econ-omy and relationship to the processes of both globalisation and European integration (cf. Hay and Rosamond 2002). It must, however, also be understood in wider terms, implying not only the protection of a model of state economic intervention or social welfare provision, but also more intangibly the protection of a 'way of life' or a sense of cultural community. In these variable senses, forms of protectionism figure prominently across the French political spectrum. Most obviously, the Euroscepticisms of both the left and the right discussed above may be understood as protectionist. Leftist projects for an 'alternative Europe' seek to protect a national social model *through* Europe. Euroscepticisms of the right too, in the French case, share these concerns, having significantly (if not uniformly) come to see a 'European preference' as a means to stem the unwanted effects of economic globalisation. At the same time, however, the Euroscepticisms of the right are also concerned with protecting French interests and practices *from* Europe – often confounding issues of European integration with those of immigration and cultural integration so as to cast themselves as the defenders of an imperilled national order.

More striking, however, than the economic and cultural protectionisms of parties towards the left and right flanks of the political spectrum is the extent to which the theme of protectionism, in various guises, figures in French mainstream political discourse. Notably, both Ségolène Royal and Nicolas Sarkozy, in their 2007 presidential electoral manifestos, spoke of the European integration project in terms of its ability to protect Europe's citizens from the putative negative effects of globalisation. The Socialist candidate's platform spoke in this vein of the need to 'construct a Europe which is more protective and more in tune with the needs of its citizens' (Royal 2007). In very similar terms, the candidate of the right argued in his platform that: 'Europe must not be the Trojan horse of a globalisation reduced to only the circulation of capital and goods, but must instead protect its peoples within the process of globalisation' (Sarkozy 2007a). Sarkozy has, moreover, continued to play on much the same register since assuming office. The President's high-profile, late intervention in the negotiations over the Lisbon Treaty, securing the deletion of the reference to 'free and undistorted competition' from the core objectives to be pursued by the Union, was a clear signal in the direction of these 'protectionist' sentiments (and 2005 'No' voters). In similar terms, it is noteworthy that Sarkozy marked the start of the 2008 French presidency of the Council of Ministers with a televised interview in which he emphasised the need 'to change profoundly the manner in which we are building Europe', so as 'to make Europe a means to protect citizens in their daily lives' (*Le Figaro*, 1 July 2008).[8]

This distinctive national European discourse, preoccupied with both 'projection' and 'protection', clearly reflects both the intellectual traditions and the substantive preoccupations of an earlier national exceptionalism – even if the discourse itself, variably advocating both domestic and European reform, is no longer literally 'exceptionalist' in the sense of seeking to distinguish France from its European counterparts. The challenges posed to French political elites by this exercise in (re-) legitimating the European project in the domestic arena are also by no means unique. In essence, French elites, like their counterparts elsewhere in the Union, must face the realisation that their traditional roles as representative mediators are being irrevocably, and uncomfortably, redefined. The classic representative role of aggregating interests within a discrete national political system is being increasingly displaced by one in which elites are called upon to act as translators or mediators between the national political arena on the one hand and wider European or international arenas on the other. Thus far, few have risen to the challenge of reshaping national political discourses and climates of expectations accordingly (Schmidt 2006), often preferring instead the short-term expediency of decrying international or European developments for which they themselves are co-responsible (Menon 2008).

It is finally in this regard that the Sarkozy presidency has opened something of a new, and potentially interesting, chapter in the French case. Perhaps rather more than any of his predecessors, or his counterparts elsewhere in the EU, Sarkozy has appeared aware of the need for a revitalisation of political communication. Certainly, his early forays onto the European stage, briefly described above, have sought directly to allay growing French anxieties about European integration and to re-establish a sense of the nation's central place in that project. Yet, at the same time, Sarkozy's European engagement, reflecting criticisms of his policy style more generally, appears bereft of a wider strategy or vision. It has been a European policy, at least thus far, of high visibility, but only rather more limited accomplishment. In this, on a markedly different basis to the past, French engagement with Europe may still serve as an important exemplar – illustrating both the possibilities, and the limits, of an activist pragmatism.

Acknowledgement

The author gratefully acknowledges the support of the British Academy (Small Grant 40300, 'The Politics of European Constitutional Ratification in France and the Netherlands'), provided while he was a member of staff at The Queen's University of Belfast.

Notes

1 Translations of quotations from the French are those of the author unless otherwise indicated.
2 Interestingly, the term 'social nationalist' has also been used, in a scathingly critical fashion, by political scientist Dominique Reynié to describe the leftist opposition to the European Constitutional Treaty. Reynié, applying an epithet which he credits to Léon Blum, describes this 'social nationalism' as characterised by 'a fierce antiliberalism, an exaltation of the State, and a nationalist discourse impregnated by xenophobia' (Reynié 2005: 15).
3 Dupont-Aignan subsequently broke with the UMP altogether, founding the self-described 'Gaullist' movement *Debout la République*. As suggested by the movement's name, Dupont-Aignan places himself firmly within the tradition of defending a 'Republican exceptionalism', attacking the constitutional development of the EU from (at least) Maastricht onwards as an 'anti-1789', with the Lisbon Treaty correspondingly dismissed as a 'coup d'État simplifié' (Dupont-Aignan 2008).
4 A *'localisme ruraliste'* may itself be seen as constituting a distinctive form of Euroscepticism or resistance to the European project in the French case. See further Rozenberg 2007: 140–3.
5 Le Pen's 2007 presidential programme, for example, called for a 'radical renegotiation' of the EU treaties. In the event that such renegotiations were to fail, a national referendum would be held in which the electorate would be asked to respond to the question: 'Should France take back its independence from the Europe of Brussels?' (Front National 2007).
6 The resonance of the renegotiation theme was clearly demonstrated in the post-referendum Eurobarometer survey, which found that fully 83 per cent of those who had voted against the Treaty expected that this would 'allow for the renegotiation of the Constitution in order to come to a more social text', a belief shared by only 30 per cent of 'Yes' voters (Eurobarometer 2005: 25).
7 Chevènement has continued vigorously to pursue much the same line of attack as regards European integration. In his most recent book, the tellingly titled *La faute de M. Monnet*, he speaks of Europe as *'tout sauf un espace républicain'*, contrasting its judicialised 'procedural democracy' with a 'republican democracy' of genuine citizen participation (Chevènement 2006: 57). He is now, however, a much less prominent figure on the French left – notably, playing at best only a rather secondary role in the 2005 'No' campaign.
8 This 'protectionist' conception of the European Union further finds strong expression in national public opinion. In a July 2008 'Opinion Way' poll, commissioned by *Le Figaro* and *La Chaîne des Informations*, fully 82 per cent of respondents expressed the view that the European Union should 'protect Europeans against globalisation'. Tellingly, however, only 24 per cent of respondents thought that it was currently doing so (*Le Figaro*, 4 July 2008).

Section III

Citizenship and the Republican Model

7
French Immigration Policy in Comparative Perspective

Martin A. Schain

What's so exceptional?

Comparison is at the very heart of any understanding of what is exceptional, whether that understanding is analysis or discourse. It is through comparison that we can see if France is indeed so different, and through additional comparison that we can begin to understand why these differences occur. If we think of comparison as limited to a number of key variables, then France can be seen as exceptional if it is consistently positioned on the far end of the range of variance for these key variables. Four variables are the focus of this volume: societal consensus/polarisation; the balance of state and society domination; the strong/weak projection of universal values and ideas in international affairs; and the integrationist/multicultural model of integration. For the purposes of this chapter I would like to add two additional variables that are linked to the first two of those listed above and that have also frequently been related to French exceptionalism. The first is political instability – both regime instability, for which France holds a record among Western democracies – and governmental instability, the record for which France vied with Italy during the Third and Fourth Republics.[1] The second is the French pattern of political change, often characterised by what Michel Crozier has called 'the bureaucratic phenomenon': blocked decision-making, and change through crisis. The literature that has dealt with both instability and crisis decision-making is linked both to ineffective decision-making and to policy *'immobilisme'*, in particular the inability of French decision-making institutions to deal with evolving requirements for policy change.[2]

For the purposes of this chapter, political instability and the bureaucratic mode of decision-making are understood as inhibiting the ability of any French government to develop and implement coherent and legitimate policy. In this chapter, we will examine the question of exceptionalism by looking at both immigration and integration policy. Immigration policy presents a real problem for the understanding of French exceptionalism. I will argue something that I had been determined to avoid: that immigration policy presents us with a double paradox:

First, I will argue that during the long period of political instability, immigration policy was developed and implemented in a relatively coherent and effective manner. On the other hand, quite the opposite was true as the political system gained legitimacy in the 1970s (as measured by public opinion and acceptance by all major political parties), and as effective policy-making became more normal as governments gained stability through stable and more or less disciplined parliamentary majorities.

Second, I will argue that the (less important, from the point of view of exceptionalism) integration policy-pattern of French Jacobinism has been improperly understood. On the national level, France has begun to develop a policy of integration only since the 1980s. Nevertheless, even before that, in important ways policy was developed and communities were recognised at the local level. By focusing on the consequences of integration policy, we can see that it has failed in important areas (compared to other countries), but that there has been unanticipated success in other areas.

I will examine the role of the state in immigration policy, first during the period of European immigration before and after the Second World War; then during the period of non-European immigration after the 1960s. I will then look at the French model of integration, often cited as different from other countries, and also compare it during these same periods. Integration policy implies primarily a domestic policy focus, although relations with other countries can have some importance, particularly with regard to aspects of citizenship.

Immigration policy

Immigration policy, we will argue, was different in degree before the war, although arguably not exceptional. Unlike Britain, France preferred immigrants for manpower, rather than labour from its colonial empire. Although, under the Third Republic, the French state has been depicted as weak, and society as deeply divided, the state remained firmly in control of an open immigration policy and societal institutions appeared to function well to integrate immigrants from other European countries.

The post-war period was different. In an attempt to maximise immigration, the French state purposely loosened its controls over entry – which is not to say that immigration was out of control. Policy remained consistent with government objectives, at least until the 1970s.

After the suspension of immigration in 1973, governments lost considerable control over immigration, as courts in France (as well as in other countries in Europe) mandated in favour of continued family unification. During the 20 years that followed, stated government objectives appeared to be increasingly at variance with realities on the ground. Although immigration levels declined substantially from those before suspension, they never approached the 'immigration zero' that governments in the 1990s were advocating. Indeed, as the state and the constitutional system grew stronger, and societal divisions seemed to become less important, the ability of the government to impose immigration policy seemed to decline. In other words, as France has become 'normalised', in terms of regime stability diminishing challenges to the regime, policy appears to have become less effective. When institutions were less stable, policy was both more effective and seemed to evolve with requirements for policy change.

Nevertheless, France did not appear to be exceptional, since every country in Western Europe developed similar policies, and seemed to have similar difficulties in implementing that policy. The exceptional country was the United States, which passed legislation that led to relatively open immigration, at the very same time that countries in Europe were doing exactly the opposite.

Administrative policy-making: coherence and low political salience

At least until the onset of the depression, the main concern of French immigration legislation was not to exclude immigrants, but to control their behaviour on French soil. Thus, in 1889, after immigration had been growing for more than 40 years, France promulgated its first legislation on naturalisation rather than immigration – in fact a major consolidation and reform of law and practice – as part of a more general effort to control and direct immigrants already within the country. The legislation was the end-product of a long process both to consolidate policy and to consider new needs that had begun to become more evident in the early part of the decade. Its principal concern was to deal with French manpower needs, and to tie immigration to settlement by firmly establishing *jus solis* as a principle of law. In the name of security, requirements became more and more exacting, however, particularly with regard to documentation. In 1912, legislation was passed that required identity documents with detailed pictures and descriptions for resident immigrants, and French administrative authorities could prevent people from crossing the frontier if '... their presence appeared dangerous' (Noiriel 1988: 89).

However, the ability of the state to mold and control immigration and immigrants was sharply limited, not by either immobilism or governmental instability, but by the weakness of the state in this area, perhaps because the priority was to facilitate, rather than inhibit, entry. As Vincent Viet has pointed out, 'On the eve of the First World War, France had no administrative organisation for immigration' (Viet 1998: 27).

This priority was accentuated by the losses during WWI, and after the war a new system was put in place that was dominated by a manpower recruitment effort that was never legislated. The post-war system was embedded in a framework of bilateral agreements with Poland, Italy and Czechoslovakia signed in 1919/1920. Within this framework, the French state recruited workers directly for the post-war reconstruction zones, but increasingly recruitment was turned over to a privately-controlled agency, the Societé générale d'immigration (SGI). Although specific departments in five different ministries were responsible for different aspects of immigration policy and control, SGI had the central responsibility for the recruitment of immigrant workers, recruitment that was deemed essential to post-war economic expansion.

The orientation of this policy remained unchallenged until the employment crisis of the depression, when state bureaucracies began to use many of the powers that had been held in abeyance before, in order to limit access of immigrant workers to the labour market. The most effective action by the state was to reimpose the frontier, and severely restrict the entry of immigrant labour. However, as the depression became more severe in 1932, legislation was passed that authorised a complex procedure that offered the possibility of imposing quotas on the employment of immigrants in various industries (but not in agriculture). As the depression wore on, increasing administrative restrictions were imposed on immigrants resident in France, and as the war approached, restrictions became more severe. Nevertheless, immigrants did not disappear from the labour force. As Cross points out, '...the regulated flow of alien labour became a permanent feature of the economies of France and later of Western Europe....A permanent reserve army of labourers emerged, defined less by their social, educa-

tional, or racial characteristics than by their legal status as immigrants'
(Cross 1983: 213).

Although what most defined immigration policy between the wars
was controlled recruitment of manpower, manpower evolved slowly
into settlement, as workers brought their families or created new ones
on French soil. The law on naturalisation eased the requirement of
residency to three years in 1927, resulting in much higher rates of
naturalisation, particularly among the more established settlements
of immigrants.

Within the French administration, there were conflicting views on
immigration, in particular how immigration should be understood and
organised. Thus, entry policy was shaped mostly by administrative action
in a problem-solving mode, that often involved different notions of
desirable and undesirable immigrants, and that often constrained the
implementation of policy. This thinking was captured in the work of
Georges Mauco, the best known expert on immigration during the inter-
war period. In a report to the League of Nations, Mauco argued that
'...among the diversity of foreign races in France, there are some...
(Asians, Africans, even Levantines) for whom assimilation is not possible,
and is, in addition, often physically and morally undesirable.' With
the aid of a survey that he had developed, he established a hierarchy of
ethnicities, with Swiss and Belgian migrants on top, and North Africans
far down at the bottom.[3]

Mauco did not draw his inspiration from the eugenics movement so
much as a deep strain of cultural racism that presumed an impenetrable
barrier to assimilation, as well as a superiority of those closest to French
ethnicity. This orientation was close to the liberal perspective on similar subjects in the United States during roughly the same period, and,
like his counterparts in the United States, he was optimistic about the
prospects of assimilation of the vast majority of immigrants in France.
Although the question continued to be framed in terms of French manpower needs, at least until the latter part of the Depression, in 1926 there
was an unsuccessful proposal to establish a French quota system similar
to the one that had been legislated in the United States two years earlier.[4]
However, in marked contrast to the United States, immigration was not a
high salience issue, and the framing of the issue tended to be dominated
by administrative concerns.

Nevertheless, the application of the 1927 legislation by the administration tended to mold naturalisation to perceived ideas of national
security and national identity with a bias against Asians, Africans and
'Levantines' – Jews (Dewhurst 2007). In practice, the administration

was less favourable to applicants for immigration who could be seen as threats to internal security, and more favourable to applicants who could contribute to conscription (Cross 1983: Ch. 8). Although there was no requirement for immigrants from North Africa to be naturalised, they were viewed as the least desirable by employers and the administration alike.

At no point during the pre-Second World War period does either the development of immigration policy or its application appear to have been 'out of control', nor did the French state seem to have difficulty dealing with immigration policy in a rapidly evolving context. Manpower was effectively recruited (along with settlement) after WWI, shaped by bilateral agreements and industrial needs. Recruitment was then restricted after 1932, but continued to flow to those sectors where it was still needed. The Third Republic was marked by acute governmental instability that gradually evolved into regime instability in the 1930s, and was increasingly incapable of dealing with the financial and economic crisis of the depression, or the foreign policy crises that began to snowball at the same time. Nevertheless, none of this appeared to apply to immigration policy-making, virtually all of which took place within the administrative system. Although there were certainly disagreements within the administration, they never overflowed into the political system. Immigration remained a low salience issue that neither emerged as a basis for coalition-building, nor as a point of contention that destroyed government coalitions.

After the war, the principles of French policy remained the same as before – the priority of manpower recruitment. Two ordinances in 1945 established the framework for post-war immigration: conditions of entry and stay; and citizenship and naturalisation. There was considerable in-fighting within the government about the criteria for entry. Population demographers (Georges Macau, Alfred Sauvy and Robert Debré) advocated 'ethnic criteria' that would facilitate integration. Labour-manpower advocates (Alexandre Parodi and Adrien Tixier), on the other hand, focused on the requirements for the economy and post-war recovery. The labour-manpower advocates won. The first ordinance once again excluded all reference to selection of manpower on the basis of national origin and established rules for entry and *séjour* in France for longer than three months. The second essentially reestablished the naturalisation requirements of the law of 1927 (Weil 1991: 54–9).[5] Perhaps most important, work permits and residency permits were entirely separate, making it possible for immigrants to remain in France even if they were not employed.

French policy also reflected many of the same concerns as the previous period. Despite the rejection of national origin criteria, the French administration – the demographers in particular – continued to be concerned with the balance between workers arriving from other countries in Europe and those from North Africa, still considered to be the least desirable recruits.

Essentially, the problem seemed to be that the framework that was established in 1945, with the Office National d'Immigration (ONI) at the centre of recruitment, increasingly failed to provide manpower sufficient for the demands of the French economy. After Algerian Muslims gained both French citizenship and free movement in mainland France in 1946 and 1947 (Weil 1991: 93), there was a surge in immigration from Algeria. In 1946, there were only 22,000 Algerians in France, a mere 1.3 per cent of the total number of residents in France from outside mainland France, and less than half the total number of North Africans in the country. By 1954, the number had increased to almost 212,000, 13 per cent of the number of immigrants (if we include Algerians as 'immigrants'), and over 90 per cent of the North Africans then in France. It was during this period of strong economic growth, between 1956 and 1962 in France and in Europe, that the French government encouraged immigrants from other parts of Europe to enter the country. This effort was often organised by private employers, and then officially recognised by the state. By the 1960s, perhaps 90 per cent of immigration was processed in this way.

That would not last, however, as the economic growth of Western Europe spread to those countries that had supplied the workers to balance those from North Africa. Ultimately, the 'internal migration' from North Africa became a foreign migration as decolonisation progressed; and the 'foreign migration' from Western Europe became linked to the process of European unification and therefore quasi internal. Nevertheless, the trend that had begun after the war was not seriously altered by decolonisation. Immigration from North Africa continued to grow, relative to that of Europe, while immigration from Western Europe grew less rapidly. Italians were replaced by Spanish, and Spanish by Portuguese, and then Portuguese by North Africans. Nevertheless, recruitment efforts in Europe were not entirely unsuccessful.

Strong efforts to recruit European (and even Turkish) workers, rather than Algerian, reflected the preferences of employers as well as those of the French administration. During the period after the Evian Accords were signed in 1962, the French and Algerian governments were in constant negotiations over the number of Algerian workers who would be permitted to enter France, with the French trying to reduce the number, and the Algerians trying to increase it. By contrast, during this same period France signed labour recruitment agreements with 16 different countries, with an increasing emphasis on the recruitment of Portuguese (Weil 1991: 95–100). These preferences reflected concerns that had been widespread within the administration since the balance of immigration began to change in the 1960s.

Among the immigrants from the Maghreb, French administrative authorities were particularly concerned about those from Algeria. At the same time that Moroccans and Tunisians had more or less free access to France – and were also given beneficial labour contracts – the French government negotiated agreements with Algeria, in 1964 and 1968, to limit by quotas the entry of Algerian nationals. These agreements were clarified in 1970 by French legislation (that specifically targeted Algerians), and the quotas were reduced by a third agreement in 1972 (Money 1999: 109–10).[6]

By the mid-1950s, administrative authorities were clearly seeking '… immigration of Latin-Christian origin'. The result was what appeared to be a period of unregulated entry and *post-hoc* regularisation, but that was undertaken as a way of balancing out the free movement of Algerians (Weil 1991). No legislation was passed, nor were there any grand debates in parliament or at party conferences. Policy evolved through a problem-solving approach that was virtually invisible, what Alexis Spire has called 'the hidden face of the state':

> Between 1945 and 1975, the legislative context of French policy on immigration hardly varied. However, the [administrative] agents of the state did not hesitate to give to this same text changing interpretations over the years….In the area of immigration, the *circulaire* occupied a preponderant place: the heads of the bureaus of immigration only occasionally referred to the ordinances of 1945 [the legal base, which was also not passed as a law], but preciously conserved the collection of *circulaires* applicable in their area of competence….The most important permitted the organisation of family immigration in 1947, the installation of action on the protection of the national labour market in 1949, the encouragement of regularisation of illegal immigrants in 1956, then to slow it down in 1972, and finally the suspension of immigration in July 1974 (Spire 2005: 13).

For 30 years state agencies dealing with immigration altered the way the problem was understood, through several hundred ministerial *circulaires* that were internal directives rather than documents with the force of law. Through these documents the frame of immigration policy moved from an understanding of immigrants as manpower for settlement, to a concern about ethnic balances, to deep concern about integration, to – finally in 1972–4 – a view that undesirable immigration must be suspended (Spire 2005: 13). Through this entire period, questions of immigration were on the agenda of administrative agencies that dealt with the issue and their changing views of the problem were under the purview of government ministers, but were not the subject of legislative debate.

Thus, throughout this period, French immigration policy continued to be decided wholly within the administration. Once again, although there were certainly conflicts, the overall objectives remained reasonably clear. Indeed, even those aspects of policy that appeared to be poorly controlled were embedded in an administrative plan. The generally unregulated immigration of the 1960s has been widely analysed, and has been related to the pressures of the labour market. However, it is reasonably clear that market forces were serving the objective of the Ministry of Labour. Thus, Minister of State for Social Affairs Jean-Marie Jeanneney noted in 1966 that: 'Illegal immigration has its uses, for if we rigidly adhere to the regulations and international agreements we would perhaps be short of labour' (Hargreaves 1995: 178–9; Miller 1981: xxx; Geddes 2003: 53). The need for labour was certainly clear, but before the opening of the frontier to immigrant workers from Europe, much of that need was being filled by migrants from Algeria and other parts of North Africa. As a result of the open door policy, by 1962, the rate of settlement of workers from Europe significantly surpassed that of Algerians.

The capstone to the administrative process was the suspension of immigration. Unlike Britain and the United States, the French government reversed policy and imposed immigration restriction by administrative action, rather than through legislation: the *circulaires* issued by the Secretary of State for Immigrant Workers on July 5 and 19, 1974. The suspension of labour and family migration took place in July 1974 during the early days of the economic crisis, and from this point of view appears to be a straightforward reaction to the change in labour-market needs. However, the decision was, in fact, far more complicated, and the consequences not at all what policy-makers had anticipated.

The problem of immigration was framed by the government in terms of the difficulty of integrating immigrants (primarily) from North

Africa, and therefore the need to limit entry of these kinds of workers. However, since immigration from other parts of Europe was declining in favour of those from North Africa, the government's decision was to suspend immigration in general. Framing the issue in these terms contributed in important ways to a broad agreement around suspension, since the main political actors in both the government and opposition shared this perspective. As in the United States during an earlier period, this perspective informed the discussions and actions of trade unions, political parties, the government and the state; and as in the United States, an emphasis on race probed the limits of the integrative capacities of the melting pot. In fact, there was no opposition to the suspension of immigration. How, then did immigration entry become such a highly charged political issue?

The breakdown of the administrative process

Certainly part of the problem was the original consensus that was developed around suspension – the undesirability of the immigrants who were entering in greater numbers. Eventually, the issue became politicised around this understanding as it became evident that – as a result of a decision of the Conseil d'Etat – French governments had only limited ability to prevent family unification (Conseil d'Etat 1978: 493). Nevertheless, governments of the Right and (after 1981) the Left tightened rules of entry, and were more or less in agreement about the desirability of strongly controlling entry. The key source of somewhat chaotic politicisation was the breakthrough of the Front National (FN) during the years between 1983 and 1986.

Indeed, increasingly after 1984, it appeared as if immigration policy was far more polarised than it was. Although very little separated left and right governments with regard to policy on immigration, the electoral stakes made immigration politics one of the great dividers between left and right. As the FN gained in electoral support, the story of immigration politics after 1984 became less about the struggle over policy orientation itself, than about the struggle by established political parties on both the Right and the Left to use policy to undermine the ability of the FN to sustain the initiative in portraying and defining these issues.

Of course, this does not mean that the electoral breakthrough of the FN was important only in terms of rhetoric. Since the mid-1980s, governments of the Right and the Left have been sensitive to the policy positions advocated by the Front National. While the more extreme positions have been resisted, other hardline FN positions have been enacted into law or promulgated by administrative actions. A 2005 analysis notes the following areas in which more restrictive policy has been linked to FN pressure: more restrictive rules for family unification and marriage, more restrictions on tourist visas, increased levels of expulsion of illegal immigrants, greater restrictions on the right of asylum, and greater requirements for naturalisation (Chambeau 2005). Of course the problem is that it is difficult to know if at least some of these more restrictive policies would have been enacted even without FN pressure. Nevertheless, at least some policy changes can be linked more directly to the competitive dynamics of electoral and party competition.

The elections of 2002 became a case study of the disruptive role of the Front National. Because the vote for the Left was splintered among several candidates in the first round of the presidential elections of 2002, Jean-Marie Le Pen, the FN candidate, came in second. The right was divided as well, with the result that Jacques Chirac was placed first, but with the lowest percentage of votes of any leading candidate in the history of the Fifth Republic, and only 2 per cent ahead of Le Pen. In the second round, Chirac won with the support of the Left, and with more than 81 per cent of the vote.

Nevertheless, for the Right, the electoral lesson seemed clear – never in the future to permit its support to be undermined by the immigration issue as used by the Front National. Thus, in the years that followed 2002, the constraints imposed by the FN remained, and were even reinforced by what had happened.

The strategy of the Right to deal with the challenge of the Front National included a combination of hard policy and actions that would demonstrate the effectiveness of the state in dealing with illegal immigration. The immigration legislation in 2003, with its emphasis on stricter visa requirements and the experimental integration contract focused French legislation on interests close to those of FN voters, while Minister of the Interior Nicolas Sarkozy, periodically employed extreme-right discourse and took action that would indicate that this government was serious about controlling the frontier. By 2005, Sarkozy was given credit by officials of the majority Right UMP for the relatively poor showing of the Front National in elections at the end of 2004 and early 2005 (*Le Monde*, June 23, 2005). The presidential and legislative victory in 2007, in part at the expense of the FN, verified the success of Sarkozy's approach (Fourquet 2008).

This success provided an opening for the recognition and elaboration of a new departure in immigration policy in 2006, termed by Sarkozy as *immigration choisie*, as opposed to *immigration subie*. It was a call for an increase of high-tech immigrants in place of those who arrive for family unification, but was also a step away from the *immigration zéro* rhetoric of a decade earlier. This new orientation, in part first elaborated under the socialists in 1998, was integrated into the 2007 legislation. It is unclear whether such a policy can be made to work, or whether reduction of family unification is even legal under existing international agreements. Indeed, the goal (that half or more of immigrants fit this category of *immigration choisie*), acknowledged as difficult to achieve, was termed 'mission impossible' by Patrick Weil, in an interview in *Le Monde* on July 10, 2007.

It is clear, however, that this is an approach that Sarkozy understands and explains in terms of the dynamics of the electoral challenge of the FN:

> *'Immigration choisie'* is practised by the quasi-totality of democracies in the world. And in these countries, racism and the extreme right are less strong than here. In short, this [proposal] is a rampart against racism. This should make us think. I want a calm and lengthy debate about the theses of the extreme right, which makes every foreigner into a delinquent, and the extreme left, for which to speak of immigration is the equivalent of xenophobia. (Interview with Sarkozy in *Le Monde*, April 28, 2006: 9)

While it is certainly true that every country has made some effort to 'choose' those that it accepts for settlement, it is less clear that this has made them more resistant to the success of the extreme right. On the other hand, the statement should probably be read for what it hypothesises about the importance of this policy for France.

Thus, in the 1980s, at a moment when French politics was becoming less and less exceptional, and the French political system was becoming increasingly stable and legitimate, immigration policy became increasingly chaotic in several different ways. First, the objectives appeared to be unrelated to the results; second, because these results created the impression of ineffectiveness, this in turn fed into support for the Front National. More to the point, French policy was becoming increasingly exceptional. As other European countries began to develop more nuanced policies on immigration in the 1990s, French law remained committed to exclusion. Under Sarkozy France has taken a half-step towards increasing labour immigration, but only by balancing this with a much harder position on family immigration and undocumented immigrants.

Integration policy

Although much has been written about the Republican model of integration – individual integration, rather than a recognition of multi-national communities – France has had very little by way of integration policy until very recently. Until the 1980s, immigrant integration was left largely to the schools (by default) and to non-governmental institutions, such as churches, trade unions and political parties.

Integration in the automatic society

One indication of the complexity within the French Republican model can be seen at the local level, as political parties attempted to integrate the post-WWI wave of European immigrants. Between the wars, among the most powerful instruments for integrating new immigrant populations were the trade union movement and the French Communist Party. Both the unions and the party sought new members (and eventually electoral support) by mobilising workers from Poland, Italy, and after the Second World War, workers from Spain. Part of the effort certainly focused on class solidarity, but mobilisation was also based on ethnic and religious solidarities.

Although the efforts of the CGTU (the Communist-dominated trade union confederation between 1922 and 1936) and the party were integrative in the sense that they represented and aggregated the interests of immigrant workers together with those of other workers, they were also supportive of the particular interests of these workers as immigrants, and in this sense contributed to the development of ethnic identity. They organised separate language groups, and the party put into place immigrant manpower commissions. Finally, the party supported ethnic organisations and demonstrations among immigrant groups that were both particularistic and more universal in nature (Wihtol de Wenden 1988: 50). The establishment of communism in immigrant communities eventually destabilised older political patterns in these same areas, but at the price of the establishment of local ethnic machines, many of which endured well into the Fifth Republic.[7]

At this level, it is difficult to separate ethnic politics from integration of ethnic solidarities into a larger, more universal political project, but two aspects of this process appear to challenge the conventional wisdom of the Republican model. The Communist Party and the CGTU not only recognised the legitimacy of immigrant collectivities, but also gave benefits to these collectivities at the local level. Thus, even during the 'golden age' of the French Jacobin melting pot, ethnic dimensions were clearly taken into account, at least by the Communist Party and the trade unions in ways that were comparable to their British and American counterparts on the left at the time.

The state intervenes

We find a similar pattern with the wave of Third World immigration after 1960. Studies on the ground provide clear evidence of the recognition of immigrant collectivities by political parties, as well as by public authorities. As during the previous period, this evidence is more obvious at the local than at the national level. Nevertheless, there are some differences, the most important of which is that the pattern of policy-making has been conditioned by what Maxim Silverman has termed the 'racialised' view of the post-1960s wave non-European immigrants in a way that has clearly differentiated them from the waves of European immigrants that preceded them; (Silverman 1992: Ch. 4) and the emphasis on race has probed the limits of the integrative capacities of the French version of the melting pot.

In contrast to the tradition of positive solidarity that Communist-governed municipalities had developed towards predominantly European immigrants, by the 1970s, many of these same local governments began to treat non-European immigrants (as well as non-white French citizens from the overseas departments), as temporary residents who must be encouraged to return home (Schain 1985). As during the earlier period, Communist municipalities tended to treat new immigrant communities as collectivities, but now in an exclusionary manner. This pattern was not, however, unique to towns governed by Communists (Grillo 1985: 125–7; Barou 1994: 24). On the initiative of local governments, the state also collaborated in establishing quotas for immigrant children in primary schools (Schain 1985: 176–81).

After 1986 the dialogue within the political elite – the discourse about the political philosophy – moved back towards a reassertion of the traditional Republican model, but the public discourse continued to be contradicted by relative open political expressions of ethnic consciousness, as well as public policies that in many ways supported this consciousness. These policies not only tolerated the public expression of ethnic differences, but, as Danièle Lochak points out, also tended to manage and institutionalise them (Feldblum 1993: 57).

Perhaps the most important change was the growth of ethnic associations after 1981. By the mid-1980s, these associations had become a network of established intermediaries for immigrant populations that negotiated with trade unions, political parties and the state at the local and national levels. By the end of the decade they numbered between three and four thousand, ranging from about a thousand Islamic associations, to the better known national groups such as SOS-Racisme and France-Plus (Wihtol de Wenden 1992). In contrast to earlier periods of immigration, these associations operated largely outside the established network of intermediary groups, which were then forced to recognise their independent existence. Even when established and more universal intermediary groups, such as trade unions, did succeed in incorporating their leadership, such incorporation remained conditional and problematic (Schain 1994).

Thus, political mobilisation on the basis of evolving categories of ethnicity, while not new in France, is now taking place in a different context, largely outside the organisational framework of established national union and party organisations, and sometimes in the context of a larger and more integrated Europe. How then, can we understand the evolution of policy on the ground, first at the local level, and then on the national level?

Perhaps the best explanation is that, as the French state has focused with greater intensity on issues of domestic security, as periodic urban riots in the early 1980s continued over more than two decades, the involvement of the state grew, and its efforts contributed to the development of ethnic organisation, as state agencies engaged in a sometimes desperate search for intermediaries among what became known as the 'second generation' (Body-Gendrot 1993: Chs. 5 and 6; Jazouli 1992). In a sometimes desperate search for *interlocuteurs valables* among the 'second generation,' both local governments and the central state have sought out and have sometimes supported whatever ethnic associations they feel can maintain social order. John McKesson cites a French Senate report on the Lyon region:

> Certain mayors are, alas!, ready to provide everything to prevent cars from burning in their towns. The public powers give in to the blackmail of the fundamentalists, who present themselves as the social actors who are best able to preserve order in difficult neighbourhoods where no policeman dares to venture (*Le Point*, August 28 1993).

In education, problems of rising dropout rates and student failures among the children of immigrants resulted in the establishment of several programmes, the most important of which was the zones of educational priority (ZEP). Many of these programmes are described in Caron 1990. The designation of these zones – which meant more money from several ministerial sources, more teachers and more, experimental programmes – relied upon criteria that focused largely on the ethnic composition of an area, but policy was not focused on immigrant children alone (Costa-Lascoux 1989: 93–5).

By 1994 it was estimated that somewhat more than 30 per cent of those benefiting from the ZEP programme were immigrant children. More 'disfavoured' native children than immigrant children have benefited from the programme (although it is not clear how many ethnic minority children benefited, since this is not a legal designation in France), but the point is that the designation of ZEPs was strongly linked to areas of immigrant concentration.

> Zones of priority, by their global vision of the problem of school failure, indicated that foreign children ought not to be treated 'as different'. However, the first government *circulaire* of July, 1981, clumsily fixed a 'quota' of 30 per cent foreign children as one of the determining indicators of such zones (Lorcerie 1994).

Yet, however clumsy these rules were, they were made necessary by the restrictions imposed by the Republican model, and a law of 1978 dealing with information. The 1978 law was further reinforced by the Constitutional Council in 2007, when it declared a section of the new immigration law that would have permitted the census and researchers to pose questions on race and ethnicity unconstitutional.[8]

The French Republican model has been under significant pressure since the Treaty of Amsterdam was signed in 1997 and two (Racial Equality and Equal Employment) directives were agreed to by the European Council in 2000 (Council Directive 2000/43/EC, 29 June 2000; and Council Directrive 2000/78/EC, 27 November 2000). By focusing on the relationship between discrimination and integration, the treaty, which came into effect in 1999, brought questions of immigration, and to some extent integration (particularly the revised Article 6a on the combat against discrimination based on sex, racial or ethnic origin, religion or belief, disability, age or sexual orientation) into the EU structure. Policy would be harmonised on the basis of proposals made by the Commission, and actions of the Council of Ministers. The directives obligated all EU countries to constitute commissions that would both monitor and act against patterns of racial discrimination. Since immigrant communities have been racialised in Europe, the emerging institutions have begun to offer them a measure of recognition and protection – but also recognition as groups. This has posed a considerable challenge for French republicanism: how to combat discrimination without recognising the legitimacy of the very groups against which discrimination is said to be directed.

In 2001 and 2002 France passed legislation banning discrimination in employment and housing, but did not pass legislation authorising an active anti-discrimination agency until 2004. The High Authority Against Discrimination and for Equality (HALDE) was established in 2005, and issued its first report in May 2006. During its first year, it received more than 2000 complaints from individuals, 45 per cent of them complaints of employment discrimination. Although the commission lacks financial resources to investigate discrimination, as well as strong legal means to pursue complaints and enforcement, it represents a new departure to deal with immigrant integration in terms of discrimination (*Le Monde*, May 4, 2006).

Thus, the French Republican model of integration, while different from approaches to integration in some other countries, Britain and the United States in particular, has never been strikingly exceptional in practice. In fact, as state involvement in the integration process has increased since the 1980s, some state policies have indeed reinforced ethnic identities, while others have represented a compromise with multiculturalism. This became more evident in recent years, when the government developed pilot programmes of affirmative action (*discrimination positive* or *égalité des chances*) using the ZEP programme as a framework. In an attempt to target ethnic communities, the government has used relatively narrow geographical criteria instead of group criteria. In this way, the Republican model had molded the way that groups are targeted, but has not prevented special programmes from being implemented.

Success and failure

French integration policy is not only different, but exceptional, however, in at least one dimension: its failure and its success. As a result of the Amsterdam Treaty, one set of standards that we can use to evaluate relative success and failure has been formalised in a list of 'Common Basic Principles for Immigrant Integration Policy in the European Union', agreed to in the Hague Programme in 2004 as part of a common programme for integration. Among the 11 agreed-upon principles, the following are the most important:

- Employment is a key part of the integration process and is central to the participation of immigrants, to the contributions immigrants make to the host society, and to making such contributions visible.

- Efforts in education are critical to preparing immigrants, and particularly their descendants, to be more successful and more active participants in society.
- Access for immigrants to institutions, as well as to public and private goods and services, on a basis equal to national citizens and in a non-discriminatory way, is a critical foundation for better integration.
- The participation of immigrants in the democratic process and in the formulation of integration policies and measures, especially at the local level, supports their integration.
- Integration is a dynamic, two-way process of mutual accommodation by all immigrants and residents of Member States (Council of the EU 2004).

Thus from these principles, we can derive several measures of integration that can give us some indication of relative success and failure. The first is that immigrants should be integrated into the economy, should be employed, and indeed should provide a crucial element of support within the economy. The second is that, over time, the educational system should be an effective instrument of integration. The third is that the political system should provide effective representation of immigrant populations. Finally, the end result should be both acceptance of immigrant populations by the host countries, and an acceptance of the host countries by the immigrant populations. If we look at two dimensions on integration – socio-economic and cultural – it will become evident that success in one does not necessarily predict success in the other. Indeed, in important cases, relative success in education and employment may correspond with evident failure in the convergence of value acceptance (see Figure 7.1).

Unemployment rates among immigrant populations have been generally higher than those of the native population throughout Europe. Compared to Britain, unemployment is higher by far among French immigrants (see Table 7.1). Moreover, youth unemployment among immigrants is more than twice the national average.

Educational attainment is more complicated. On one hand, educational attainment among immigrant populations at the university level is as great as or greater than that of the native population in all three countries. On the other hand, the proportion of immigrants who drop out, or who never get to upper secondary education (a prerequisite for good jobs in most Western societies), is disastrously high in France, but comparatively low in Britain (see Table 7.2). Therefore, in terms of employment and education, the outcomes for British

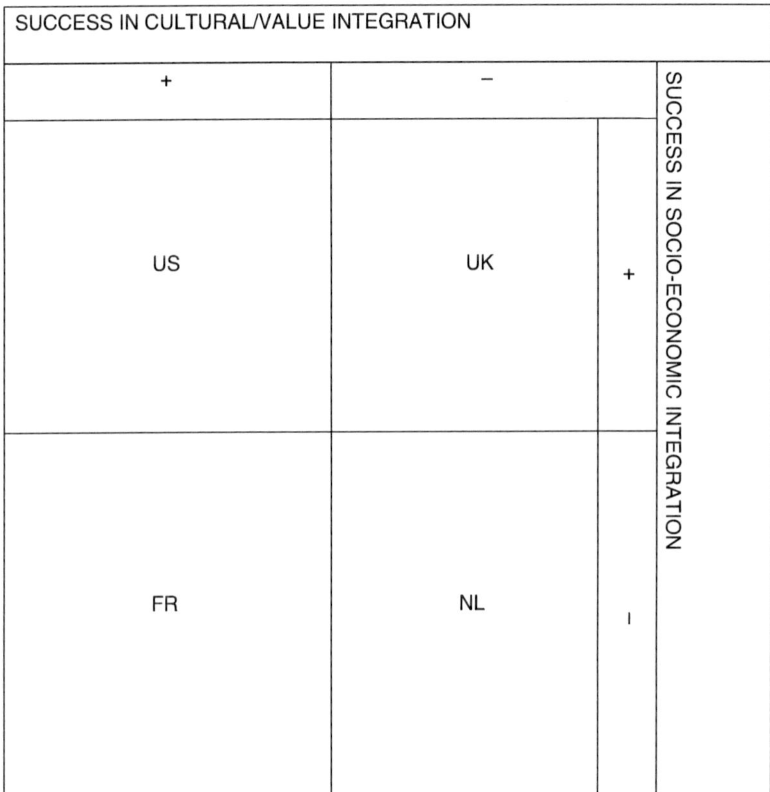

Figure 7.1 Two dimensions of integration success/failure

Table 7.1 **Unemployment rates for immigrants and natives in 2004**

	Immigrants	Non-immigrants
France	13.8%	8.0%
Britain	7.3	4.7
NL	10.3	3.6
US	5.8	6.9

Sources: Data from OECD, *International Migration Outlook* (Washington DC, OECD, 2006), p. 73; European Community Labour Force Survey.

Table 7.2   Educational attainment of immigrant populations, 2004

| | Less than upper-secondary education* | | University degree or greater | |
	Native-born	Foreign-born	Native-born	Foreign-born
France	35%	56%**	13%	12%
Britain	49	45**	20	28
NL	34		24	
US	12.5	32.8	27	27

*UK = no qualification – GCSE; France = BEPC (first cycle high school)
**no qualification: UK = 10%; France = 50%
Sources: (US, NL, France and Britain): OECD in Figures, 2005, p. 65; European Community Labour Force Survey; INSEE, Enquête emploi de 2005; University College London, CreAm, Christian Dustmann, and Nikolous Theordoropoulos, 'Ethnic Minority Immigrants and their Children in Britain,' CDP 10/06, p. 20. US: US Bureau of the Census,US Congress, CBO, *A Description of the Immigrant Population*, November, 2004.

immigrants have been quite good, especially compared with the outcomes in France.

These differences are confirmed by an analysis of achievement scores in reading, maths and science among immigrant children in ten countries, including France and Britain, compared with native children of the same age. The differences were almost 40 per cent higher in France, compared with Britain. Some of this difference can be accounted for by differences in socio-economic status (SES), but in France, even if we control for SES, lack of achievement at the lower levels continues to be significant. If we control for SES in Britain, first generation immigrant children do as well (or as poorly) as others of the same age. (Schnepf 2004: 12, 23, 33, 40, 34–6).

This is important because educational attainment has a strong impact on unemployment rates for immigrants (for natives as well). However, the impact is far greater in Britain than in France. The reduction of unemployment rates is brought down only 36 per cent in France by higher education, compared with 66 per cent for Britain (see Table 7.3).

Political representation can be understood as integration through politics, As Richard Alba and Nancy Foner have noted, election of immigrant candidates to political office is a measure of their integration '… in the same sense that entry by minority individuals into high-status occupations is. It is an indication of a diminishment, however modest, in differentials in life chances that exist between majority and minority.' Representation also gives them a voice in the distribution of public

Table 7.3   Unemployment rates of foreign-born populations, by level of education attainment, 2003–2004

	Low education	Medium Education	High Education	Diff lo/hi
France	18.4	14.4	11.8	–36%
Britain	12.2	7.9	4.2	–66%
NL	6.5	7.3	3.3	–49%
US	9.1	5.7	4.3	–53%

Source: Data from OECD, *International Migration Outlook* (Washington DC, OECD, 2006), p. 53.

goods, as well as the ability to control the spatial zones in which they live. Finally, achievement of elective office gives groups control over both patronage and influence over decisions made by civil servants (decisions that are disproportionately important for immigrants).

> The Irish of the United States offer a compelling historical example, as they used their leadership of Democratic political machines that ruled many US cities a century ago to bring about massive municipal employment of their co-ethnics (Alba and Foner 2009).

Table 7.4 indicates that immigrant representation is roughly similar for all three countries at the local/state levels, but sharply different at the national level, where the more porous American system has generally succeeded in providing better access than either Britain or France. France has consistently had the worst record by far in this area. In the British case, where there are concentrations of ethnic minorities, representation has been more significant, and has grown substantially at the local level over time (Anwar 2001).

Table 7.4   Political integration of immigrant populations, 2004

	% Population	% Electorate	% State/local representatives	% National representation
France	5%	2.7%	3.3%	0% NA 0.6% Senate
Britain	7.9	6.6	2.6	2.3

Source: Alba and Foner 2009.

Table 7.5   Attitudes *towards* immigrants and Muslims

	Unfavourable view of Muslims	A good thing people from Middle East and North Africa coming to your country	Immigration having good influence only our country	Muslims in your country mostly want to adapt to national customs	No conflict between being a devout Muslim and living in modern society	Growing Islamic identity – good
French resp	34	58	46	45	74	11
British resp	14	57	43	22	35	27
Spanish resp	37	62	45	21	36	13
German resp	47	34	47	17	26	11
NL	51	46				
US	22		52	33	42	37

Source: Pew 2006 3, 6, 8, 10; Pew Global Attitudes Project 2006; IPSOS 2006.

Nevertheless, attitudinal surveys indicate that by several measures, France has been at least as accepting as Britain, and by others, even more accepting. Indeed the idea that 'immigration is having a good influence' is (perhaps surprisingly) accepted in Europe and the confidence that Muslim immigrants seek to adapt to customs in their country, and that there is no conflict between devout Muslim practice and living in modern society, is far more strongly held in France than in other countries (see Table 7.5).

These societal attitudes are reflected in attitudinal patterns among the immigrant population who identify as Muslim. French Muslims are, by far, the most integrative in their orientation, and the least conflicted between their Muslim and national identities (see Table 7.6).

In addition, a recent study of Muslim elites in Europe indicates a similar pattern. Jytte Klausen has developed a typology of four preferences as modes of integration for Muslim populations:

Secular Integrationist: respondents believe that Islam is compatible with Western value and that the organisation of Islamic practice should be integrated into existing frameworks of church-state relations (Klausen 2005: 87).

Neo-Orthodox respondents believe that Islam is not compatible and should not be integrated into existing frameworks.

Voluntarist respondents believe that Islam is compatible in terms of values, but should not be integrated into existing frameworks.

Anticlerical respondents believe that Islam is not compatible in terms of values, but should be integrated into existing church-state relations.

The responses of Muslim elites by country are indicated in Table 7.7. The two most strikingly different patterns are those of French and the British sub-samples, each of which overwhelmingly fits into a single category. While the support of French elites for 'secular integration' largely conforms to French norms on church-state relations, the strong support for 'voluntarist policies' indicates a distrust of the state but an acceptance of the compatibility of French and Islamic values. It is also worth noting that the French sample had the lowest 'neo-orthodox' response of any of the European groups studied by Klausen. On the other hand, the support of British Muslim elites for the 'neo-orthodox'

Table 7.6   Muslims in Europe: Attitudes towards identity, fellow citizens and modernity

	Positive views of Christians	Positive views of Jews	No conflict between being a devout Muslim and living in modern society	Consider yourself first: a citizen of *your country*/ Muslim	Muslims in your country want to adopt national customs
French Muslims	91%	71%	72%	*42%* /46%	78%
British Muslims	71	32	49	*7* /81	41
Spanish Muslims	82	28	71	*3* /89	53
German Muslims	69	38	57	*13* /66	38

Source: Pew 2006: 3, 11–12; Pew Global Attitudes Project 2006.

Table 7.7   Policy choice for integration of Islam of Muslim elites, by country of residence

	Denmark %	Sweden %	France %	Germany %	NL %	UK %	Total %
Secular							
Integrationist	20.8	37.5	60.0	25.0	13.6	10.7	23.5
Voluntarist	33.3	37.5	30.0	30.6	59.1	17.9	33.8
Anticlericals	33.3	12.5	0.0	22.2	9.1	0.0	14.7
Neo-Orthodox	12.5	12.5	10.0	22.2	18.2	71.4	27.9
Total	100	100	100	100	100	100	100

Source: Klausen 2005: 95.

pattern indicates a strong sense of isolation from British norms that makes Britain different from every other country studied by Klausen.

Thus, the British record of economic integration of immigrant populations is far better than that of France. These figures, combined with periodic urban violence, have left the impression that French immigration policy has failed, in comparison with policy in the past, and compared with other countries (Britain, for example). The British record of educational integration appears to have been relatively successful (even if we control for SES); the French record, however, is far worse. No doubt the poor French economic performance is linked to the failures of the educational system, where almost two-thirds of immigrants did not attain the level of upper secondary school, and 50 per cent simply dropped out without any degree (INSEE 2005).

Nevertheless, among immigrant groups in Europe, French people who identify as Muslim, appear to be the most 'European'. As a minority community, they have the most positive views of their compatriots who are Christian (and Jewish), and are among the least sympathetic to radical Islam.[9] They are the most supportive of ideas that are consistent with the French Republican model. Among Muslim elites, there is a consensus about the compatibility of Islam and Western state values, which, in Klausen's study, clearly differentiates Muslim elites in France from those in every other major country in Europe (see Table 7.6). Within Europe, Muslim immigrants in France of Islamic origin have the strongest national identity and are the most inclined towards integration.

In the charts in this table, the gaps in unemployment rates and education between native and immigrant populations for the Netherlands generally resemble those of France. The value gap, however, is closer to that of Britain, but with a twist. Muslim values are generally more accommodating than those in Britain, but native rejection rates seem to be far higher than the British rates. Therefore the 'gap' is due more to majority attitudes than to those of the immigrant minority (Pew 2006: 3, 6, 8, 10; Pew Global Attitudes 2006; IPOS 2006).

Conclusion

This chapter raises many questions about the usefulness of the framework of French exceptionalism. On one hand, it was certainly possible to develop coherent and effective policy on immigration during a long period when the instability of the French political system appeared to be more or less exceptional in Europe. Despite governmental instability within regimes that were frequently under threat from within and without, stable administrative policy-making and implementation defied the political environment within which it took place. The incoherence of immigration policy has been a product of the political salience of immigration issues. As immigration has become politicised in France, the dynamics of the party system in particular have been the primary influence over policy and policy implementation. The 'puzzling' of policy has given way to the more open and chaotic politics of policy formation within the political arena. While I know of no evidence that political instability was responsible for moving the immigration issue into the administrative arena, or the reverse, I would argue that the arena of policy formation is far more important for determining the stability of policy than the stability of the political system.

The exceptionalism of integration policy, on the other hand, has been less exceptional in practice than in principle. Moreover, there has been a growing pattern of convergence of policy within Europe, in part as a result of the application of the Treaty of Amsterdam, around a version of civic integration that looks increasingly Jacobin in content and anti-discrimination measures based on the Anglo-Saxon experience. This does not mean that the Republican model is no longer relevant, but it does mean that the French approach tends to mold and form this process of convergence.

Finally, the French approach is indeed exceptional in terms of indices of failure and success of integration policy. Arguably, the biases of the Republican model are responsible for the poor results in education of immigrant populations, as well as the lack of economic and political advancement. On the other hand, France is a strong positive model for civic integration, compared to other large countries in Europe.

Notes

1 The first four chapters of Philip Williams' seminal book on the Fourth Republic (Williams 1964), are probably the best single exposition of the long period of political instability under the Third and Fourth Republics. Nicholas Wahl then presented this phenomenon to American undergraduates in the first edition of Beer and Ulam (Beer and Ulam 1958); and Stanley Hoffmann then linked instability to what he called 'the paradox of immobility', and more general political weakness, in 'Paradoxes of the French Political Community', in Hoffmann *et al* 1963: 1–118).

2 Michel Crozier developed these ideas in two notable volumes. The first (Crozier 1964) had a strong influence of how the French system was understood in the United States. The second (Crozier 1970) was an elaboration of the earlier ideas, and strongly influenced by the events of 1968.

3 Mauco is cited by Weil 1991: 44–6. The key table from the report is in Annex
   III of Weil's book. Mauco, however, went well beyond cultural racism during
   the war, when he gave intellectual support to Vichy's anti-semitic policies.
   See Weil 1991: 65–75.
4 The effort was led by Charles Lambert, a Radical deputy from Lyons, who
   strongly influenced by both the American debate and the American legislation of 1924. However, the proposal never gained much political support,
   and ended when the government shifted to the (pro-business) right in 1926.
   For a useful account, see Cross 1983: 173–4.
5 Weil notes, however, that ethnic and racial criteria – together with a quota
   system modelled after the system then in force in the United States – were
   seriously considered, and advocated by Alfred Sauvy and Robert Debré (p. 56).
6 The legislation was an amendment to the Labour Code, that made it illegal to
   employ workers who lacked 'a permit to do salaried work in France', a category
   that applied only to Algerians and Francophone Africans.
7 I have looked at the relationship between immigrant mobilisation and the
   rise and decline of the PCF in Schain 1996.
8 The legislation that authorises the prohibition against the collection of ethnic
   data is the *Loi no. 78–17 du 6 Janvier 1978 relative à l'informatique, aux fichiers
   et aux libertés*. However, this law was modified in 2004, and the National Commission on Computers and Liberty lists seven criteria that could be used to
   measure 'diversity'. See: www.cnil.fr/index.php?id=1844. The decision of the
   Constitutional Council is elaborated in *Le Monde*, November 25 2007.
9 They are, for example, the only Muslim group in Europe in which a majority
   believes the attacks of September 11, 2001 were carried out by Arabs (Pew
   2006: 4).

8
France, Islam and *Laïcité*: Colonial Exceptions, Contemporary Reinventions and European Convergence

Natalya Vince

The 2004 law banning 'ostentatious' symbols of religious belonging from being worn in French state schools claimed to reaffirm the principle of *laïcité* and put an end to two decades of controversy and inconsistent approaches. Whilst hijabs, turbans, skullcaps and large crosses were all prohibited, it is clear that the Muslim headscarf was the main target. The passionate debate which the 'law on the veil' provoked was followed by a relatively uneventful implementation, but the place of Islam within the 'Republican model' continues to be a burning topic of intellectual, political and popular discussion. Despite occasional concerns about Evangelical attempts to find new adherents in the *banlieue* and a small media furore in 2004 when then Interior Minister Nicolas Sarkozy met movie star and Scientologist Tom Cruise, when the cry of '*laïcité* in danger' goes out in 21st century France, the menace is usually a Muslim one.[1]

This chapter seeks to explore the meaning of *laïcité* in France today, in particular in relation to Islam, and in comparison with France's European neighbours. We begin by situating *laïcité* in its historical context and considering how the application of this so-called 'French exception' has always had its own exceptions. The place of *laïcité* in the French colonies, and notably Algeria, is a particularly significant example. Migration from former North African colonies from the 1960s onwards largely explains why France is today home to one of the highest percentages of Muslims in Europe: an estimated 3.65 to six million people, equivalent to around 6 to 10 per cent of the total population (Laurence and Vaisse 2006: 17).[2] Secondly, this chapter examines the creation of the Conseil Français du Culte Musulman (CFCM) in 2003 and President Sarkozy's discourse on a 'new' '*laïcité positive*'. Thirdly, we consider two events in 2008 which provoked controversy:

the annulment of the marriage of a young Muslim couple of Moroccan origin in Lille because the wife had lied about her virginity and the refusal of French nationality to a woman who wore a niqab. Finally, this chapter analyses the ways in which *laïcité* has been reinvented since the late 1980s, and examines how current debates and policy developments concerning relations between the State and religious minorities reflect shifts across the French and European political landscape.

Lost translations and received ideas

In the strictest sense, *laïcité* is the separation of Church and State: one shall neither run, influence nor finance the other. Its English-language equivalent, secularism, is a much less precise term, which can refer to the separation of Church and State, but also the decline in religious practice and/or belief within society – this latter meaning is inferred by the French *sécularisation*. One can thus be *laïque* without being secular. This chapter uses the French term *laïcité* in recognition of this distinction, whilst also demonstrating how within and beyond France's borders there is no consensus on what *laïcité* means or should mean.

The 'French Republican model' of *laïcité* is often contrasted with the 'Anglo-Saxon model' of multiculturalism. The Anglo-Saxon model is characterised as a liberal, laissez-faire approach to integrating minority groups: individuals and communities are free to adopt whatever beliefs and practices they choose, as long as these do not harm others. Multiculturalism (in English) is the belief that cultural differences should be accommodated, in order for society as a whole to function harmoniously. The French Republican model is seen as centralising and homogenising, requiring individuals to conform to a specific set of political, social and cultural values defined by the State. *Multiculturalisme* (in French) is seen as a danger to the direct and exclusive relationship between the State and citizen, opening the door to the fragmentation of the nation into interest groups divided by race, religion and previous nationalities – this is what is pejoratively termed *communautarisme*. In practice, these two models of integration have never been diametrically opposed. The United States and the United Kingdom have always required that individuals and groups respect the law of the land, which is based on mainstream social and cultural norms. At a local level in France, new cultures have been accommodated and differences negotiated: local town halls have provided prayer space, Muslim cemeteries exist and there are Muslim chaplains in prisons and the army. Since the start of the 21st century, the boundaries between the 'French model' and the 'Anglo-Saxon' model have become even more blurred, as will be shown.

In political and popular discourse, Islam is often presented by both non-Muslims and Muslims in an essentialising way, as unchanging and homogenous. The diversity of its theological forms, daily practices and internal debates amongst contemporary followers are rarely foregrounded. Islam has been depicted as a crusading and 'totalising' religion, making no distinction between the public and private spheres and thus posing particular problems for secular European states. Aside from this being only one possible interpretation, we should be wary of assuming that religion is the driving force in the political and cultural behaviour of 'Muslims', above other determining factors such as class, gender, age, political affiliation and nationality. The vision of a united, transnational Muslim *umma* (community of believers) masks a far more complex picture, in which distinctions need to be made between practising and non-practising Muslims, between believers and non-believers who are of Muslim culture and between those who choose to define themselves as Muslim and those who prefer alternative categories of self-identification. The limited usefulness of the term 'French Muslims' has been underlined by a number of scholarly studies which highlight the diversity of France's Muslim population(s).[3] The focus of this chapter is not on the multiple forms of identification of those who might choose – or not – to define themselves as Muslim, but rather on the interactions of the French State with organisations which claim to represent Islam in France and mainstream political discourse on 'Muslims in France'.

Historical background and colonial exceptions

In the last two decades of the 19th century, the Third Republic steadily chipped away at the influence of the Catholic Church on French politics and society. In 1884 divorce was legalised, measures were taken to reduce the number of religious personnel in French hospitals and a series of laws in the 1880s established universal, free and secular education. The reaction of the Catholic Church to these measures was, unsurprisingly, hostile and religion was a key area of Franco-French conflict at the turn of the century. The 1905 law on the separation of Church and State trod a third way between free thinkers who wanted to save minds from the reactionary influence of the Church, and Catholics who wanted to save souls from the godless Republicanism of anti-clericals. Amongst *laïcs*, Jean Baubérot underlines that there were two distinct tendencies. In the more radical camp were those who wished to promote a

Rousseau-inspired 'civil religion' by actively secularising religious devotees and converting them into citizens with a new set of non-Christian symbols such as 14 July, the Marseillaise and the Enlightenment *philosophes*. However, the form of *laïcité* which was eventually concretised in the 1905 law was of a far more conciliatory nature, promoting not freedom from religion, but neutrality towards and equality between religions. The missionary, crusading elements of *laïcité* as a civil religion were absent. As politician Aristide Briand argued: 'The *laïque* State must remain neutral with regard to all religious denominations. It is not anti-religious... It is areligious' (Baubérot 2007: 8–9).

The law of 1905 contains three key principles. Firstly, the Republic guarantees freedom of conscience and the freedom to practise one's religion. Secondly, the Republic neither recognises nor funds any one religion – State and Church are independent of the other's influence. The State, civil service and civil servants are neutral bodies. Thirdly, although exercised freely, religions must respect public order and the individual, and places of worship should not become political forums. The 1905 law aroused violent opposition from the Catholic Church until at least 1914. The three departments of Alsace and Moselle, which became once again part of French territory in 1918, have maintained a different status because they were not part of France when the *laïcité* laws were passed, and France's overseas possessions (the DOM-TOM) also have different rules regulating religion in public life. After the fall of France to the invading German army in 1940 and the creation of the authoritarian Vichy regime under Philippe Pétain, the Catholic Church seized upon the opportunity to reassert its authority, albeit briefly, in the educational sphere. Following the Liberation of France, *laïcité* was inscribed in the French constitutions of 1946 and 1958. By the mid-20th century the 'two Frances', anti-clerical France and practising Catholic France, had largely been reconciled, although we should not minimise the passions of confrontations between Catholics and *laïcs* in 1959, 1984 and 1994 on issues surrounding the existence and state funding of private Catholic schools.

Yet when we talk about 'France', until at least 1960, we are also referring to a vast colonial empire. Algeria presents an interesting example when considering the application of *laïcité* because it was not considered a colony but, since 1848, an integral part of mainland France, under the responsibility of the Minister for the Interior, not the Minister for Colonies. The vast majority of the autochthonous population of Algeria was Muslim. From 1865 onwards, the Muslim inhabitants of Algeria were considered to be French subjects, but not citizens. In order to obtain citizenship, individuals had to renounce their 'Muslim personal status' in civil law matters such as marriage and inheritance and go through a lengthy naturalisation process (Weil 2004: 352–9). If they did not reject this part of their religious identity, they had to accept that, because of their 'cultural differences', they would remain second-class citizens. Moreover, the instrumentalisation of Islam was perceived by the French State as a key tool in maintaining control of the Muslim population of Algeria. The early stages of the colonisation of Algeria in the 1830s and 1840s had seen the confiscation of much of the land and property of Muslim religious organisations. The Second Empire (1852–1870) set about creating a 'Muslim clergy' – even though this was a paradox in Sunni Islam which has no one leader or centralised hierarchy of religious bodies. Qu'ranic schools were set up by the State in order to supervise and control the training of personnel for a 'French Islam' which, it was hoped, would prevent religious institutions becoming centres of anti-colonial resistance.

Given that the manipulation and surveillance of Islam, from the choice of imams to the censorship of sermons, played such an important part in controlling the autochthonous population, it is hardly surprising that *laïcité* remained a dead letter in colonial Algeria. A decree of 1907 which laid out how the 1905 law was to be applied to different religions in Algeria made so many exceptions that the original text was emptied of its substance. From 1947 until Algerian independence in 1962, various attempts to make the Muslim religion independent from the French State failed, as Michel Renard underlines, due to the authorities' fear of the political consequences, divisions amongst Muslim leaders and the fact that Muslim clergy had often been chosen on the basis of their usefulness as police informers rather than their theological competence. In 1953, the Conseil d'Etat declared that there was a fundamental legal problem: to create a single, independent Algerian Islam, it would be necessary to create a central body to receive donations and other income – which, the Conseil declared, was illegal, as it did not respect the 1905 law. This, argues Renard (2000: 85), was largely an excuse to hide a lack of political will.

The relationship of the French State with Islam in Algeria thus remained, right up until independence in 1962, *concordataire* rather than *laïque*,[4] despite a number of Muslims in Algeria from the 1930s onwards campaigning for an independent Muslim religion and the enforcement of the 1905 law. The French State saw Islam as a means of controlling a population whom they were not prepared to accord equal rights to, in defiance of any Republican 'model' of liberty, equality, fraternity or *laïcité*. For Anna Bozzo (2005: 81), the current relationship between Islam and the French Republic has been significantly shaped by this colonial period 'upon the abstract basis of Republican values which were not applied'. This colonial history will be particularly pertinent when we examine the CFCM and controversies surrounding the creation of a 21st century 'French Islam'.

As Baubérot (2007: 3) highlights, the characterisation of French *laïcité* as an 'exception' in contemporary Europe is in many ways inaccurate. He underlines that the principal authors of the 1905 law did not see France as an exception, instead viewing other nations as *laïque* in different degrees. Olivier Roy (2005: 5) similarly argues that it is simplistic to think about *laïcité* solely as a description of Church-State relations, as the term implies a much broader range of ideas about how societies define themselves and religions play a key role in shaping all societies: 'There are therefore different histories of laicisation and of secularisation and there is no point trying to established a definitive model'. Joel Fetzer and Christopher Soper (2005: 15–16) argue that different histories of Church-State relations have had an important impact on shaping responses to the arrival of Islam. Whilst in France *laïcité* denotes the removal of religious influence from political life, in Belgium and the Netherlands State neutrality involves recognising key religions and structuring civil society around this pluralism. In the United Kingdom there is an established (state) religion and theocratic elements of government remain within the political system: the monarch is the 'supreme governor' and 'defender of the faith' of the Church of England and unelected Anglican bishops sit in the House of Lords. However, Britain is also a multicultural society in which religious plurality is recognised. Whilst there are many different models of State-religion organisations within the countries of the EU, all share characteristics of the secular state: freedom of conscience is guaranteed, the State does not interfere in daily worship and political decisions are generally not made under the influence of religious organisations.

Jean-Paul Willaime (2007: 40) summarises why French *laïcité* has nevertheless been seen as having a number of singularities compared to its European and global counterparts. Firstly, the separation of Church and State in France emerged in a context of conflict more acute than elsewhere, creating major divisions within French society. Secondly, discussions of *laïcité* are highly ideologised with philosophers and political theorists playing an important role in orientating debates. Thirdly, the French State accords itself a very specific role – as an emancipating, enlightening and homogenising force. Finally, religion in France is seen as belonging exclusively to the private sphere in a much stricter way than elsewhere. In the course of the 19th and 20th centuries, these 'specificities' have largely held true in relation to France and *laïcité*. At the same time, as Willaime underlines, these particularities are becoming increasingly blurred around the edges.

A new approach to *laïcité*? Institutionalising Islam and European comparisons

The creation of the Conseil Français du Culte Musulman in 2003 was 'the culmination of a 15-year political and bureaucratic process' (Laurence 2005: 2). Since the late 1980s when the growing number of Muslims living in France became increasingly visible and permanent, a range of 'issues' began to emerge such as the funding of mosques, the training of imams and the creation of representative bodies for the 'Muslim community'.

Under the terms of the 1905 law and subsequent related legislation in 1907 and 1908, religious buildings constructed before 1905 became the property of the State and therefore the responsibility of the State to maintain, although significantly, the Church kept control of their usage. Places of worship built after 1905 receive no state funding. Following the arrival of significant numbers of Muslim immigrants from the mid-20th century onwards, the French authorities relied on individual initiatives and funding from the governments of immigrants' countries of origin to pay imams and establish mosques and prayer space, often in privately-owned basements and garages. There were a range of accommodations through which practising Muslims and local authorities came to arrangements within the 1905 law or circumvented its limits: for example, town halls providing prayer space in public buildings on long term leases for minimum rent. The building of mosques was more controversial. A rare exception to this is the Grande Mosquée de Paris (GMP), inaugurated in 1926 and financed by the French State in honour of the many Muslims from the colonies who died for France during the First World War.

From the late 1980s onwards, the presence of Islam in France began to attract political and public attention not just because of the practical needs of practising Muslims. Across Europe, sections of second generation immigrants whose parents were from Muslim countries increasingly assumed and openly affirmed a 'Muslim' identity. These younger generations could not claim to be Algerian, Pakistani or Turkish as their parents could, but faced with racism and discrimination they were not accepted as French, British or German either. Being 'Muslim' provided an alternative identity. At the same time the practice of Islam by some of these young people took a more radical, scripture-based form than that of their parents (Laurence and Vaisse 2006: 92–3; Cesari 2005a: 3).

The lack of French State involvement in Islam in the 1970s and 1980s was not just a 'principle of *laïcité*', it is representative of a general laissez-faire attitude towards Muslims by European states during this period. However, this 'hands-off' approach, foreign influence in the funding of European Islam and radicalisation of some members of the younger generation came to be seen in France, as elsewhere in Europe, as a threat to national cohesion and breeding ground for extremism. The idea of developing a 'French Islam', with the State playing a role in regulating and organising the representation of Islam in France thus developed, hence the emergence of the CFCM in 2003 and the creation in March 2005 of a Fondation pour les Oeuvres de l'Islam de France, to centralise and distribute funding. The CFCM is both a national and regional interface for Islam in France, with 25 regional departments involved in the organisation of religious celebrations, the building of mosques and Muslim burial grounds, the training of imams and the presence of chaplains in prisons, hospitals and the army.

Responses to the CFCM and the Foundation have been mixed. The Foundation could potentially provide Muslim organisations with financial autonomy, and thus be entirely coherent with the spirit of the 1905 law, or could be used by the State to police sources of finance for religious projects, which is certainly not an expression of *laïcité*. In practical terms, it remains ambiguous how the Foundation will function and what resources it has access to. The CFCM has been seen by some commentators as a positive move towards the political and social recognition of Islam in France in return for Islam recognising the Republic. In this vision, the CFCM is an interlocutor with a similar role to that of the Catholic Conférence des Evêques de France, the Jewish Consistoire Central and the Fédération Protestante de France. Others have denounced the CFCM as an attempt to 'clericise' Islam in France, as in colonial Algeria (Bozzo 2005: 77). It perhaps does not help that a number of figures in the CFCM have the reputation of being well regarded by the French political elite but with no real popular base. Dalil Boubakeur, the first president of the CFCM (2003–08) and head of the GMP, came from a family of Algerian *notables* well-integrated into the colonial regime. Boubakeur has cultivated his image as a loyal government collaborator promoting a 'moderate Islam' in France.

Since its inception, the CFCM has been riddled with factional divisions and external criticisms of its legitimacy. The number of electors who vote for members is tiny compared to the Muslim population of France, the electorate consisting of a few thousand delegates from prayer spaces. The CFCM is made up of a heterogeneous collection of organisations attempting to parcel out power between them. These organisations are under significant influence from the Algerian and Moroccan national governments, whose support the French government has regularly sought in order to bolster the CFCM. Serious rifts have emerged between Boubakeur's Fédération Nationale de la Grande Mosquée de Paris (FNGMP) which is seen as the 'Algerian Camp' and is financed by Algeria, the *Rassemblement des Musulmans de France* (RMF), created in January 2006 with the support of Morocco and a splinter group of the Fédération Nationale des Musulmans de France (FNMF) which played an important role in the creation of the CFCM, and the Union des Organisations Islamiques de France (UOIF), which has been accused of representing the interests of radical Islam in France. The UOIF is the French branch of the Federation of Islamic Organisations in Europe (FIOE) and presented itself in the 2005 elections as the only genuinely 'French' Muslim organisation (as opposed to those under the influence of foreign governments) (Laurence and Vaisse 2006: xi).[5] The conflicts within the CFCM highlight the difficulties of trying to locate a homogenous 'Muslim community' in France and underline the fallacy of taking at face value the concept of a transnational Muslim *umma*. Nationality and North African rivalries remain important parameters of identity, as does social status – it is understandably difficult to see the relevance of political horsetrading between personally ambitious Muslim *notables* to the daily lives of Muslims often living in the most deprived socio-economic areas in France.

Despite the so far limited scope of its activities, the underlying thinking behind the creation of the CFCM is that it will serve as a tool to integrate minorities into the Republic. This aspiration goes far beyond the boundaries of the 1905 law, whose key principle was the neutrality and non-interference of the State in religious affairs. As we have seen, this is not without historical precedent: in the 19th century there was a comparable attempt to institutionalise Islam in colonial Algeria. The creation of the CFCM fits in with a general move across European countries since the 1990s to develop intermediary organisations through which Muslim minorities can be brought under State authority. In 1992, the Spanish government formed the Islamic Commission of Spain and Germany set up the Central Council of Muslims in 1994. In the UK, the

Muslim Council of Britain (MCB) emerged in 1997 with a semi-official status. Silvio Ferrari (2005) underlines that European states have faced similar problems in 'institutionalising' Islam, including State demands that one organisation incorporates all Muslims despite the diversity of Muslim inhabitants, delaying tactics by public administrators and the lack of institutional organisations within Islam. As in France, other European states are increasingly seeking to enter into contact with 'minority groups' through these religiously-defined bodies, rather than through older representative organisations such as trade unions, anti-racist groups, groups representing immigrant workers and political parties.

Before and after his election as president in May 2007, much was made of Sarkozy's proclaimed 'new' approach *laïcité*. In September 2005, at a conference to mark the centenary of the 1905 legislation, he claimed that the law needed 'tidying up'. At a speech in Saint-Jean-de-Latran in December 2007, Sarkozy pleaded for a *'laïcité positive'*, underlining the importance of religion to the individual and infuriating *laïque* activists by declaring that: 'In the transmission of values and in the teaching of the difference between good and evil, the teacher can never replace the priest or the pastor.' Another speech in January 2008 in Saudi Arabia reiterated similarly controversial themes (*Les déclarations de Nicolas Sarkozy sur les religions* 2008).

Like so much in Sarkozy's proclaimed *rupture tranquille*, his declarations on *laïcité* have been more rhetoric than precursors of any concrete readjustment of the 1905 law. Despite his emphasis on the importance of religion in daily life, Sarkozy has repeated his support for the separation of Church and State. He played a key role in launching the CFCM when Interior Minister in 2003, but this can be seen as the culmination of a decade of cross-party support for such an institution. Sarkozy's *'laïcité positive'* is a prominently articulated discourse which represents a quieter shift in the last decade amongst *some*, but by no means all, French intellectuals and politicians towards a more pluralist model, which interprets *laïcité* as more about religious freedom and mutual understanding than religious separation. In 1998, leading Catholic intellectual René Rémond argued that *laïcité* had become 'almost a synonym of pluralism' (Bedouelle and Costa 1998: 2). In 2001, Socialist Education Minister Jack Lang asked the philosopher Régis Debray to study the teaching of religion in schools, which was not part of the curriculum. Debray distinguished between a *'laïcité* of incompetence' (religion is not studied) and a *'laïcité* of intelligence' (where the fact that religions exist, their history and sociology are part of the school programme). The subject provoked debate, but the Debray report was largely welcomed and today the history and sociology of religions is part of certain teacher training programmes (Willaime 2007: 44). Philosopher Alain Renaut argues that *laïcité* should follow a 'logic of inclusion' (Renaut, Touraine 2005: 23) accepting that differences exist, rather the kind of exclusionary *laïcité* which expelled girls who wore headscarves to school without putting in place alternative educational provision (Bowen 2007: 91).

What is the cause of 'new approach' to *laïcité*? Is this an example of the influence of European integration scratching away at French specificities? The EU, with its focus on economic goals, has paid relatively little attention to its cultural project until recently, although the controversy over the potential inclusion of a reference to Europe's Christian heritage in the preamble to the failed European Constitution Treaty may be seen as a forerunner of future debates. The EU as an institution has no jurisdiction in Church-State relations and cases which have been brought to the European Court of Human Rights relating to freedom of religious practice or freedom to express anti-religious opinions have met with varied outcomes depending on the individual case. What we are seeing is not a 'European influence' on France, but more of a convergence of member states towards what Jonathan Laurence and Justin Vaisse (2006: 138) term 'secularist pragmatism' mixed with concerns about national security and a desire to develop diplomatic links with the Arab world. This has led to the establishment of bodies to represent 'Islam' and 'Muslims' (whether or not these are representative) and taking greater control of the training of imams and the financing of Muslim organisations, whilst accommodating requests for day-to-day issues such as prayer space, religious instruction, the provision of cemeteries and the regulation of halal meat. Journalist Fouad Bahri (2008) puts this 'secularist pragmatism' rather more pithily, describing it as *'Realpolitik sécuritaire'*: a security-minded practical approach to reducing the terrorist threat from Muslim extremists and appeasing potential sources of resentment amongst Muslim minorities. This *'Realpolitik sécuritaire'* is far from being a French, or a European, exception.

Why, then, is it often argued that France's approach to dealing with religious minorities is exceptional? Partly the answer is because the French model of *laïcité* historically has had distinctive specificities, although these have perhaps been exaggerated. Baubérot makes an important point when he highlights that the expression *'laïcité exception française'* first began to be used in the 1990s, after the first 'headscarf affairs' (2007: 13). This phrase, he argues, suggests a unified French 'vision' which sweeps under the carpet vigorous debates in France both between Catholics and *laïcs* and amongst *laïcs*, misleadingly suggesting that *laïcité* is something consensual, threatened by outside influences from the 'Anglo-Saxons' and the EU and challenged internally by Muslim 'Others'. It is perhaps because the French model is no longer so distinctive that certain sections of French society are so keen to assert that it is different. The way in which religion is dealt with in the public sphere has become, Willaime argues, much more nuanced with the French State playing a mediating role between religions rather than attempting to replace them: 'The State is no longer the *recteur* of civil society, it is becoming the *animateur*' (2007: 54). The choice of the term *recteur*, which can mean head of the local educational authority or a priest is significant, hinting perhaps at a Republican 'civil religion' which saw the school teacher as its missionary. The word *animateur* is equally loaded, meaning organiser or indeed showbiz compere – suggesting that the French State is not only having its role in society squeezed from above (through decision-making power being shifted to the EU) and below (through regional demands for decentralisation and the recognition of local identities), but in some way has lost its aura and *mystique*, is now just the equivalent of a TV show host whose lines are scripted elsewhere. In this perspective, debates about *laïcité* are a smoke-screen masking the diminishing importance of the nation-state and the increasing meaningless of 'national identity'.

Somewhat in contrast to this post-ideology, post-nation-state, view of *laïcité* as evolving towards a practical 'management' issue, Baubérot (2007) argues that 'Republican values' still maintain a talismanic status within French discourse. Whilst Americans regularly invoke God in polit-ical speeches, their French counterparts call upon Republican values in a similar omnipresent, untouchable way. This, argues Baubérot, is evidence that a sense of *laïcité* as a civil religion still exists, albeit in an unspoken and unspeakable way. The sacred connotations attached to *laïcité* have been suggested in the work of a number of authors who use terms such as 'a holy *laïque* alliance' (Roy 2005: 12) and describe the 'excommun-ication' of veiled girls from schools (Houziaux 2004: 16). The vestiges of these sacred connotations perhaps go some way to explaining why debates about *laïcité* in France arouse such intense passions, and indeed a reinvigorated missionary zeal to protect individuals from the claims of religion (Scott 2007: 98).

The reinvention of *laïcité*: semantic shifts and political positioning

2008 saw two *faits divers* become *affaires d'Etat*. In May, the annulment of the marriage of a young Muslim couple of Moroccan origin in Lille led to conflict within the judiciary, National Assembly uproar and a media frenzy. The annulment had been granted on the grounds that the wife had lied to her husband about her virginity, this lie thus constituting, according to the French *Code Civil*: 'an error on an essential quality of the spouse.' The incident became variously interpreted as an attack on women's rights, an attempt to introduce *shari'a* law into France and further proof of the incompatibility between Muslim values and those of the French Republic. The fact that the tribunal argued that the annulment was based on the deceit rather than the lack of virginity of the bride, that nothing in Islamic scripture demands that wives be virgins before marriage and that both spouses were seeking the annulment to avoid a lengthier and costlier divorce were nuances largely drowned out in the wave of indignation that followed. Justice Minister Rachida Dati, the first child of North African immigrants to occupy a senior position in the cabinet, initially seemed reluctant to condemn the decision. In the early 1990s, she had used an annulment to terminate a marriage which she had been pressurised into by her family. In the face of the uproar, however, Dati requested that the public prosecutor of Lille appeal. In November 2008, the couple was 'remarried' with the Douai court of appeal ruling that if the lie did not relate to an 'essential quality' then the marriage could not be annulled, and that virginity was not an essential quality. Thus emerged a rather surreal situation in which a woman was remarried to a man whom she no longer wanted to be married to, in order to protect women's rights (and *laïcité*) by rejecting outmoded ('religious') ideas about spousal virginity.

Swiftly following the *affaire de Lille* came the so-called *affaire de la burqa*. In June 2008, the Conseil d'Etat confirmed the decision to refuse French nationality to a woman of Moroccan origin who wore the niqab, a type of clothing common in parts of the Middle East, in which a woman's body is entirely covered apart from her eyes. The niqab is not in fact the same as a burqa, in which the face is totally covered. The difference might seem insignificant, but the connotations of the word 'burqa' are far stronger – this is the type of clothing which the Taliban forces Afghan women to wear. The semantic 'slip' thus conjures up a more powerful image of hidden faces, foreign influence and male domination. Refusals of nationality to those who are already married to a French national, as was the case of 'Faiza M.', are rare, but the ruling argued that she demonstrated a 'lack of assimilation' to the fundamental values of French society through her dresswear and submissive status in relations with her husband. It was alleged that, during interviews with social services, Faiza M. had 'no idea about *laïcité* or the right to vote' (La burqa 2008). The judgment thus stated that the applicant demonstrated: 'a radical practice of religion incompatible with the essential values of the French community' (Refus de national-ité 2008). The decision to refuse her French nationality was welcomed by both Junior Minister Fadela Amara, feminist founder of Ni putes ni soumises and the Front national which deplored that courts were being forced to deal with 'unprecedented communitarianism in French society' (Femme en burqa 2008).

Both the *affaire de Lille* and the *affaire de la burqa* are in many ways minor incidents with unwarranted importance attached to their signifi-cance. However, they highlight three key aspects of how debates about *laïcité* are framed in current French discourse. Firstly, the convergence of opinion across the political spectrum on the importance of actively reject-ing perceived threats to *laïcité*. Furthermore, debates about *laïcité* are con-sidered to be popular politics: every politician from left to extreme right jumps on the bandwagon and has something to say, often for reasons of political expediency rather than a desire to engage in a serious debate about 'Republican values' or define what *laïcité* means.

This brings us onto the second point. Whilst the assimilationist aspect of the Republican citizenship model invites comparison with 19th-century France, many of the core ideas being promoted from the 1980s onwards as 'fundamental' Republican values – *mixité*, gender equality – are what Hobsbawm might term 'invented traditions' (see also Roy 2005; Bowen 2007; Gauchet 1998). Republican politicians on the right and left during the Third Republic consistently resisted attempts to enfranchise women, fearing what they saw as their reactionary tenden-cies, Church-going habits and inability to reason as rational citizens. French women were amongst the last in Europe to obtain the vote, in 1944. *Mixité* between men and women has only recently been considered a key aspect of *laïcité* and a 'Republican principle'; *mixité* becoming the norm in French schools after May '68. Legislative advances in women's access to economic equality and contraceptive rights in the 1960s and 1970s coincided with worldwide movements in favour of gender equal-ity and their emergence is neither particularly French nor Republican, although many supporters of the legislation legalising abortion used the language of *laïcité* and the free choice of the individual in their arguments (Rochefort 2007). This highlights the dangers of seeing *laïcité* as in some way a 'fundamental' Republican tradition. It is and has always been a flexible concept whose meaning has constantly been adapted to present exigencies and in response to external as well as internal pressures.

The third key point that these 2008 *affaires* illustrate is thus a semantic shift from *laïcité* as a core Republican value to women's rights as a key Republican ideal. The discourse in support of rejecting both the marriage annulment and Faiza M.'s bid for French nationality referred to the principle of *laïcité* and the importance of upholding gender equality. Faïza M.'s application was not acceptable because she wore a strict form of Muslim dress and because she was labelled a submissive woman unaware of her rights. The marriage annulment was unacceptable because it was based on an outmoded and discriminatory view of women's sexuality which, it was suggested, was based on religious beliefs. Headscarves were banned in 2004 because they did not respect the principle of religious neutrality in schools and because they were widely interpreted (rightly or wrongly) as a symbol of women's oppression. The discourse around all of these examples often falsely suggested that gender inequality was a particularly Muslim problem and here we fall back on an old cliché of the colonial period of bad Muslim men and oppressed Muslim women (Clancy-Smith 1998; Seferdjeli 2004). Nacira Guénif-Souilamas (2006) underlines the pernicious and widespread use of the stereotype of the violent, oppressive Arab/Black male versus the assimilated *beurette* (young woman of North African origin), which she argues ignores both the wider social and economic problems of deprived areas with populations of predominantly immigrant origin and the voices of young Muslim women themselves. Anna Kemp (2009: 21) highlights the 'seemingly emancipatory but in fact deeply regressive vision of femininity' which surrounds discussions of gender, Islam and the *banlieue*, underlining that the 'feminism' being promoted is a commercialised and sexualised version, in which the sole markers of emancipation are tight clothes and heavy makeup. The convergence of two discourses – one on gender equality and one on religion – is perhaps deliberately ambiguous. It could be interpreted as an attempt to distract attention from an ethnicised interpretation of these exclusions, emphasising that the rejection is based on a political model of integration, not on blood, thus pre-empting accusations of racism. However, these subtleties are largely lost in the public debate where Muslim–immigrant–sexism–social problems are all too easily conjugated. The reactions and responses generated hint at the unrealistic belief that if immigrants somehow became less Muslim all kinds of other problems – socio-economic inequalities, exclusion, discrimination and violence against women – would disappear.

The French left is split on issues such as the headscarf law and the burqa and marriage affairs. The anti-racist, anti-colonialist left are more open to Islam, arguing that there are socio-economic explanations for what seems to be a radical rejection of Republican principles by some Muslims in France. Other sections of the left view Islam as a totalitarian threat, a danger to women, free speech and gay rights which must be met with a firm hand and not naïve cultural relativism (see Laurence and Vaisse 2006: 57; Roy 2005: 10–11). These splits within the left are also evident in European countries which have embraced 'multicultural' models, such as the UK and the Netherlands. Jocelyne Cesari (2005b: 45) argues that post-9/11 discussions about the place of Islam in Europe 'are accompanied by the often aggressive revaluation of multiculturalism as a social policy and practice'. Tariq Modood (2002: 118–19) dates the British left's discomfort with a politicised, religious identity and divisions in the UK between rival versions of multiculturalism back to the uproar surrounding the publication of Salman Rushdie's *Satanic Verses* two decades ago: Muslim anger found no echo in the anti-racist movement. New Labour's 'faith schools', by which all religions, and notably Islam, are given access to state funding to build their own educational establishments is a logical step towards equality between religions in a country which has a high number of state-funded Anglican and Catholic schools, but one which makes many of those on the left who fought for Britain's multicultural identity to be recognised in the 1970s and 1980s uneasy, as it suggests separate existences. More generally, all European states are now demanding that immigrants and Muslims, and in particular Muslim immigrants, prove their loyalty to the nation and their preparedness to give up 'cultural specificities': the introduction of citizenship tests in Germany (2008) and the UK (2005) indicates a move towards a more 'French' model of integration in which newcomers are required to demonstrate their knowledge of language and life in the country to which they have migrated.

Conclusion

This chapter has sought to demonstrate that *laïcité* in France has never been as 'exceptional' as its supporters or detractors have claimed, and that this 'exceptionality' has often been emphasised for political and ideological reasons: as a Republican shield against Papal condemnation, as a way of appearing to maintain an independent path faced with Anglo-Saxon influence and as a means of refuting accusations of racism and exclusionary politics. Since the 19th century, *laïcité* has been redefined and reimagined in response to internal and external social and political change, and the current definition of *laïcité* as promoting gender equality, pluralism and social mixing is only the most recent version. As a number of authors have underlined, Islam is not a threat to *laïcité*, instead it puts a magnifying glass upon debates about what *laïcité* is.

During the colonial period, Islam was used by Republican France as a tool to control indigenous populations and maintain them in a position of subservience; the attachment of autochthonous populations to Islam was the justification for refusing full citizenship and equality. As relatively recent immigrants, France's Muslims today are more likely to live in socio-economically deprived areas, are less likely to access the most sought after educational and employment opportunities and are more likely to end up in prison. Michel Wieviorka (2002: 142) argues: 'Today the Republic would seem to demand of those who find themselves in a minority and excluded – ethnicised and despised for their religion – that they recognise themselves in its abstract universalism.'

The recent turn to an 'interventionist' approach to Islam in France, with the creation of the CFCM and its associated Foundation, and a more proactive attitude towards the provision of prayer spaces, halal meat and training for imams, finds echoes across all European countries with significant Muslim minorities, anxious about the perceived threat of Islamic fundamentalism within and beyond Europe's borders. European states feel vulnerable that they do not know who is funding their mosques, that the majority of imams are trained outside Europe, that the Internet allows dissatisfaction with European domestic and foreign policy to be relayed around the globe instantaneously, that a tiny minority of European-born Muslims feel so disillusioned with 'Western society' that they are prepared to explode themselves on buses, trains and aeroplanes.

These issues are seen of major importance in states across the Western world, regardless of their model of Church-State relations. This perhaps demonstrates the failure of both the 'French model' of assimilation and the 'Anglo-Saxon model' of multiculturalism in integrating minorities and managing diversity: the former refuses to recognise difference and imposes a monocultural model, the latter essentialises cultural difference, reducing individuals to the limited confines of racial or religious identities. And whilst focusing on cultural 'integration' and 'identity issues', more far-reaching, long-term and expensive socio-economic integration has been overshadowed. There is a convergence across Europe towards similar positions on Church-State relations and attitudes towards Islam, but the basis for these policy shifts is suspicion and fear rather than a positive re-evaluation of how societies negotiate difference and welcome newcomers.

Notes

1 Although the French state does consider religious movements which it classes as sects, such as Scientology, as a serious challenge – hence the 2001 About-Picard law 'Against Sect movements damaging to the Rights of Man'.
2 North African immigration accounts for the majority of Muslims in France, but there are also significant minorities from former colonies in sub-Saharan Africa, and from Turkey, which is not a former colony.
3 Some recent publications include: Cesari, J. 1998. *Musulmans et républicains: les jeunes, l'islam et la France* (Brussels: Editions Complexe); Flanquart, H. 2003. *Croyances et valeurs chez les jeunes Maghrébins* (Brussels: Editions Complexe); Hajji, S. and Marteau, S. 2005. *Voyage dans la France musulman* (Paris: Plon); Khosrokhavar, F. 1997. *L'Islam des jeunes* (Paris: Flammarion); Tietze, N. 2002. *Jeunes musulmans de France et d'Allemagne: les constructions subjectives de l'identité* (Paris: L'Harmattan); Venel, N. 2004. *Musulmans et citoyens* (Paris: PUF).
4 I.e. echoing Napoleon I's 1801 Concordat with the Catholic Church, in which the civil war between anti-clericals and Catholics engendered by the French Revolution was resolved through state recognition of Catholicism as France's main religion and state funding (and thus also significant control) of religious institutions.
5 Other (smaller) organisations involved in the CFCM include the Comité de Coordination des Musulmans Turcs de France (CCMTF), an organisation for Turkish Muslims in France, and the Fédération Française des Associations Islamiques d'Afrique, des Comores et des Antilles, for African and Caribbean Muslims.

9

From Private Lives to Intimate Revelations: Politicians and the Media in Contemporary France

Raymond Kuhn

Until recently France was widely regarded as quite distinct, even exceptional, among advanced liberal democracies in the way in which a clear boundary between the private and public spheres was maintained in both politicians' mediated communication and journalists' coverage of political issues and events (Kuhn 2004). French exceptionalism in this respect was underpinned by the norms of the national political culture, with its particular mix of Roman Catholic and secular Republican values, and by the universalist rules of the one and indivisible Republic that posited a particular ideal-type relationship between state and citizen based on a formal codification of the rights and responsibilities of each. It is now apparent that such a well-delineated boundary between the private and public spheres no longer exists in either the realm of political communication (content released into the public sphere under the control of politicians) or the world of political journalism (information and comment mediated by journalists).

The traditional French approach was based on a shared understanding of certain practices and norms of behaviour among three sets of actors: first, politicians, government officials and their communication advisers; second, media professionals, notably journalists, but also including proprietors and newsroom managers; and, finally, the public as citizens, voters and media users. This understanding was based on the following elements. First, elite political actors did not seek to project their private lives into the public realm. Instead, they maintained a distinction between their private lives and their public careers, with the result that they did not seek to exploit the former for electoral gain. Second, the news media did not intrude into the private lives of politicians. Indeed, even where it could be argued that certain aspects of what politicians sought to retain in the private sphere might well have merited media coverage in the public interest, news outlets frequently imposed on themselves an embargo of self-restraint. The lack of an Anglo-American style tabloid culture among mainstream news media was particularly evident in France. Finally, French public opinion did not consider a politician's private life to be an appropriate matter for media scrutiny or a relevant criterion in electoral evaluation.

This shared understanding between politicians, news media and the public was in turn shored up by a fourth factor, namely the existence of some of the toughest privacy legislation to be found in an advanced democratic society anywhere in the world. In France politicians who considered that their private lives had been infringed by media exposure could seek recompense in the courts. In turn, the knowledge of the existence of this body of law had an impact on the behaviour of the news media, encouraging caution, circumspection and even self-censorship. The argument of this chapter is that the first two elements of this traditional approach – politicians' self-denial and journalists' self-restraint – have to a significant extent collapsed, possibly irreparably, while the third – public indifference to politicians' private behaviour – is under strain. Only the legal framework protecting individual privacy is still fully in place, although even here the judicial process inevitably has to take some account of changing elite behaviour, media practices and social norms in forming a judgement.

This chapter examines selected features of this changing public/private interface in the mediatisation of French politicians in the Fifth Republic, including the two main contenders in the 2007 presidential election, Nicolas Sarkozy and Ségolène Royal. The chapter is divided into three sections. The first part looks at the way in which politicians have increasingly accepted the desirability of marketing aspects of their private lives via the media for electoral purposes. Part two focuses on the structures and functioning of the contemporary media landscape in France, emphasising the competition for audiences and revenue that is driving changes in media content and a more intimate form of political coverage. The third section examines the inter-relationship between politicians and journalists, where well-embedded and extant practices of collusion between the two sets of actors (for example, over Mitterrand and the Mazarine affair) have not prevented the emergence of a critical journalistic culture of revelation, even if this is still relatively tame by the standards of Anglo-American 'attack journalism'.

Politics: marketing the personal

French politicians have traditionally kept a clear dividing line between their private lives and public careers. The introduction in 1962 of direct election to the presidency by a single national constituency of voters certainly increased media and public attention on the personal characteristics and leadership skills of candidates to the supreme office. The nationwide take-up of television during the de Gaulle presidency allowed politicians, especially among the ranks of the governing majority, to enter voters' living rooms via the 'small screen'. The advent and routinisation of television as a mass medium in the 1960s ushered in fundamental changes to the nature of election campaigning that are still in evidence today. In addition, the expansion of opinion polling further encouraged the personalisation of presidential electoral competition, with respondents being asked to comment on the 'sincerity', 'honesty' and 'integrity' of candidates. Yet despite the confluence of these changes in the electoral system, the media and voter survey methods, for several years this personalisation of electoral competition did not extend into the controlled mediatisation of politicians' private lives into the public sphere.

De Gaulle is the archetype in this respect. His campaigning in elections and referenda focused on what he regarded as the key issues facing the country. The strength of his views and his self-belief were rarely in doubt. Yet he never sought to make any association between his political career and his private life in his campaigns, while during his presidency his wife Yvonne remained largely out of the public gaze. In the intervening years several other major candidates for the presidency have followed this Gaullian tradition of keeping their spouse and family out of the public spotlight. For reasons which were later to become apparent (see below) François Mitterrand could not have projected a political image based on his role as a loving and faithful husband even if he had wanted to. Other leading presidential candidates including Raymond Barre (1988), Edouard Balladur (1995), Lionel Jospin (1995 and 2002) and, to a lesser extent, François Bayrou (2007) did not make much reference to their private or family lives in their electoral campaigning.

In contrast, in the 1974 presidential campaign Valéry Giscard d'Estaing was the first major candidate to use his wife and family as an integral part of his electoral marketing in an attempt to humanise his image as a technocratic egg-head. In the run-up to the 2002 presidential contest Jacques Chirac benefited from the direct input of his wife, Bernadette, who pitched in to aid her husband's re–election through the publication of a best-selling book that revealed aspects of their relationship as a couple (Chirac 2001), while she also made highly popular appearances on television chat shows. In similar vein the two main candidates in the 2007 presidential election – Royal and Sarkozy – experienced no reluctance in using aspects of their private lives for the purpose of constructing their images as serious *présidentiables*.

One of the axes of Royal's campaign was to present herself as a maternal figure, compassionate and understanding (clearly seeking to contrast herself with Sarkozy). For example, during a prime-time television debate with 'ordinary citizens' (*J'ai une question à vous poser* on TF1) she left the podium and walked across to comfort a disabled person in what was to become one of the most talked about aspects of the programme in the next day's newspapers. Prior to the campaign Royal had overtly related her sex, and in particular her role as a mother, to the stance she adopted on certain political issues, such as her opposition to pornography on television and violence in schools. In 2007 she presented herself as someone who not only understood but also empathised with the insecurities and anxieties of the French electorate, responding to them with policies that emphasised the importance of 'tough love'. She was also willing to use her family in the pre-campaign period, posing for photos in *Paris Match* with her daughter. During her time as a government minister in the early 1990s Royal had famously publicised her role as a 'working mother' by allowing the press and the main private national television network, TF1, to photograph her in hospital shortly after the birth of her fourth child as she continued to work on ministerial correspondence. Royal, in short, has a long track record of being willing to mediatise her status as a woman and her role as a mother as an integral part of her constructed public image.

Until their marital problems became the big news story of the summer of 2005, the close relationship between Sarkozy and his wife Cécilia had been mediatised at length by the government minister. Even their young son, Louis, was mobilised in the effort to help his father's presidential ambitions through an appearance on video footage at the UMP rally in November 2004 which marked Sarkozy's takeover of the party leadership: 'Bonne chance mon papa' (Artufel and Duroux 2006: 43–50). Promotion of a spouse and family – especially in the case of male politicians – can help provide a more rounded, human image to the public, especially women voters who in 2007 constituted more than half of the total electorate. This image softening may be particularly useful for a politician such as Sarkozy who needed to counterbalance those aspects of his public image based on a projection of 'firmness' and 'order'.

The high point of this marketing of the personal by Sarkozy came after his election victory and involved the early months of his new relationship with Carla Bruni. In the wake of his divorce from Cécilia only a few months after entering the Elysée, Sarkozy entered into a whirlwind romance with the singer and former model that he was only too keen to publicise. Staged photo opportunities for the media were arranged at Disneyland Paris, in Egypt and in Jordan, while at his presidential press conference in January 2008 Sarkozy was at pains to remark that his new relationship was not a light-hearted fling: 'C'est du sérieux'. In short, for a few months in late 2007/early 2008 the French President unashamedly played up his new romantic relationship, keen to propagate the fairy tale of a French version of John F. Kennedy's 'Camelot' years in the US White House at the start of the 1960s.

Mediatisation of spouse and family as part of a politician's public communication strategy can, however, be dangerous territory with considerable rebound potential from the media and public opinion. Sarkozy had previously discovered the downside of marketing the personal when Cécilia left him in 2005 and was then seen in a new relationship which was itself covered in depth by certain media (Aubry and Pleynet 2006: 201–51). Sarkozy responded by stopping the publication of a biography of his wife through exerting pressure on the publisher, and while the book was later published by a different publisher, it now took the form of a thinly veiled fictional romance which had little media or public impact (Domain 2006). Sarkozy also complained to the owner of *Paris Match*, Arnaud Lagardère, about the magazine's coverage of Cécilia's liaison with her new male companion, Richard Attias. Later, the editor of the magazine, Alain Genestar, who had approved a cover picture featuring Cécilia and Attias, was removed from his post in a move widely interpreted as Sarkozy exacting his revenge (Genestar 2008).

Moreover, even when there is cooperation between politicians and media in the construction of the story – as in the early coverage of Sarkozy's romance with Bruni – there is always the risk of a critical public response. The President's opinion poll ratings plummeted in early 2008, with one of the principal reasons for the decline in his popularity, especially among older voters, being the perception that he was too focused on his private life at the expense of his public responsibilities. In the light of the poll findings Sarkozy's advisers urged him to readjust the thrust of his public utterances away from his personal life and towards more conventional political issues.

News media: chasing audiences

While one of the drivers contributing to the blurring of the public-private divide has come from the marketing activities of politicians, another is the product of changes in the news media landscape. France has intensely competitive media markets as a result of an explosion in outlets and the advent of a 24/7 news culture. This has led to a relentless pursuit of both audiences and advertising revenue, with media outlets seeking to exploit changes in popular taste for commercial gain. Developments in three media sectors in particular – print media, television and online – can be linked to the changing nature of the public/private interface in contemporary political journalism.

Among print media, general information newspapers such as *Libération* and *Le Monde* are in decline, some would say in crisis, as circulations and advertising revenue slide in the face of competition from free newspapers and internet websites. In contrast, the magazine sector is generally healthy. The strong sales figures of celebrity magazines (*la presse people*) such as *Voici* and *Gala*, competing with more established photonews weeklies such as *Paris Match*, are particularly noteworthy (Lutaud and Dromard 2006). Every week about 2.5 million people in France buy a 'celebrity' publication and more than 13 million people read them. Cover stories featuring high profile politicians frequently increase circulation figures. In turn, the popularity of photonews and celebrity magazines makes them attractive vehicles for advertisers, while allowing politicians to target sections of the electorate who are low users of general information newspapers.

Both Sarkozy couples (Nicolas/Cécilia and Nicolas/Carla Bruni) have featured on the front cover and inside pages of *Gala* and *Paris Match* on several occasions in the past few years with carefully arranged photos purporting to show the 'authentic persona' behind the professional politician. The French public's appetite for information about the intimate lives of their politicians has even affected the journalism of mainstream news magazines. For example, in the summer of 2007 *Le Nouvel Observateur* featured President Sarkozy's wife, Cécilia, on its front cover and devoted no fewer than ten pages to the so-called 'enigma' of France's new first lady: 'woman of power or fragile spouse?'. (The answer turned out to be neither).

Across the news media as a whole, free-to-air television continues to provide the most important channels of political information to reach a mass audience. In particular, the evening news programmes of TF1 and France 2 are the main sources of national news for much of the electorate, even if their hold over audiences is now under threat in the multi-channel digital broadcasting environment. Traditional political debate programmes, however, have become less common on French television since the 1990s, with such programmes no longer regarded by television management as audience pullers – rather the reverse. The decline in this genre of programming has been particularly marked in the commercial sector. Outside of election campaigns, TF1 and M6 have virtually given up on coverage of national politics except as part of news programmes. Moreover, although they may have greater regulatory obligations than their private sector competitors, even public service channels are not immune from audience maximising pressures.

The power of ratings in a zapping televisual culture has meant that politics has to sell itself in the competition for scheduling space with other content on mainstream free-to-air channels. In terms of style of coverage broadcasters are constantly looking at new ways of covering politics to attract the kinds of audiences that advertisers wish to attract. These commercial pressures on television scheduling have encouraged politicians to appear on non-traditional programme formats such as television chat shows in an attempt to flesh out their image and get their message across in a less adversarial setting than political debate programmes. In the 1990s and early 2000s chat shows such as *Tout le monde en parle*, *On ne peut pas plaire à tout le monde* and *Vivement Dimanche* welcomed politicians on to their programmes, but only on condition that they refrained from discussing the politics of the public realm (issues and policies) and instead concentrated on aspects of their private lives (Neveu 2005).

Alongside chat shows, the other development in television's political coverage worthy of note has been the increased attention to process journalism, whereby politics is presented as a narrative, drama and spectacle, with recognisable *dramatis personae* and a plot constructed around the theme of personal ambition. One manifestation of this trend is the popularity of 'behind-the-scenes' (*coulisses*) type programmes, where issues are presented through a focus on the 'human' side of politics and the emotional consequences for the protagonists.

In his extended essay *La fin de la télévision* (2006) Jean-Louis Missika outlines what he regards as the essential characteristics of political information in the current stage of television's development. These include: the rise of infotainment (i.e. a mix of information and entertainment) content and genres in contrast to a more serious, rational form of news; a focus on the wings and backstage of politics, on the tactics and strategies of politicians; and a tendency towards a more intimate, personal and emotional register in reporting. Missika argues that when these three tendencies of what he calls the 'post-television' era are combined, it is possible to understand why the politician as a person has become a news topic of the first order.

Other academic researchers have written about the explosion in the 'television of intimacy' in France since the early 1990s (Mehl 1996), evident in various television reality shows, including France's first version of the *Big Brother* format, *Loft Story*. The growth of reality television in its different forms has allowed and even encouraged audiences to engage in a voyeuristic relationship with a show's participants, as certain psychological traits are revealed before the cameras. In this context of the deprivatisation of the sphere of intimacy via television, it is tempting for media executives and politicians to see a mutually beneficial gap in the market. A political version of a reality show to be screened on TF1 and entitled *36 Heures* was mooted at the start of Chirac's second presidential term. While the project was finally blocked by the government, the fact that the concept was considered marketable by TF1 management and that some leading politicians expressed an interest in participating indicated the extent to which both media and political elites were willing to consider 'politainment' genres (i.e. politics as entertainment) for their own respective ends of audience maximisation and electoral outreach.

Finally, there is the multi-faceted impact of the internet to change both rules and practices. The trend on the part of politicians towards the mediatisation of their private lives has been amplified by the routinisation of the internet as a medium of political communication and information, and in particular by the onward march of the blog. The 2007 presidential election was the first in which the internet played a major role – including official candidate websites such as Royal's *Désirs d'avenir* and an array of political blogs. The blog allows a politician to bypass the traditional intermediary filters and journalistic gatekeepers of the mainstream news media. In terms of process, the production of the blog is fully under the control of the politician as source and the resultant output can be put into the public sphere without any intermediation. With regard to content, the nature of the blog allows for a mix of public and private information to be disseminated at will: politicians may not only give their views on public events, but can also control the release of more personalised information, including elements of their private lives if they so choose.

There is, however, also the possibility of 'blog backlash', with politicians open to information about their private lives being put on the web by their political opponents, journalists or amateur bloggers. This happened to Royal in the 2007 presidential campaign, when information about her property holdings and alleged tax avoidance originated on the internet and then became a story in the mainstream news media. While the accuracy of the information was contested by the candidate, the capacity of a blog for spreading rumour and gossip – as well as accurate information – is a new potentially destabilising element that politicians now have to incorporate into their rebuttal communication strategy.

Politicians and journalists: collusion and revelation

It is not just image construction by politicians or commercial pressures and technological changes in the news media that are responsible for the blurring of the dividing line between public and private in political communication and journalism in contemporary France. A third element lies in the interdependent relationship between politicians and journalists, that may be characterised as an unequal mix of collusion and revelation. In France top politicians and leading political journalists inhabit the same milieu and get to know each other well. Indeed, affairs of the heart, including marriages, between politicians (male) and journalists (female) are not uncommon: Dominique Strauss-Kahn/Anne Sinclair, Jean-Louis Borloo/Béatrice Schonberg and François Baroin/Marie Drucker are some recent examples of the personal interlinkages between the two milieus. Perhaps the highest profile relationship of this type is that of Bernard Kouchner, the 'French doctor' and current Minister of Foreign Affairs, and Christine Ockrent, a former news anchor and more recently presenter of a political magazine programme on the public service network, FR3. In this context it is hardly surprising that Sarkozy sought solace with a female journalist from the conservative daily *Le Figaro*, Anne Fulda, when his marriage with Cécilia was in difficulty in 2005, while the then leader of the Socialist Party, François Hollande, was photographed with a journalist from *Paris Match*, Valérie Trierweiler, in the weeks following his split with Royal in the summer of 2007.

Sarkozy has for a long time enjoyed a good relationship with news media professionals. He is a friend of various media proprietors including Arnaud Lagardère (*Paris Match*), Bernard Arnault (*Les Echos*), Serge Dassault (*Le Figaro*) and Martin Bouygues (TF1) (Farbiaz and Mamère 2009: 55–88). Sarkozy has also cultivated media managers and news editors, such as Jean-Pierre Elkabbach (Radio Europe 1). He both bullies journalists – he has been reported issuing blatant threats – and tries to win them over, using their first names and breaking convention by often using the more intimate form of 'you' ('tu' instead of 'vous') as part of a process of cooption. Since his election to the Elysée Sarkozy has paid close attention to news management, with the President apparently seeking to emulate many of the agenda building and issue framing techniques of the early years of the Blair premiership in Britain.

Traditionally in France the relationship between politicians and journalists has been marked by a high level of deference on the part of the latter, most notably in broadcast interviews, and by close cooperation, even connivance between the two sets of actors (Carton 2003). In this interdependent relationship the professional cultural norms of the journalistic milieu are central. Deference on the part of journalists to politicians may well be on the wane in France. However, it still remains more of a feature of the French political communication system than in Anglo-American democracies where a journalistic tradition of adversarial contestation, critical watchdog and 'Fourth Estate' thinking is more firmly implanted. For instance, French television interviews between leading politicians and broadcast journalists often seem tame compared to the cut-and-thrust of their equivalents in Britain, with the French President in particular generally accorded deferential treatment by interviewers who are usually reluctant to push home their interrogative advantage.

Part of the normative accord between politicians and journalists is that sexual relationships, including marital infidelity, belong to the private sphere and are off-limits to media coverage. The most notorious example of media reticence in the face of a politician's extra-marital affair was Mitterrand's relationship with his mistress, Anne Pingeot, and in particular the product of their union, their daughter Mazarine. It has been argued that not only did several journalists know about the existence of Mitterrand's illegitimate daughter well before this information was revealed to the public, but that some journalists even cooperated with the Elysée in keeping the information a secret (Chemin and Catalano 2005: 109–25). Throughout her childhood and teenage years Mazarine thus inhabited a shadowy world in which her status was hidden to many, partly disclosed to some, and fully revealed to only a select few (Pingeot 2005). It was not until November 1994, when Mazarine was already nearly 20 years old and Mitterrand had been head of state for 13 years, that the President's private secret was made fully public by *Paris Match*, with the requisite photos to illustrate the shocking news (Chemin and Catalano 2005: 225–43). By this time Mitterrand was coming to the end of his second seven year term in office, was in the advanced stages of the cancer that would kill him barely over a year later and was seeking to control how his life and career would be represented and evaluated after his death. The revelation of Mazarine's existence, so long zealously protected by Mitterrand, now became part of his bid to impose on posterity a positive framing of his legacy.

Accustomed to detailed and salacious media coverage of the sexual indiscretions of their own politicians, Anglo-American audiences may be tempted to regard respect by the French news media for this aspect of Mitterrand's presidential tenure as a commendable feature of French journalism. Was this not a private matter with no public interest? Yet before one rushes to praise the restraint of the French news media in this respect or the desirable impact of strong privacy legislation, two caveats are worthy of note. First, neither Anne nor Mazarine was simply an element of Mitterrand's private life: both benefited from accommodation and security protection paid for out of the public purse. The existence of Mitterrand's 'second family' was, during his time at the Elysée at least, a matter of legitimate public interest. The reluctance of Mitterrand and of the mainstream news media to go public with the information may be understandable and, in the eyes of some, even defensible: Mitterrand wished to protect his daughter and mistress from intrusive media publicity. Such a concern would have weighed particularly heavily when Mazarine remained a minor, during which time her protection from unwarranted media attention would have depended on a deal being struck between the Elysée, media owners and journalists. What is clear is that the case in support of the public concealment of Mazarine's identity cannot be based on the grounds that her existence was simply part of Mitterrand's private life. Second, to ensure the secrecy surrounding Mazarine, the Elysée indulged in practices which represented a misuse, indeed abuse, of presidential authority. For example, the writer Jean-Edern Hallier was the victim of telephone tappings and financial threats against his publishing ventures (Palou 2007). Hallier's private life and professional career were grossly interfered in so as to protect Mitterrand's secret.

The Mazarine case is one of the prime examples of news media coverage of politicians that has been called a *journalisme de révérence* (Halimi 2005: 17–48). In the light of this culture of journalistic deference to top politicians and especially the president, it is perhaps not surprising that Sarkozy was so taken aback by a question from a foreign correspondent about the state of his marriage to Cécilia in the early weeks of his own presidency. Sarkozy's unilateral and premature termination of the interview with the American CBS journalist was described as follows (*Sour Sarkozy storms out of TV interview* 2007):

Mr Sarkozy's smile froze. 'If I had to say something about Cécilia, I would certainly not do so here', he said before taking off his microphone.

'What was unfair?' Mrs Stahl [the correspondent] stammered. 'Au revoir, merci et bon courage (Good-bye, thank-you and good luck)', said the President over his shoulder as he walked out.

The incident illustrated Mr Sarkozy's sensitivity over his divorce. A French journalist who asked about the marriage at a press conference received similarly short shrift, with Mr Sarkozy denouncing the media's 'inelegance' in pursuing the issue.

However, alongside this tradition of deference and collusion, there has also emerged a practice of exposure journalism: a journalism of irreverence – or what Ramonet calls a *journalisme de révélation* (in contrast to a *journalisme d'investigation*) which focuses on 'the private lives of public personalities and scandals linked to corruption and political racketeering' (Ramonet 2007: 25). Such coverage has not been confined to the 'usual suspect' of *Le Canard enchaîné*, whose irreverence is legendary and whose revelations in the area of political scandal has frequently set the agenda for mainstream news outlets (Martin 2005). Exposure journalism has spilled over to embrace mainstream outlets such as *Le Monde* and *L'Express*. For instance, Chirac's first presidential term was dogged by newspaper coverage of apparent financial malpractice during his period as mayor of Paris (1977–95) and President (1995–2002).

There has even emerged a French variant of the Anglo-American practice of personalised 'attack journalism' (Sabato 2000), albeit more usually found in books than in daily or weekly news media. The publication in 2006 of *La Tragédie du président* (Giesbert 2006) marked the culmination of a series of critical books about Chirac by leading journalists (Colombani 1998; Jeambar 2005; Gattegno 2006). Amid the sustained political attack, Giesbert somewhat bizarrely devotes a chapter to the alleged gargantuan appetite of the then President (2006: 26–31) – an apt illustration of the way in which previously private aspects of a politician's life have now become raw material for the journalistic enterprise. What purpose is served by the detailed description of Chirac's daily intake of food and drink? Giesbert is here establishing his credentials as an authoritative commentator – if he can write with such authority about the president's dietary habits, then the reader may reasonably infer that the journalist has enjoyed first rate access backstage to all the political manoeuvring at the Elysée. The as yet unanswered question is whether such personalised adversarial commentary will migrate across into other genres and outlets of daily and weekly political journalism – as has long been the case in Britain. In an age when in terms of prestige the presidential office has lost its sacerdotal dimension of heroic leadership and the media are competing for revenue and audiences, such a development certainly cannot be ruled out.

Conclusion

It is important to contextualise the phenomenon of the mediatisation of the private lives of contemporary French politicians both under controlled conditions and through journalistic commentary. First, some aspects of the phenomenon are not as novel as one might imagine. In 1954, for instance, René Coty's wife was photographed by *Paris Match* performing a variety of domestic tasks at the Elysée following her husband's accession to the presidency, while among the featured photos from the new president's 'family album' was one showing him posing in a swimming costume alongside his similarly attired daughter.

Second, and in contrast, by no means all contemporary politicians have been happy or even willing to mediatise aspects of their private lives for electoral purposes. Some, especially among the older generation, have been reticent and uncomfortable in the face of the altered rules of the political communication game. Third, ideas and values continue to inform candidates' political communication, while issue-oriented forms of political journalism still exist. Electoral politics in France has not been reduced to a simple personality contest, nor is 'policy lite' the only form of political journalism available.

Finally, and most obviously, the phenomenon is by no means unique to France. On the contrary, in many respects France is only catching up with aspects of media and political behaviour which are considered commonplace in other advanced liberal democracies (Seaton 2003; Stanyer and Wring 2004). Although aspects of the French situation, notably strong privacy laws, continue to constitute an important element of difference, there is much in French political communication and journalism which seems to be bringing the French experience more in line with that of comparable advanced democracies.

If so, the apparently well-entrenched notion of French exceptionalism in this area of public life now has to be subject to significant qualification. It is not the case that France now has a political-media culture exactly similar to that of the UK or US. However, it is certainly true that it is now more difficult than previously to analyse the French experience without taking into account the transfer of practices – for instance in politicians' image projection – across national boundaries. As a result, it may now be less appropriate to talk of a French model in this sphere of mediated politics and more useful to think in terms of a French variant of a transnational template.

It is clear that the personalisation of electoral politics has grown in France in recent years and that this has led to a less well-defined boundary between private and public in the mediatisation of politicians both by themselves and by journalists. While the phenomenon may not be new in itself, what is striking is the reduction in the degree of control that a political figure can now exert over what becomes public when compared to only a few years ago, notwithstanding the tough privacy legislation. The younger generation of French politicians is learning to embrace these developments, aware that there is little chance of the clock being turned back. In the mediatisation of the private lives of politicians, the public/private interface will continue to be a territory of ill-defined and fluid frontiers, where the imperatives of voter outreach, the impact of technological developments, the pressures of media markets and the desire of the public for revelation will combine to make it ever more difficult for politicians and the media not to indulge in the mediation of intimacy and the exposure of secrets.

Section IV

France as a Universal Model

10
France, Europe and the Limits of Exceptionalism

Helen Drake

Introduction

> France is a country unlike any other. It has special responsibilities inherited from its history and the universal values that it has helped to forge.
>
> (....)
>
> France must insist that Europe is powerful, political and upholds our social model.[1]

In these few words, delivered on television in his valedictory speech to the French nation on 11 March 2007, former President Jacques Chirac summed up what has come to be deemed exceptional in France's relations with the European Union (EU). First is the claim made by a succession of French political leaders that France is unlike any other country in the EU or indeed, as in Chirac's statement, any other country on earth. Second is a set of interlocking strategic objectives for France in Europe that appear exceptionally inflexible and, in some respects anachronistic. These strategies revolve around the ambition for a European entity that is a *powerful* world actor, that is constructed by a *political* process, and which has a distinct *identity* in the global capitalist system.

In what follows we offer a critical appreciation of this bundle of strategic principles that underpins France's European policy, with a view to grasping any 'exceptional' quality it might have. We begin, first, by reminding ourselves of the journey that France has taken between Robert Schuman's declaration of 9 May 1950 and the present day, when French national identity itself is predicated upon France's centrality to the EU and *vice versa*. Significant milestones passed *en route* have come to constitute in France a unique narrative of *la construction européenne* that itself feeds a distinct rationale for French EU membership. We then, second, consider how these stories have hardened into a strategic political discourse that has evolved remarkably little over time, despite the EU's dramatically altered circumstances, notably the reunification of Germany and the EU's enlargement, especially eastwards, to 27 member states and counting. This common language is couched in terms of concepts of power, politics and identity that are also central to contemporary French republicanism. Third, we entertain the likelihood that the so-called French exception in the EU constitutes a political orthodoxy that is both potent yet vacuous, a possibility not lost on the French opponents of the EU's constitutional treaty in the French referendum of 2005, and a viewpoint shared by several observers. We see that President Sarkozy has already offered a limited critique of these politics of exceptionalism, and is perhaps on his way to bursting the bubble in favour of a more grounded appreciation of France's role in the EU. In this respect France is certainly not exceptional compared to other EU member states – notably but not exclusively the United Kingdom – which experience ongoing and extraordinary difficulties in sustaining a convincing rationale and consensus for EU membership in their own country.

French tales of France in Europe since 1950

Strategy in foreign affairs and international relations is the product of many factors. These include a definition of the national interest based on specific interpretations of history, events and circumstances as well as, invariably, a set of symbols and myths relating to national identity. It is these latter intangibles that can be most resilient to change, however dramatically times may change. For Flynn, writing of French foreign policy in 1995 at a time of momentous change in Europe: 'A symbol arguably becomes an element of identity when it becomes so powerful that either it may not be changed by successive governments, or it can prevent a party that rejects the symbol from being elected, or taken into coalition. Independence and grandeur clearly meet this particular test.' (Flynn 1995: 238) Sonntag goes as far as to conceive of French diplomacy towards Europe as '[t]rapped within the prison walls' of a political culture which struggles to challenge the symbols and values of the past, including the Gaullist legacy in foreign affairs (2008). An overview of France's journey towards today's European Union demonstrates that tales from France's Gaullist past are not the only myths to have fused into a set of seemingly immutable laws governing French strategy towards Europe. Schmidt joins these commentators in her conviction that French elites seem uniquely 'trapped in the old discourse, unable to develop new ideas capable of legitimising France and Europe in the world.' (Schmidt 2007: 992).

Indeed, where EU member states are most distinct from one another – most themselves, in other words – is in the stories that they tell themselves in order to justify and sustain membership and, just as important, how these stories fit into broader narratives of national identity. Each member state has its own *raison d'être* or rationale for joining the EU in the first place, and staying there, inevitably at the cost of domestic sacrifice. Thus the Central and East European countries which joined the EU in 2004 and 2007 rationalise their membership, broadly-speaking, in terms of their post-Communist transition to democracy and an overdue and deserved 'return to Europe'. Germany, for its part, joined the European Union in the 1950s as a condition and guarantee of its slow return to legitimacy as an independent and sovereign state: to save itself from itself. The UK is still trying to formulate a rationale for membership to puncture the scepticism and cynicism that characterises British attitudes towards 'the continent'. In these terms, France is notable for the extent to which its post-war national identity hinges upon the telling of tales about the uniqueness of France's role, duty and destiny in what has become the EU, as exemplified in the above extracts from Jacques Chirac's 2007 farewell address to the French. Such tales have a habit of turning into dysfunctional membership myths and empty rhetoric, which run the risk of miring France in nostalgia (Lequesne 2008: 13) for a golden age of French influence in the EU which never quite existed (Floch 2004). Tales from France's experience of European integration relate, we will see, to broader narratives of French Republican identity.

Journey without end

Each and every member state of the European Union (EU) has a unique history of EU membership upon which its European strategy is predicated, and France is no exception to this rule. The journey for all member states begins with a political decision to join 'the club', which itself necessitates the formulation of a political discourse intended domestically to justify this decision, quell opposition, and ideally, generate a stable, national consensus in favour of the decision taken. The adventure continues with the negotiation of conditions of entry that are acceptable to important domestic constituencies and partner EU member states alike. Domestic adjustments to membership usually begin before entry itself, and they certainly continue indefinitely *post-hoc*; collectively, these adjustments are invariably described as the Europeanisation of the domestic setting. This is a veritable journey without end. Its destination is indeed unknown (Schonfield 1973), and the route itself is ever-changing: another day could mean another treaty, another member, another crisis of policy, another vote, almost certainly, another law. Under these difficult conditions, member states must maintain popular and political support for the expedition, ensure that it is properly resourced, and work to influence its outcome. What were the milestones on France's journey; how did these shape its strategic objectives; and what myths did they generate?

The French role as co-founder of the European Coal and Steel Community (ECSC), was sealed by Foreign Minister Robert Schuman's '*coup d'état*' against the establishment of the Fourth French Republic (Bossuat 2005: 48–52) in the name of the transformation of the post-war French economy, and putting a stop to France's warring with Germany. This act of statesmanship laid down a strategic sediment in which 'Europe' was synonymous with socio-economic modernisation and progress on the one hand; and with the definitive taming of Germany by friendship, on the other, informed by a sense of equality, at last (if not French superiority) between German and French power in the international system. It was an ambush against the traditional principles that had guided French policy towards Europe, and it succeeded thanks to the exceptional circumstances in which France found itself (see Parsons 2000, 2003), and the influence of extraordinary figures.

In Hayward's terms, '…the person who shaped the conceptual context in which France's "German problem" could be practically approached was Jean Monnet. He persuaded Schuman that the way to end nationalist war between the two countries for ever, at a time when the American government was pressing for German rearmament directed against the Soviet threat, was to pool sovereignty over the industrial sinews of war, coal and steel, by creating a supranational authority' (Hayward 2007: 335). This was not a defensive manoeuvre but a forward-looking and hopeful gesture, sentiments that still underpin French public attitudes to the EU. Three years later in 1954, the rejection by the French Parliament of the European Defence Community (EDC) reflected the victory of a more traditional seam of political argument in France, as alluded to above: highly defensive in the face of German rearmament, and lacking the imagination to imagine a post-national French identity. Here was the defence of national sovereignty that is still traded as valuable currency in today's French political debates – and votes – on European integration, such as the near-miss of the 'yes' vote (a bare 51 per cent of votes cast) in the September 1992 referendum in France on the Maastricht Treaty.

In 1957–78, it was Prime Minister Guy Mollet's decision to override significant opposition to membership within his government and their departments; and his success *vis-à-vis* the other five member states (Germany, Italy and the Benelux countries) in negotiating favourable terms for France (covering, amongst other things, workers' rights, agricultural policy, and trade with France's overseas territories) that clinched French membership of the EEC, a venture that was certainly not a French initiative at the outset (Bossuat 2005: 57–81; Chopin 2008: 31; Hayward 2007: 338).[2] Here undoubtedly were sown seeds of today's French Socialist Party's internal dilemmas over the marketisation aspect of European integration that were so potent in mobilising fear of the EU's Constitutional Treaty in the French referendum campaign of 2005. But Chopin underlines (*ibid*) that French agreement to the Treaty of Rome in 1957 was in fact couched in terms of a vision of French participation in a common market that stopped well short of British demands at the time; in Bossuat's terms: 'The unification of Europe would occur by means of the Communities, and not the British free-trade zone, lacking in political ambition.' (Bossuat *ibid*: 80) We see below that this balance continues to elude French policy towards the EU in practice, but is characteristic of its aims.

De Gaulle's outright challenges to the Treaty of Rome in the early mid-1960s, in the name of the independence, *grandeur* and rank of France, constituted a significant dimension of what Sonntag has called 'the burdensome politics of prestige' that today still act as a drag on France's current ability to 'adapt to a changing world (2008 *ibid:* 84). Sonntag sees Gaullist 'dogma' in foreign and European matters as a 'cultural legacy shared across party lines' (*ibid:* 85). This dogma emphasises rank over influence, where rank is defined as 'the prestige derived from a seemingly inalterable hierarchical position that [is] self-proclaimed and deemed self-evident' (*ibid:* 77). De Gaulle would not disagree with this analysis: in his own famous terms, France was only herself if in the 'front rank'.

This preoccupation with prestige was translated into De Gaulle's conviction that states and only states, in the name of their sovereign peoples (*les patries*), were the building blocks for any European cooperative venture. His blueprint for an alternative to the Treaties of Paris and Rome accordingly, was entitled 'A Union of States'. These so-called Fouchet plans came to nothing in the face of opposition from France's partner member states (based on the absence of the UK from the plans, and the challenge they represented to US leadership of the Cold War western camp), but they nevertheless laid down a marker still evident in today's French approach to the EU, better known as intergovernmentalism. This is a process conceived of as inherently *political*, meaning, for de Gaulle, decisions taken unanimously by national political representatives invested with national sovereignty and political will, able to agree – or disagree – amongst themselves, on the basis of the reciprocity of any concessions. The Fouchet plans themselves would have relegated the European Commission to a mere bureau (the 'Political Commission') with strictly administrative functions. This high-handed tone towards the European Commission, and by proxy the supranationality of the 1950s European Communities, has been a regular feature of French political rhetoric ever since these days, although cooperation in practice is often far smoother than the language would suggest; this is certainly true of Nicolas Sarkozy's government in the present day, as we shall see below.

Yet the ambitions for the Fouchet plans were far-reaching. Where Monnet and Schuman proposed project-based European construction (*les solidarités de fait*), President de Gaulle envisioned ambitious common European policies in defence, foreign affairs, culture and the economy, based on the values of European civilisation as he saw them, and designed to turn Europe into a superpower in its own right, capable of defending itself against external threats. The 'spectacular short-term failure' of the Fouchet Plans (Hill and Smith 2000: 47) did not prevent de Gaulle from making further spirited efforts (notably, the 1965 'empty chair' crisis) to entrench intergovernmentalism as the working method of the Communities that France was saddled with, and he was influential in this respect. Ultimately, however this sharp Gaullist turn in France's European strategy led to something of an impasse in France's journey towards a united Europe. De Gaulle's ambitions for European cooperation were far-reaching, and enjoyed broad political support, but he rejected absolutely the authority of the Community institutions that he had inherited. At the same time, he was unable to persuade his EU counterparts, especially the Germans, and especially in the absence of the UK, to start again from scratch, and his successors were left with this state of affairs, for better or for worse.

This vision of a powerful and political Europe, exclusively European in its geography and culture, and explicitly imagined as an alternative to an 'Anglo-American counter-identity' (Hayward 2007: 1), therefore forms a further element of the strategic architecture of France's contemporary European policy, even though we see that it was unrealistic and unworkable in its own day, as visions tend to be, even – or especially – under de Gaulle's leadership. Haywood describes de Gaulle's belief in Europe as a way for France to recover a leading role in the world as 'an illusion in pursuit of an anachronism' (*ibid* 2007: 342); for Schmidt, 'President Charles de Gaulle's discourse could be seen as the foundational paradigm for French discourse about Europe, setting the path along which other leaders' discourse would build incrementally, whether by adding new layers of meaning or reinterpreting earlier ideas' (Schmidt 2007: 998). Gaullism, then, along with Schuman's triumph in 1950 over the French diplomatic establishment, and Guy Mollet's decisive act of 1957, form the keystones of the edifice of French strategy in Europe.

The practice of French 'exceptionalism' in Europe: power, politics and identity

The case made over at least the last decade (Flynn 1995; Schmidt 2007; Sonntag 2008) is that these tales of France in Europe have hardened into a dominant political discourse which has proved resistant to change, and which has trapped or imprisoned its users – the French foreign policy-making elite. Analytically, we can view this discourse in terms of three sets of interlocking principles and problems; each of which has generated distinct discursive mantras and terminology.

Power

When Jacques Chirac reminded the French of his insistence, on their behalf, on a '*Europe puissance*,' he was referring to the predominantly Gaullist notion, seen above, that 'Europe' must exist in its own right as *a* power within the international system. David Yost, with only some exaggeration, has defined this ambition as the French desire for Europe as an 'autonomous, nuclear, armed power bloc.' (Yost 2006: 719); and Sonntag (2008: 79) defines it as an expression 'assigning a strategic objective to the European Union and implying a vision of it as a self-conscious political actor providing a counterweight to American power'.

From these perspectives, the EU is seen first, as having the quality of 'actorness' in the international system, alongside states – notably the US. This implies military capability as well as the ability to project the 'soft' power of cultural diplomacy (Sonntag *ibid)*; and the political will and the structural instruments to take and operationalise common positions towards world events. These were precisely the attributes that de Gaulle wished for in the case of his 'Union of States' and which have taken shape since in practical terms in the form of consistent French support – and initiatives – for a common foreign and security policy (CFSP) for the EU and, latterly, a European security and defence policy (ESDP). Crucially and unsurprisingly, these ambitions have been contained by the equally pressing French preference for the intergovernmental mode of decision-making in this field; and by the wariness that characterises the Franco-British relationship in this regard despite the historic accord reached in December 1998 at St Malo (and reaffirmed a decade later), which proclaimed a shared ambition for an 'autonomous' EU defence capability.

Second, and logically, *l'Europe puissance* thus defined would provide a stage for the exercise and projection of French power in conjunction with other willing pioneers. In this respect, Hayward has described French policy as a reversal of traditional alliances, away from the UK and towards Germany: a 'Franco-Saxon' Europe (Hayward 2007: 335). However, the Franco-German *directoire*, even in de Gaulle's own day, has proved insufficient to mobilise support for the sort of ambitions implied by the goal of Europe as a power bloc. NATO, not a European nuclear power bloc, to reuse Yost's terminology, has been the goal for virtually all EU member states, including Germany, in matters of collective security.

Third, the pursuit of a *Europe-puissance* has primed France to fear and resist every single enlargement that the EU has undertaken, beginning with the 1973 accession of the United Kingdom; de Gaulle for his part having unilaterally halted negotiations on UK entry throughout the 1960s. Enlargement is seen from this perspective as blurring the edges of 'Europe', with at least two damaging consequences for Europe's potential as an independent actor. First, enlargement imports values, ideas and norms into the existing community; these potentially dilute what French leaders have portrayed as the inherently 'European' characteristics of civilisation, to use de Gaulle's terminology. This is clearly a highly subjective point of contention within the EU, as the prospect of EU Turkish membership demonstrates: French public opinion is consistently negative on this point, along with Germany and Austria. Moreover, in the case of the 2004 enlargements, French reticence was notoriously immortalised in President Chirac's rebuke to the (then) candidate countries of East and Central Europe that they had no place airing their views – favourable to the UK–US alliance – over the matter of Iraq. François Mitterrand had, over a decade earlier, lost face (and the argument) when his proposal for a 'European Confederation' was construed as a ploy indefinitely to postpone eastwards enlargement (Lequesne 2008: 48).

Second, enlargement is deemed to slow down the decision-making process (which it has not) or, more accurately, challenge Franco-German leadership, already complex in a Europe of Six, fraught in a Europe of 27. The Franco-German relationship in the Cold War was vulnerable, as seen from Paris, to the pull of Germany's other friendships, loyalties and commitments – with the US, with East Germany and beyond; in the post-Cold War era, these attractions are no less strong. Enlargement therefore dilutes the resources critical to French influence in the EU, namely, the power of ideas; the power of a special rapport with neighbour Germany; and the power of the vote and voice. This latter dimension is all the more important when we consider the second of our strategic principles: politics.

Politics

The second of Jacques Chirac's goals highlighted above (*une Europe politique*) refers to three interrelated ideas: first, the distribution of power in EU decision-making; second, the conceptual confusion this has sown in French political discourse on the EU's institutional design; and third, the 'project' or purpose of European integration in the broader sense. First, 'political Europe' denotes the process by which EU member states reach decisions, and thus refers to the power to decide, and in whose name. If Europe is to be an independent actor, it needs institutions that are both legitimate and powerful. The French preference here for a 'political' process relates to the right of politicians elected by sovereign peoples to exercise political will (*volonté*) over and above what President Sarkozy has called 'automatic' rules and procedures, by which he means supranational authority. The French hand in the creation of the European Council is one manifestation of this priority. The crux of the issue here is the right of member states to preserve and exercise their sovereignty within the Community of member states, and to retain control over their national citizens, yet enable the EU to move ahead collectively – as an international actor. The 1958 French Constitution explicitly states that the French people are sovereign; but EU membership and in particular the extension of EU-level policy competence has required equally explicit 'transfers of power' to be written into the French Constitution in the form of constitutional amendments under the provisions of Article 89, which in turn has brought 'Europe' into the forefront of political debate, not least by the referendums of 1992 and 2005.

This takes us straight back to the long-standing tension inherited in French strategy from the superimposing of de Gaulle's preferences on the existing European Communities, with their provisions for supranational decision-making (by qualified majority); and to François Mitterrand's accommodations with increased supranational authority in the form, first of the Single Market Programme in the 1980s, and then the single currency in the 1990s. The 1992 Maastricht Treaty also undercut the traditional republican link between nationality on the one hand, and citizenship on the other. Under the terms of the treaty, EU nationals have certain rights in any member state of the EU, including the right to vote and stand for election in local and European Parliament elections. This was a controversial clause in France, derided by the 'sovereignist' opponents of the Maastricht Treaty.

Second, an unfortunate outcome of these tensions over institutions in France has been to dodge the political and philosophical question of the EU's nature as a federal polity. Robert Schuman bequeathed a 'federal vocation' to the Community process; Charles de Gaulle turned France's back on this notion so alien to French republican notions of state sovereignty. François Mitterrand did indeed strike a more daring compromise between state, nation and Europe. Frédéric Bozo has portrayed the Maastricht Treaty as a clash between Mitterrand's 'federalist declaratory policy', and a 'confederalist operational approach' (1995: 217). Jacques Chirac for his part campaigned in the 2002 presidential election in favour of an oxymoronic 'European Federation of Nation States', as did his Prime Minister at the time, Socialist Lionel Jospin. We shall see below that President Sarkozy has gone some way to closing this gap by means of a language that is explicit about the institutional options for the future of Europe.

Third, 'political Europe' relates to Europe having a *'projet'* or even a *'finalite'* which is not reduced to economic notions of free trade and open markets (a vision typically associated in France with the UK's idea of Europe, and known as *Europe-espace).* The notion of a *'projet de société'* is commonplace in French political culture as the expression of a 'grand vision of what the nation should do' (Hall 2006: 20). Scaled up to the European level, the thinking is that Europe itself has a distinct identity related specifically to values deemed by France to trump other global forces in the world, particularly those emanating from world capitalist markets and their 'Anglo-American' supporters.

Identity

The third and final of Chirac's objectives for Europe was that it should uphold the 'French social model'. This takes us to the heart of the debate in France over Europe's identity, namely that the EU should constitute a variant of capitalism which manages (*maîtriser)* and 'humanises' market forces on behalf of its member states. This is a vision where Europe is perceived as a genuine alternative to what Chirac himself dubbed the 'Anglo-Saxon' style of neo-liberalism that he and his successors consider not only to have become orthodoxy in the EU, but to have fuelled French opposition to the EU's Constitutional Treaty in 2005. Instrumentalising 'Europe' to explain national problems is not new in France. Since the EU's single market initiative of the mid-1980s, and the staged transition to Economic and Monetary Union in the late 1990s, the scope for state intervention at the national level in competition, industrial or monetary policy is strictly regulated. EMU has removed exchange rate control from domestic governments and required them to adhere to strict financial discipline in the form of low inflation and public deficit targets. These 'Maastricht criteria' have become associated in France with austerity measures or, more accurately, cut-backs in state spending (on state employee pensions for example). In practice, the SEA and EMU have provided tactical opportunities for successive French governments of both left and right to scale back the public ownership of economic and industrial resources, making way for privatisation deals of considerable financial benefit to the state coffers. These developments have been controversial in a country where the notion of 'public service' is closely associated with state activity.

In addition, French politicians are used to justifying the sacrifices involved in adjusting to 'Europe' by arguing that EU membership has bolstered France's identity as a modernised post-war nation-state; that French leadership of the EU has fulfilled France's ambitions to be a world power of global significance; and that *la construction européenne* has buffered France from the forces of globalisation. President Sarkozy depicts the European Union, still, as a 'Europe that protects' all of its citizens from global forces. It was in precisely these functions that French opponents to the 2005 Constitutional Treaty deemed the EU – and their own government – to have failed. These doubts over the EU's identity as an economic actor and, in this capacity, its relevance to France and the French, inevitably generate scepticism if not fear about French national identity itself; as we saw above, the post-war transformation of France was not only contemporaneous, but virtually synonymous with *la construction européenne*.

Turning the page on 'exceptionalism'?

The French people have spoken. They have chosen to break with the ideas, habits and behaviours of the past.

(...)

> My fellow countrymen and women, together we will write a new
> page in our history.[3]

We looked above at the strategic principles underlying France's action
in Europe, the foundations on which they rest, and their application in
practice, in policy and discourse. We saw from the referendum vote in
May 2005 that the French are no longer convinced by these politics of
exceptionalism; and academic debate seems to converge on the argument that French elites should mind the gap between their rhetoric on
Europe and the realities faced by French citizens. We remind ourselves
too of Flynn's warning that politicians smash symbols and icons at
their peril; this is particularly pertinent given how far 'Europe' is symbolic of French national identity in the Fifth Republic. We ask in this
penultimate section what might be stopping French elites from constructing a new political discourse for France in Europe, whether there
is evidence of change in this regard; and how the whole process relates to
the broader question of the republican identity of contemporary France.

French tales of Europe have congealed into a seemingly impermeable
discourse because they are so tightly bound to conceptions of French
national identity, which itself turns on the republican tryptich of *liberté,
égalité* and *fraternité,* not to mention the imagery of claims to exceptionalism such as Jacques Chirac's. As Sonntag puts it, French republicanism is 'nothing short of a dogma whose principles must never
be called into question by anyone bent on a political career' (2008: 85). It
is not the values themselves, such as *laïcité* or the *indivisibilité* of the
Republic, or the republican motto itself, that constitute this 'second
prison wall' of the 'politics of prestige', but 'the absoluteness with which
they are defended in the political discourse' (2008: 85). Yet President
Sarkozy's declarations made on the night of his electoral victory on
6 May 2008 as highlighted above signalled an explicit intention to smash
any number of taboos, tradition and dogma.

In relation to Europe, and taking the first of our strategic principles
– *l'Europe puissance,* we can already see evidence of the pursuit of change
begun, in fact, under Sarkozy's predecessor, Jacques Chirac. Sarkozy for
example has continued the overhaul and review of France's European and
foreign policy structures, which are not to escape the spending cuts
raining down on other parts of the French state. Strategically too, France's
defence and security policies have been reviewed and significant cuts and
changes envisaged here.[4] Just as significant, Sarkozy manoeuvred France
into NATO's integrated command structures in April 2009 against considerable political opposition at home. These developments suggest an

awareness of the urgency of updating strategic planning assumptions, and aligning them with domestic reform programmes. Relations with the UK, moreover, are not only cordial but fraternal, and the behind-the-scenes cooperation on military and defence is central to the gradual steps being taken towards greater EU capacity in ESDP (Drake 2009).

On enlargement, Sarkozy's France has projected a more mixed message. On the one hand, for example, President Sarkozy remains explicit in his personal and categorical opposition to Turkish membership of the EU. On the other hand, his Foreign Minister Bernard Kouchner is explicitly in favour of Turkish entry, and no French bloc has been put on the ongoing negotiations with Turkey over the various chapters of the Community *acquis*. The case of the Union of the Mediterranean, launched under the French EU Council Presidency in July 2008, demonstrates the ambiguity of the French position. This was initially proposed by France to EU partners as a prototype of the sort of special relationship which could be constructed between certain EU states and their neighbours who, seen from Paris, are not European – not geographically nor culturally. Ultimately the proposal was brought back under the existing 'Barcelona process' (the Euro-Mediterranean partnership) under pressure from France's EU partners, and in particular Germany: here, as elsewhere, Sarkozy has respected the Franco-German relationship in practice if not symbolically. Sarkozy has in addition insisted that there can be no further enlargement without institutional reform – and his team threw themselves into the negotiation of the Lisbon Treaty with some success in pursuit of this goal.

In terms of Europe's *political* nature, the tension between a federal and an intergovernmental Europe persist, although Sarkozy's proposals whilst still presidential candidate suggest that France is inching further still towards support for collective (QMV) decision-making and away from unanimity, in favour of 'super-majorities' in the Council; this itself translates Sarkozy's interest in a 'big 6' consortium for EU leadership (France, Germany, Italy, Spain, Poland and the UK). Yet we also see President Sarkozy taking on the mantle of all of his predecessors, and most of their Prime Ministers, in criticising the Commission – or just as often, individual Commissioners. In Sarkozy's case, he publicly berated British ex-trade Commission, Peter Mandelson in June 2008, for example, for surpassing his authority in world trade talks – as Sarkozy saw it. He has also maintained the consistent French critique of the imbalance between the European Central Bank (ECB) on the one hand, and the Eurozone's finance ministers on the other. France is also a rule-breaker: of the 2010 deadline for eliminating France's budget deficit (to make good manifesto tax cut pledges), for example. At the same time, cooperation and exchange between the French diplomatic service and the European Commission, and European Parliament, is routine; and France maintains a significant presence in the EU's senior civil service at Council and Commission level.

But domestically the problem of Europe's political nature is far from resolved. 'Europe' has become a political issue in France since at least the Maastricht Treaty, and this has exposed French policy and discourse on Europe, not only to the scrutiny of the 'street' by referendum, but gradually to greater parliamentary oversight, particularly when French commitments to EU developments require constitutional amendment, as was the case with the Constitutional and Lisbon treaties. Moreover, 34 per cent of no voters in 2005 said they had not understood the Constitutional Treaty; 34 per cent deemed it too 'liberal'; and 46 per cent thought that it would worsen unemployment (Exit Poll 2005). This reminds us of Europe's problematic identity as seen from the French perspective.

In terms of Europe's *identity* in relation to global forces, President Sarkozy has adopted the notion of 'protection' as his guiding principle for action on Europe; this was the slogan of the French EU Council Presidency in 2008 ('a Europe that protects'), and it related to protecting EU citizens from global forces such as climate change, unlimited immigration and the global financial crisis that worsened during those months. Even before then, in June 2007 during the negotiation of the Lisbon Treaty, Sarkozy successfully argued for the removal of 'fair and free competition' from the statement of the EU's founding principles in the treaty text proper; the language would, however, remain in the existing EU treaties, and a protocol to the Lisbon Treaty underlines the single market rule that 'competition is not distorted'. This was most definitely a rhetorical victory for domestic consumption; French proposals, made from the EU Council presidency chair in 2008 in the throes of the world financial crisis, for a new 'Bretton Woods' of market regulation, arguably conveys more substance, and enjoyed support from key EU partners including the UK.

So perhaps these are further signs of an ongoing French challenge to its own strategic paradigm. Yet Sonntag identified two further 'prison walls' encasing French diplomacy in its past, namely the straitjackets of the elitist educational system, which channels a narrow elite into the service of the state; and the cultural tics of deference, refinement, 'elegance and *esprit* in interpersonal relations' that underpin what we have already described as a 'French obsession with distinction, hierarchy and rank' (2008: 87). Here too though we learn of generational change; and of declining support amongst middle class children for public service in general, and public service in France in particular (Drake and Lequesne 2009). Perhaps President Sarkozy was responding to what Bozo calls the 'challenge of empiricism' posed by the post-Cold War years to France's foreign policy: '[g]iven the highly theorized (to say Cartesian would be a cliché) nature of French policy in the past decades, the new situation confronts France with the need for something approximating a cultural revolution' (Bozo in Flynn 1995: 221–2). We saw above that Sarkozy certainly portrays himself as an iconoclast, unbound by dogma (such as the EU's competition policy), or taboo (economic protectionism).

Conclusions

Grossman has suggested that 'strategic ambiguity' is a 'characteristic feature of EU policy-making in France' (2007: 988). From a different perspective, we have depicted a strategic edifice whose foundations have stiffened into a discursive house of cards, and whose exceptionalism is very much in the eye of the beholder. Even in the days of de Gaulle's presidency, the claim to French exceptionalism in Europe was an anachronistic ideal. The legacy of such strategy has bequeathed a set of problems to France's current leaders that reach into the essence of French identity itself: problems of sovereignty, citizenship, market liberalism and even social structures, if the radicalisation of opposition to 'Europe' seen in the French 'no' vote of 29th May 2005 is anything to go by.

President Sarkozy thus faces the challenge of constructing a new rationale for French membership of the EU that makes room for both the extraordinary – exceptional – nature of the French commitment and contribution to building a European Union; and the more ordinary costs and compromises that this 50-year old decision entails in a fast-enlarging Europe. At stake is France's credibility as a founder member state, and its own democratic credentials with the nation. The distinctiveness of the French experience of *la construction européenne* does not in itself guarantee that France is exceptionally well-qualified to guide the EU into the near future. France, more so than many other member states, is highly Europeanised in the important sense that its Europeanness is a crucial prop of national identity. This fact in itself throws the flaws and contradictions of this republican identity into sharp relief. In Chopin's terms, EU membership has brought out the worst in the Fifth Republic – such as the opportunity for its elites to dominate public opinion, which understandably rebels, or for the political executive to undermine parliamentary democracy – or to stand as proxy for complaints in these regards.

Perhaps all that is truly exceptional in this tale of France in the EU is that France took the step it did in 1950 so soon after the close of WWII, especially in the form of its structured friendship, at elite and popular level, with Germany. The UK, by way of contrast, has never taken a comparable step in refreshing or refashioning its national identity; in this respect, the story of France in Europe is *sans pareil*.

Notes

1 Jacques Chirac, valedictory speech, broadcast 11 March 2007 www.elysee.fr/ elysee/elysee.fr/francais_archives/interventions/interviews_articles_ de_presse_et_interventions_televisees/2007/mars/declaration_televisee_de_m_ja cques_chirac_president_de_la_republique.74076.html

2 And see www.assemblee-nationale.fr/histoire/traites_de_rome/sommaire.asp for a summary of the debates that took place in the French National Assembly over the negotiation of the Treaty of Rome. See also, for Prime Minister Mollet's defence of the Treaty of Rome to Parliament on 22 January, 1957, www. traitederome.fr/fr/histoire-du-traite-de-rome/archives-diplomatiques/ la-conference-intergouvernementale-juin-1956-mars-1957/guy-mollet-defend-le-marche-commun-a-l-assemblee-nationale-janvier-1957.html; and, for a range of documents from the archives of this period, www.traitederome.fr/fr/histoire-du-traite-de-rome/archives-diplomatiques.html#c435.

3 President Sarkozy's short speech delivered on the night of his election victory, 6 May 2007, Salle Gaveau, Paris. www.support-sarkozy-france.com/nicolas_ sarkozy/victory_speech.php and news.bbc.co.uk/1/hi/world/europe/6631125. stm

4 See the 2008 White Papers (Security and Defence; European and Foreign Policy) as follows: *The French White Paper on Defence and Security*. Accessible (with overview) at www.ambafrance-uk.org/New-French-White-Paper-on-defence.html; *Livre blanc sur la politique étrangère et européenne de la France 2008-2020*. And www.diplomatie.gouv.fr/fr/ministere_817/modernisation_12824/livre-blanc-sur-politique-etrangere-europeenne-france_18407/remise-du-livre-blanc-m.-bernard-kouchner-11.07.08_64433.html; also www.premier-ministre.gouv.fr/ en/information/latest_news_97/the_white_paper_on_61264.html for an overview in English.

11
Back to the Future? Franco-African Relations in the Shadow of France's Colonial Past

Margaret A. Majumdar and Tony Chafer

France can no longer claim, as Louis de Guiringaud did in 1979, to be able to 'change the course of history [in Africa] with 500 men' (quoted in D'Epenoux and Hoche, 1979: 38). Yet, 30 years on, France still lays claim to a 'special relationship' with Africa (Chafer 2002), the 'exceptional' nature of which differentiates it from other 'special relationships'. This exceptionalism hinges, to a large extent, on the importance of idealist, universalist ideology in rationalising these particular relations and the disjunction between this rhetoric and the underlying realities (Majumdar 2004). With respect to Africa, the relationship is thus exceptional in two ways: first, in the way in which France articulates its special relationship with its ex-colonies in Africa, for example through the discourse of 'Francophonie', and, linked to this, the use of Africa as a privileged arena for France to claim a universal role; and secondly, the methods that it uses to give substance to that claim. This latter refers in particular to the networks or *'réseaux'* that France has traditionally maintained in order to sustain its 'exceptional' relationship with Africa. The present chapter examines recent developments in this exceptional relationship in the light of difficulties France experiences in confronting its colonial past, as well as its attempts to overcome accusations of 'neocolonialism' by revising its discourse about Africa and 'multilateralising' its interventions on the continent. Yet these efforts are accompanied by a continuing policy of acting either unilaterally or alongside others, in a way that ultimately sustains certain exceptional features of the Franco-African special relationship.

Of course, France shares much the same history as other European colonial powers in Africa. However, not only did France develop its own specific colonial ideology, it also offered a distinctive response to the success of African nationalist movements in the wake of the Second

World War. Indeed, with the loss of power and influence, France continued to see its African hinterland as a vital bulwark to its position on the world stage. The notion of 'Eurafrique', a European-African organic entity linked through close geographical proximity, interdependent economic relations and shared historical ties (Martin 1982), inspired much of French policy through the Fourth Republic. Then, in the Fifth Republic, 'France-Afrique' really came into its own, with the Franco-African connection seen as a safeguard against swamping by one or other of the global superpowers. On the one hand, the old colonial relations were reworked into a neo-colonialist framework, sporting the rhetorical banner of 'coopération' and the fine idealism of the developing Francophone movement, built on shared cultural and political values, and the common French language (Bossuat 2003). On the other hand, the underbelly consisted of economic, military and financial relations, working to the mutual advantage of France and minority African elites, kept sweet through a network of personal dependencies, financial aid and military assistance, forged between autocratic leaders and their French sponsors (Keese 2007). This combination of high-minded rhetoric and corrupt self-interest kept the system afloat, even though the fundamentally unequal relations were clearly skewed to France's benefit. Moreover, until relatively recently, France's right to its own sphere of influence, or *'chasse gardée'*, in Africa was largely respected by other world powers.

The first part of this chapter deals with the particularly problematic relations between France and Algeria before moving on, in the second part, to discuss relations between France and sub-Saharan Africa. The third part examines the impact of Sarkozy's policies in this area since May 2007 and assesses how far he has fulfilled his promise to bring about a *'rupture'* (*Le Monde* 29 July 2007) by putting relations on a new footing and how far his visions of 'Eurafrique' and a Mediterranean Union hark back to the period of French colonial rule.

From 'Françafrique' to 'Eurafrique': new discourse, old realities

The change of terminology under President Sarkozy, from 'Françafrique' to 'Eurafrique', was not accidental. It was intended to denote a break – *'rupture'* – from the old-style relationship between France and Africa, characterised by corruption and illegality and overly redolent of an increasingly contested colonial past. Yet the notion of 'Eurafrique' itself dates back to the 1930s, before its enthusiastic revival by French and African politicians under the Fourth Republic. A key proponent of 'Eurafrique' in the 1950s was Pierre Nord, who saw it as an answer to Europe's political, strategic and economic problems in a world dominated by the Cold War rivalry between the US and the Soviet Union. Within a Eurafrican alliance, Africa would provide raw materials and manpower, which, combined with European technological and industrial capability, would give Europe a real chance of competing effectively with the world's two superpowers (Nord 1955: 1–11).

The notion of 'Eurafrique' was subsequently abandoned under De Gaulle, as it implied an unacceptable sharing of French sovereignty. It also harked back to a difficult colonial past that had become a millstone round France's neck, preventing the country from embracing the modern era (Chafer and Evans 2008: 249). Moreover, as African countries moved towards independence, it was important to stress the firmness of the links with France, so the term France-Afrique was preferred (Chipman 1989: 84), thereby underlining the new 'state-to-state' partnership between France and Africa that would characterise the new, post-colonial era. De Gaulle always eschewed the term 'political independence' for France's former African colonies, preferring instead to describe them attaining 'international sovereignty'. A new discourse of '*coopération*' was also developed to emphasise that the new relationship would be between equal, sovereign partners (Bossuat 2003). A Ministry of Cooperation was even created out of the former colonial ministry to manage relations between France and its former colonies in sub-Saharan Africa, although the relationship was never purely an inter-state one as the Franco-African 'special relationship' was always underpinned by a dense network of personal relations (Chafer 2002: 346–7). It was only much later, in the 1990s, that France-Afrique became 'Françafrique', a term that was used to refer both to the close, family-like relationship between France and Africa and the corruption, abuses and illicit practices that had become a feature of Franco-African relations (Verschave 1998).

Against this background, Sarkozy's use of the term 'Eurafrique' indicates his intention to move towards a healthier, multilateral relationship between Europe and Africa operating to the benefit of both continents: 'What Africa wants to do together with France is to prepare the way for "Eurafrica", this great shared destiny that awaits Europe and Africa' (Sarkozy 2007e). The term 'Eurafrique' also represents the vision of a more inclusive relationship, embracing relations with *both* north and sub-Saharan Africa. Yet it is ironic that the term used by President Sarkozy to describe this new relationship harks back to an old colonial vision of an alliance between the two continents. Moreover, as we shall see, turning this vision into reality, in both regions, has proved problematic.

Franco-Algerian relations in the post-colonial world

Within the context of the exceptional relationship between France and Africa, the country with which relations have been most problematic is Algeria. This is because of specific political and historical circumstances resulting from the bitter colonial past, which have meant that Algeria has not on the whole signed up to the rhetoric suffusing other Franco-African relations, in spite of the closeness of the ties with France into the postcolonial period. Indeed, some argue that 'the post-colonial predicament [...] unites Algeria and France into a single trans-political space' (Silverstein 2004: 2). There is certainly a human trans-Mediterranean dimension to this space, with the diasporic Franco-Algerian population, along with repatriated Europeans and *harkis*. Important 'transnational' relations also operate on economic, social and cultural levels. The focus here, however, is on relations between the two states and the discourses through which they are articulated. This will involve a consideration of the security dimension, as well as the politics of commemoration and the instrumentalisation of history.

The impetus to progress to a new stage in Franco-Algerian relations was first given by Abdelaziz Bouteflika, whose overriding ambition at the start of his presidency in 1999, was to end Algeria's isolation. In Jacques Chirac, he found a willing partner, also motivated to draw a line under the contentious past, through the signing of a Friendship Treaty between France and Algeria, in what may be interpreted as an attempt to emulate de Gaulle's 1963 Franco-German Treaty.

In June 2000, Bouteflika made the first full state visit to France by an Algerian president. Its significance was largely symbolic and concrete results deemed meagre, not least by Bouteflika himself who is reported as saying that he was 'departing empty-handed' (Roberts 2003: 283). Despite their close ties, with France as Algeria's main creditor and trading partner at the time, Bouteflika hinted that if France could not deliver the investment Algeria needed, then he would look elsewhere (Roberts 2003: 284). Evidence that the US, in particular, was strongly interested in developing military and economic cooperation, had been there since 1998, visibly keeping the French on their toes (Roberts 2003: 285). The Americans were keen to develop commercial interests based on hydrocarbons, as well as to extend their military involvement in the region (Mellah and Rivoire 2005: 4–5). After 9/11 this interest increased (Keenan 2006: 269–96), when Algeria became a firm collaborator in the 'war against terror'. The opening of a new American Embassy in Algiers, with a great rhetorical fanfare in May 2008, gave a new political boost to these relations.

Clearly, the US was not the only player in the game, with Russia and China both heavily involved in projects with Algeria. Apart from security concerns that enabled Algeria to emerge from its pariah status, the main attraction was the oil and gas production of a country with the third largest reserves in Africa. France nonetheless had several cards in its favour. Chirac visited Algeria in March 2003 to launch the Friendship Treaty. Bolstered by his opposition to the Iraq war, the French President received an extremely warm welcome in Algiers. The visit culminated with the signing of the 'déclaration d'Alger', committing to signing the Treaty in 2005 to establish a special partnership, *'un parténariat d'exception'*, covering economic, cultural, scientific, human and military exchanges and cooperation (Mellah and Rivoire 2005: 4–5). In parallel, there were hopes that Algeria would finally join the Francophone club, the *Organisation Internationale de la Francophonie*. Bouteflika had attended the 2002 Beirut Francophone Summit and the 2004 Ouagadougou Summit as a special guest, without taking the leap of joining the organisation. With increasing tensions, Bouteflika boycotted the 2006 Bucharest Summit, sending the Foreign Minister instead.

Chirac's hoped-for Treaty did not, in fact, materialise in the last years of his presidency, for several reasons. Perhaps most importantly, his efforts were sabotaged by UMP members, determined to keep alive the interests of the pro-colonial lobby, the supporters of *Algérie française*, the *rapatriés* and, to a lesser extent, the *harkis*. The law voted on 23 February 2005 stymied attempts to turn the page on Franco-Algerian history. The law was framed to recognise the contribution of those who fought alongside the French in the Algerian War and to provide them with aid. In fact, the most remarkable part of the text was the section dealing with the teaching of French colonial history. Article 4 stated that 'academic research programmes devote to the history of the French presence overseas and particularly in North Africa the attention it deserves.' More tendentiously, it continued: 'The school curriculum recognises the positive role of the French presence overseas, particularly in North Africa, and gives the due prominence to the history and the sacrifices of those members of the French Armed Forces who originated in those lands, to which they are entitled.' This provoked outcry, particularly amongst French historians, who claimed the law gave backing to a revisionist version of colonial history and renewed legitimacy to such discredited organisations as the OAS.

The controversy dragged on for months and was an important back-drop to the riots that November. On 8 November, legislation first enacted in 1955 to establish a state of emergency during the Algerian war was reactivated, imposing a curfew in the French suburbs, which were populated by many of North African origin. This was seen as a further provocation and roundly condemned in the Algerian press (*Le Monde* 30 December 2005). The rejection of a socialist proposal to amend Article 4 of the 23 February law and the success of General Schmitt's appeal in connection with his actions during the Algerian war (Beaugé and Bernard 19 March 2005), added to the mounting feeling that the French establishment was siding firmly with the supporters of *Algérie française*.

Chirac's response was to distance himself from the law. He finally prevailed upon the Conseil Constitutionnel to intervene, removing the second paragraph of Article 4 in January 2006. However, Chirac also made clear that he, and France, were only prepared to go so far. On 11 November 1996, at the inauguration of a monument to the dead of the Algerian War, he himself had stressed the positive side to French colonialism in Algeria (quoted in Bertrand 2006: 9).

A full apology or act of penitence was never on the cards, though some government representatives made significant steps in that direction. Chirac, himself, during a visit to Madagascar in July 2005, expressed his regret for the '*dérives*' ['excesses'] of the 1947 repression. In Algeria, the 60th anniversary of the Sétif massacres that followed the 8 May 1945 nationalist demonstrations, a hugely symbolic event in the history of Algerian nationalism, was marked by a break in French silence on the matter, notably by French Foreign Minister, Michel Barnier (Metaoui 2005). The French ambassador in Algiers, Hubert Colin de Verdière, had already deplored the Sétif massacres earlier in the year, as an 'inexcusable tragedy' (Le Monde 19 September 2005). That all of France was not behind this gesture became clear. An association of North African war veterans, amongst others, justified the French repression as 'a necessary measure to re-establish order' (Metaoui 2005).

Algerian reaction to the 23 February law was delayed. However, when it came, in a highly charged speech by President Bouteflika on the eve of the Sétif anniversary, it was a virulent condemnation of France's brutal colonial past and a clear attack on revisionist and negationist interpret-ations of colonial history (Metaoui 2005; *Le Monde* 19 September 2005). He asserted that nothing less than an apology for all acts committed during the colonial period would suffice. On the one hand, Bouteflika seemed to be reigniting the anti-colonial issue for domestic reasons, to detract from other issues. On the other hand, the battery of laws and governmental measures taken in France throughout 2005 was undoubtedly seen in Algeria as an escalating series of insults and provocations, which managed to turn the friendship shown to France, and Jacques Chirac in particular, into resentment and hostility.

There were also foreign policy objectives to be served, reminding France that Algeria had other options and was no longer tied to a purely bilateral relationship with France. In any event, the reluctance of French firms to invest in Algeria had provided further fuel for those opposed to placing much credence in this 'special relationship'. This was brought home sharply, when Mohamed Bedjaoui, the Algerian Foreign Minister, remarked during a visit to the US in 2006, 'Compared to the US, France does not carry the same weight in Algeria' (*Le Monde* 9 July 2007).

This suspicion was intensified by the failure of the Euro-Mediterranean partnership, launched by the Barcelona agreement of 1995, to take off in any significant manner. An association agreement between the EU and Algeria was only finally signed in December 2001. Although the different priorities of northern European states no doubt contributed to this disappointing result (Roberts 2003: 239–40), Euro-Mediterranean policy had been largely determined by French influence and interests, with a recognition that the Maghreb was, to all intents and purposes, part of France's '*domaine réservé*' (Roberts 2003: 338–9). In any event, it appeared to many Algerians as a continuation of the old unequal ties of the French colonial period, whereas France interpreted the ineffectiveness of European policy as further reason to pursue bilateral, as opposed to multilateral, ties.

It is clear that, for both sides, the Friendship Treaty was to be largely symbolic. This is not to say that very real interests were not involved. Despite losing ground to other nations, France's policy of encouraging more investment has produced some results. From 49 million dollars in 2000, investment increased to 294 million by 2006, making France the second largest investor in Algeria, though largest in the non-hydrocarbon-related sector (*Le Monde* 9 July 2007). Although the US, with 369 million dollars in 2006, is now the largest investor, mainly in the oil sector, and the largest trading partner with 14 US billion dollars of Algerian imports, France remains the largest importer into the country – 4.3 billion dollars in 2006 or 20 per cent of the market (*Le Monde* 9 July 2007). For France, the promotion of a special relationship, transcending the unequal relations of the colonial past, was considered vital to the protection of those interests. The Treaty was viewed as a significant element in the stabilisation of this relationship.

The special relationship was based not just on the geographical proximity of the two countries, which, in any case, had been greatly exaggerated in the colonial period, particularly through the typical slogan of the colonists, proclaiming that 'La Méditerranée traverse la France comme la Seine traverse Paris'. It was founded far more on the notion of a shared history, in which past conflicts were sometimes acknowledged and sometimes obscured behind a rose-tinted view of mutual affection and attraction (Girardet 1993: 84). Of course, this argument of a shared past had been pressed into service by supporters of French colonialism in Algeria, who developed the notion of '*Afrique latine*', to highlight trans-Mediterranean links between Europe and Africa, going back to Roman times (Silverstein 2004: 60–6, 222–8). When Michel Debré visited Algeria in 1959, Frantz Fanon reported him stating: 'The authority of France in Algeria is a requirement of history, of nature, of morality' (Fanon 1970: 168). Fanon also quoted Debré's claim that the geographic link between France and Algeria was needed for reasons of security (Fanon 1970: 169–70).

It was in the area of security that other players' involvement became of paramount importance. US involvement in Algeria has encompassed military training and equipment, a new air facility at Tamanrasset and the so-called PSI (Pan-Sahel Initiative), later renamed as TSCTI (Trans-Saharan Counter-Terrorism Initiative) (Keenan 2006: 274, 292, n.7; Mellah and Rivoire 2005: 4–5; *Le Monde* 12 April 2007). American involvement has been partly in response to the so-called 'Banana' theory of terrorism, in which fighters uprooted from Afghanistan following the overthrow of the Taliban were dispersed into the Horn of Africa, to spread across the Sahara and the Sahel into North Africa, in a movement supposedly resembling a banana-shaped curve, threatening not just the Maghreb but also Europe (Keenan 2006: 274–5). Some argued that the kidnapping of Europeans in the Sahara in 2003 was staged to give credence to this theory and facilitate US input into the 'war on terror' in the region.

Jeremy Keenan has questioned why France allowed US penetration into territory traditionally regarded as its own preserve, without an apparent 'beep', and why it maintained silence on the kidnapping and hostage-taking (Keenan 2006: 277). He claims that France's silence was determined by complicity in these events, as was revealed when the *Washington Post* published a report on intelligence relations between the US and France on 3 July 2005 (Priest 2005). This detailed close collaboration, involving the joint establishment of a covert intelligence and operations base in Paris in 2002, code-named 'Alliance Base' – or 'The Base', funded by the CIA's Counterterrorism Center, but headed by a French general from the Directorate-General for External Security (DGSE) and including officers from other countries. France's contribution is said to include surveillance of Muslim networks, intelligence links to former colonies, particularly with Algeria's military intelligence services, and collaboration in operations, including, it is claimed, staged incidents and orchestrated provocations (Keenan 2006: 278–9).

The overarching importance of misinformation and bogus ideology in the context of Franco-Algerian relations cannot be overestimated (Keenan 2006: 291; Roberts 2003: 219), particularly regarding matters related to security and terrorism where it is often difficult to determine the real facts. Thus, there has been much cynical speculation around the identity of the real culprits for particular atrocities and the motives behind them.

Ideology is just as predominant in the political sphere, with the same disjuncture between reality and the dominant discourse. In spite of lip service paid to democratisation and the principles of good governance, embodied in the African development initiative, the New Partnership for Africa's Development (NEPAD), in which Algeria is a leading player, the reality is that the multiparty political system is largely a façade, manipulated by power-brokers behind the scenes.

Real power, based on an oil- and gas-rich rentier economy that gives employment to only a fraction of the population, is concentrated in the hands of a small clique, whose power base is the higher echelons of the intelligence services (Addi 2006: 6–7). The importance of foreign support, in particular that of France, is explained not just by the need to keep this group in power, but also to safeguard against eventual prosecutions for crimes committed during the years of bloody conflict. This immunity had already been secured within Algeria, through the amnesty measures of the charter for national reconciliation, approved by referendum in September 2005. However, these measures have no international standing and prosecutions by external jurisdictions are not excluded. Indeed, the family of Father Lebreton, one of the Tibéhirine monks murdered in 1996, began a legal case in Paris in December 2003 to bring those responsible to justice. As Lahouari Addi has affirmed, fear of such prosecutions was a main motive behind Algeria's original willingness to sign the Friendship Treaty, which, he says, was also supposed 'to be accompanied by unwritten clauses, guaranteeing the immunity of those in power from prosecution (Addi 2006: 6–7).

Thus, although both sides saw some benefit in the Treaty, it became evident that the attempt to pin Franco-Algerian relations on the notion of a shared past, a special relationship, alternately favouring repentance or revisionism, had had its day. In the event, Jacques Chirac would not see the Friendship Treaty signed under his presidency.

Relations between France and sub-Saharan Africa

French relations with sub-Saharan Africa have lacked the bitterness that has defined Franco-Algerian relations during much of the post-colonial period. This difference is a direct result of the decolonisation process in French Africa where, unlike in Algeria, the transition from colonial rule to independence passed off smoothly, largely without bloodshed. Indeed this mostly peaceful transfer of power enabled the development of a family-like 'special relationship' that only began to change significantly after the 1994 Rwanda genocide (Chafer 2002: 347–9). By this time, as we have seen, the term 'Françafrique' had ceased to be simply a description of the Franco-African special relationship, symbolising the special sense of solidarity and understanding and the particular affinities that French and African politicians proclaimed bound France to Africa, or more precisely to its former African colonies. Instead it became a pejorative term, connoting the illicit, often corrupt nature of the special relationship. It was in this sense that François-Xavier Verschave used the term in his books: *La Françafrique. Le plus long scandale de la République* (1998) and *Noir Silence. Qui arrêtera la Françafrique?* (2000).

As in the section on Franco-Algerian relations, the focus here is on inter-state relations and the changing discourses through which they are articulated. Moreover the security dimension, as well as the politics of commemoration and the instrumentalisation of history, are once again significant themes in the evolving relationship between France and its former colonies in sub-Saharan Africa.

The continuing strategic importance of Africa to France was underlined by the dense network of links that continued to bind France to the continent after independence and by the discourse of 'cooperation' underpinning it. The Franc zone pegged the currency of the former French colonies to the French franc at a fixed rate; the Ministry of Cooperation became effectively a ministry for francophone sub-Saharan Africa; and France signed a series of cultural, technical and military cooperation accords with its former colonies. Cultural cooperation served French interests by propagating the French language and culture, while French public development aid reinforced ties with its African *pré carré*, maintained dependency and gave privileged access to African markets and raw materials. The defence and military cooperation accords were the springboard for a succession of French military interventions on the continent in the post-colonial period, furthering the continuing projection of French power and influence in Africa (Charbonneau 2008a: 61–72). There were also the annual Franco-African summits, initiated in 1973, that traditionally brought together French and African political leaders, but had no published agenda and made no formal policy recommendations, thus resembling more informal family gatherings than official intergovernmental meetings. Just as important as these official links were the non-institutionalised forms of the relationship, in particular the close personal links between members of France's governing elites and African political leaders that had in many cases been forged during the Fourth Republic. These links continued into the post-colonial era and Nicolas Sarkozy is the first French president since 1958 not to have developed such personal links to African political leaders before his election. Moreover, African policy has in effect formed part of the president's *'domaine réservé'* since 1958. Each president has had his own personal adviser on African affairs as part of an Africa 'cell' operating outside normal government channels, accountable neither to the government or parliament.

This Franco-African special relationship came under challenge in the 1990s, initially from specialists who noted in a series of articles and books that over 30 years of *'cooperation'* had apparently done little or nothing to promote African development.[1] They also questioned its supposed benefits to France (Adda and Smouts 1989; Chesnault 1990; Brunel 1993). French implication in events leading up to the 1994 Rwanda genocide, criticism of its intervention, code-named Operation Turquoise, after the genocide, and its support for the Zairean dictator, President Mobutu, when his leadership was threatened by the ensuing regional war, made a wide-ranging reassessment of French African policy inevitable. Certainly, criticism of France's role in the region from international NGOs and African leaders played a role in forcing this reorientation, but even more important was the fact that African policy was no longer seen to be serving French national interests; even worse, French loss of credibility in Africa was undermining French interests and potentially threatened its long-term future role on the continent.

France stood accused of using its military, economic and diplomatic power to prop up African dictators, simply because they were friendly towards France, and of failing to support moves towards greater democracy, initiated across the continent after the end of the Cold War in 1990. During the Cold War the strategic importance of maintaining France's African *'pré carré'* in the Western camp had taken precedence over concerns about the lack of development and democracy, but the new international political order after 1990 brought these latter concerns to the forefront. The new international context attached central importance to promoting development and democracy and the granting of new aid was made conditional on economic and political reform. This change was noted by President Mitterrand at the 1990 La Baule Franco-African summit, when he stated that France would in future give priority in its development aid programme to those countries making the greatest progress towards democracy (Chafer 2005: 14). However, aid conditionality posed a particular problem for France as this new approach did not sit well with France's traditional policy of *'coopération'*, rooted in the notion of inter-state cooperation and based on the principle of respect for each partner's international sovereignty. It was no doubt partly for this reason that the implementation of the new policy of aid conditionality was so uneven (Cumming 2001: 104–10). Moreover, the practice of *'coopération'* was far more ambiguous than the foregoing suggests, if only because of the history of French military intervention on the continent in the post-colonial period. However, French African policy after 1960 was built on the foundation stone of *'coopération'* and the myth of respect for international sovereignty was maintained through the claim that such interventions were at the request of the national government or in order to protect its nationals. This was the basis for their legitimacy.

A further criticism of French African policy, increasingly heard in the late 1990s, was that it was neo-colonial. In 1999 France initially refused to intervene to save its ally, President Konan Bédié of Côte d'Ivoire, following a military coup. However, three years later a mutiny broke out in Abidjan, rebel forces took control of the north of the country and prepared to march on the capital. Fearing for the future of more than 20,000 French citizens and many more foreign nationals in the country, France sent troops to the centre of the country to establish a demarcation line between government and rebel forces and prevent the latter from marching on the capital. France became further embroiled in the crisis in January 2003 when it called the belligerents to a conference in Linas-Marcoussis near Paris, where it imposed on the Gbagbo government a power-sharing agreement providing for the appointment of government ministers from the rebel forces. Immediately afterwards, anti-French demonstrations erupted in Abidjan. The situation deteriorated further the following year, after President Chirac ordered the destruction of the entire Ivoirian air force following an attack on French soldiers in the country. Banners appeared on the streets of Abidjan proclaiming 'Chirac go home, Bush welcome', 'Vive la Côte d'Ivoire indépendante'. This was followed by widespread criticism of France across the continent for its support for African dictators, its failure to promote human rights and development and its general interference in African affairs (Ould Mohamedou 2005; Lecoutre and Kambudzi 2006; Leymarie 2006).

France's response to these criticisms has been a concerted effort to 'multilateralise' its African policy. In an attempt to defuse accusations of neo-colonialism, steps were taken to move away from the traditional French unilateral approach to Africa and share the burdens, and risks, of African policy. Just as the Abidjan doctrine, announced by Balladur in 1993, sought to share the economic cost of supporting Africa with the International Monetary Fund and World Bank, so the Reinforcement of African Peace-keeping Capacities (RECAMP) initiative sought to share the burdens and risks of French military policy on the continent (Chafer 2008: 46). Launched by France in 1997, the RECAMP programme provided support to African forces with the aim of enabling them to take greater responsibility for peace-keeping and the maintenance of security on the continent. At the 1998 Franco-British summit, both governments announced their intention of cooperating more closely on African policy. In the same year the Ministry of Cooperation was abolished and its activities transferred to the Ministry of Foreign Affairs. France also sought to distance itself from the notion of a French *'pré carré'* in Africa by establishing a 'zone de solidarité prioritaire' for its aid budget that covers the whole of Africa, rather than only those countries that were part of its traditional 'pré carré'. Furthermore, it has since 2003 sought to invite every African president, not just those from the 'pré carré', to its Franco-African summits. Other developments, such as the fact that the CFA franc is no longer pegged to the French franc but to the euro, have also had an impact on the exclusivity of France's relationship with its *'pré carré'*. On the military front, France has sought to obtain international backing for its interventions, for example from the UN (Côte d'Ivoire 2004) or the EU (Chad/CAR 2008), and RECAMP was 'Europeanised' in 1998, to become 'Euro-Recamp'.

Nonetheless France's relationship with Africa remains in many ways a special one. First, Africa continues to be strategically important to France's role as a global power and as an arena for French *'rayonnement'*. It maintains over 4,000 troops permanently stationed on the continent (8,000 if we count those based on La Réunion), which can be supported if necessary by a rapid reaction force based in France; it continues to intervene militarily on the continent, albeit as one of the 'lead nations' in a UN or EU operation rather than acting alone. However, as Bruno Charbonneau has remarked: 'the French colonial tradition of military intervention is not necessarily incompatible with a multilateral approach' (2008b: 293). Moreover, France has significant economic interests in Africa, notably in oil, its major firms have done well out of the privatisation of public services such as water, electricity and telephony, and it is the continent with the highest number of countries using French as their official language.

Second, France remains unable to escape its colonial past in Africa. Other EU member states remain wary of French motives in seeking to 'Europeanise' its African policy and accusations of French neo-colonialism have not gone away, as African reaction to Sarkozy's Dakar speech in July 2007 demonstrated (Ligue des Droits de l'Homme, n. d.). However, whereas in Algeria it was the 23 February 2005 law that killed attempts to turn the page on Franco-Algerian history, in sub-Saharan Africa a range of issues have prevented France and Francophone Africa from burying the colonial past. French interventionism is often resented and seen as redolent of an outdated paternalism. The difficulty of obtaining entry visas to France is a constant source of resentment, as is the treatment of immigrants resident in France: the discrimination suffered by African immigrants has been attacked as a form of 'internal' colonialism. There is also the ongoing issue of African war veterans' pensions: these had been frozen since 1959, but the issue gained new prominence, when Amadou Diop took his case to the Conseil d'Etat in 2001 and won a ruling that African war veterans should be paid the same pensions as French veterans. This did not lead to any immediate change in French policy, however. The campaign for equal treatment rumbled on and became linked to the question of remembering African troops' role in the liberation of France. It culminated in President Chirac belatedly recognising their role, in a speech to mark the 60th anniversary of the Allied landings on 15 August 2004 (Chirac 2004). Official French amnesia surrounding their role was also highlighted by the film 'Indigènes', which won the Cannes Film Festival award for best male actor in 2006.[2] At the same time, public commemoration of their role remains an issue in Africa. For example, in 2004, the Senegalese president, Abdoulaye Wade, declared 23 August the 'Day of the Tirailleur' and this annual event provides an opportunity to highlight and remember the French government's wretched treatment of its African troops. This relates not only to the pensions issue, but also to the massacre of 35 returning

African ex-POWs and the injuring of another 35 by French troops at the Thiaroye military camp near Dakar in December 1944, following their demonstration to demand the pay arrears and discharge allowances they were owed.

A change in problematic under Sarkozy, 'l'homme de la rupture'?

Although Sarkozy had not cultivated personal relationships with African leaders before 2007, he had nonetheless been actively involved with questions affecting Franco-African relations, especially during his time as Interior Minister. His anti-immigration policies, his restrictions on visas for Africans, his provocative comments on the 'scum' of the suburbs, his ambivalent support for 'positive discrimination' policies, his conflict with Equal Opportunities Minister, Azouz Begag (Begag 2007), all this played to the gallery of potential Front National supporters, while also offering a more pragmatic discourse, in which immigration would be fine-tuned to the needs of the economy.

Much of his victory speech on 6 May 2007 was devoted to foreign policy. Significantly, no mention was made of Francophonie, which had hitherto provided a rhetorical vehicle for much of the high-sounding French discourse of human rights, cultural diversity and anti-hegemonic view of global power relations, used by previous presidents, including Chirac, to define France's exceptionalism on the world stage. Instead, the underlying theme was how the new President intended to restore France to greatness. This would be achieved not by France going it alone, but at the head of a series of alliances, set out in a ranked order of priority, in stark contrast to the Chiraquian rhetoric of multipolarity.

As first priority, Sarkozy reiterated France's role in Europe as its primary sphere of operation. As for relations with the US, France would be a major ally, but he implied that the two allies would not only agree to differ, but would also respect their different spheres of influence. Second came his proposal for a Mediterranean Union, involving all countries bordering the Mediterranean, 'that was at the heart of everything that was at stake' (Sarkozy, 2007f). Next, he came to Africa as a whole, where he also saw France as a leading partner in the development of the continent.

The speech thus suggested a pyramidal, hierarchical approach to foreign policy, in which the principal axis of France's influence would extend south from Europe, through the Mediterranean basin and North Africa, to the rest of Africa. This was soon confirmed, when the new President devoted his first foreign visit outside Europe to a brief trip to Algeria and Tunis, on 10 July 2007, where he once again reiterated his proposals for a Mediterranean Union, in what he termed 'our second area of solidarity after Europe' (*Le Monde* 9–10 July 2007).

Sarkozy made clear that he represented a new generation with a new approach.[3] History did not weigh upon him, as it did for the generation of the Algerian War. His attention was focused on the future, not the past. While acknowledging the dark side of French colonialism in Africa, he also asserted that there was another side. He favoured an objective examination of the facts, not apologies. Repentance was a religious notion that had no place in inter-state relations. Meanwhile, the 'young generations' on both sides of the Mediterranean were impatient to move towards the future and only interested in concrete outcomes.

Just as the Franco-Algerian Friendship Treaty had been Chirac's attempt to put relations on a new footing, following the stalling of the Barcelona process, the Mediterranean Union project appears to address the same failure, arising from two key difficulties: firstly, the concentration on trade, without tackling the root problems of economic and social development in those countries on the southern shore; secondly, the lack of real will on the part of the EU to give real momentum to the process. The Mediterranean Union project thus began its life as a mission to inject active French leadership into a more wide-ranging and effective cooperation process.

Its form, however, presupposed a multilateral structure from the outset, even if it was primarily conceived to put France's relations with the Maghreb on a new footing, wiping the slate clean and avoiding any further talk of memory/repentance. It reasserted France's primacy in the region, whilst also seeking to provide a better framework for dealing with issues of immigration and security and possibly offer an alternative to Turkey's full membership of the EU.

In the event, the opposition of the European Commission and other members of the EU, notably Germany, fearful of the unilateralism of French leadership ambitions in this area and of the potential costs of the project for Europe, extended the multilateral dimension of the project, through the involvement of all members of the EU, not just those countries bordering the Mediterranean. The newly retitled Union for the Mediterranean, is now incorporated as an extension of the Barcelona Process, under the aegis of the European Union as a whole, with a much reduced initial agenda for action, concentrating on Mediterranean pollution, civil defence, transport and solar energy (*Le Monde* 20 May 2008). With the Franco-Algerian Friendship Treaty now confined to the dustbin, it seems that relations will move forward on the political front, if at all, through this new multilateral framework.

There has no doubt been a break. The question is where this break is to be situated and what is its significance. Clearly, Sarkozy would have us believe that there has been a break with the past, literally in terms of a change of generation, but also a break with a certain type of ideological approach, linked to the politics of memory. Some have interpreted his new stance as a break with the paternalism of Chirac and the old relations of 'Françafrique'. Indeed, in his New Year speech on 15 January 2008, Jean-Marie Bockel, at that time Minister for Coopération and Francophonie, was outspoken about his intention to 'sign the death warrant of Françafrique' and to put an end to France's support for corrupt politicians and practices (*Le Monde* 16 January 2008). However, this speech provoked the fury of a number of African leaders, notably the late president Bongo of Gabon, and President Sarkozy subsequently moved Bockel to a less prominent post within the government. Others have concluded that Sarkozy is more interested in a pragmatic approach, putting France's interests first, in spite of fine-sounding words about promoting a 'healthier relationship' and welcoming the intervention of other world powers in Africa, as evidenced, for instance, by his intervention at the UN on 25 September 2007 (*Le Monde* 30 September 2007) and his speech in South Africa on 28 February 2008 (*Le Monde* 1 March 2008; Dolek 2008), while reserving France's right to intervene in parts of non-francophone Africa outside its traditional sphere of influence.

From what we have heard from him so far, however, he seems to be just as fond of fine speeches as his predecessors, or as Florence Beaugé and Philippe Ridet put it, 'this incantatory, verbose diplomacy so dear to the new French president' (*Le Monde* 10 July 2007). Certainly, on one level the discourse has changed and, in that sense, there has been a break. However, a change in discourse does not in itself lead to a change in global realities and there is a clear gulf between the rhetoric and the reality, as there is between the hyperactive launching of initiatives and the real politics of the situation.

Moreover, it is clear that there is a strong tendency for the old historical ideological baggage to reassert itself and one has only to scratch just below the surface, for echoes of ideas put forward during the colonial period to emerge. There was clear evidence of this retrograde tendency in Sarkozy's disastrous speech to students at Dakar University on 28 July 2007, in which he based his remarks on an obsolescent Eurocentric, Hegelian approach to Africa (Robert 2007: 32). Moreover, we have seen that even the attempt to bring France's relations with Africa into the broader context of European relations with Africa in fact draws on ideas that hark back to the colonialist past in the shape of the vision of 'Eurafrique' (Dolek 2008). Thus, Sarkozy may wish to move on, but his progress appears to be severely limited by the weight of the outmoded baggage he is still carrying in his retinue.

Notes

1 *'Coopération'* in this context cannot be translated simply as 'cooperation'. From political independence until 1997 France had a ministry of cooperation (successor of the former colonial ministry), which was largely responsible for maintaining the whole range of France's relations with its former colonies in Africa. Based in principle on the notion of respect for international sovereignty, the policy of cooperation in practice provided the platform for continuing French intervention in its former African colonies after independence.
2 The film *Indigènes* tells the story of North African soldiers who helped to liberate France in the Second World War.
3 See in particular President Sarkozy's speech to the South African parliament, 28 February 2008, available from www.ambafrance-uk.org/President-Sarkozy-s-speech-to-the.html

Section V

The French Exception Seen from Abroad

12
A View from the South. France in African Eyes: Universalism and Francophonie Reassessed

Abdoulaye Gueye

To deal with the 'French exception' in regards to African writers and thinkers[1] is first and foremost to explore the journey of a discourse in the Other's imaginary and intellectual territory. Indeed, French exceptionalism, at least at the moment of its inception, was a discourse, but not any kind of discourse. It was (and still is) to a certain extent, a performative discourse, in Austin's sense (Austin 1975). As such, it aimed at putting into action words whose capacity for being *real-ised* rests, as Bourdieu shows, on them being uttered within institutions vested with the authority and power to enable them (1991). Even though the notion of French exceptionalism has appeared only in the last 20 years (Godin and Chafer 2005), the idea itself is apparently contemporary with the foundation of the French nation. Already in the late 18th century, authoritative politicians and organic intellectuals of the modern French state like Abbé Grégoire (Sepinwall 2005) and Jules Michelet (Hewlett 2005) sketched out its meaning in their own writings. Only more recently has a body of scholarly research appeared which is less concerned with manufacturing the exceptionalism of France than unveiling the fundamentals on which the purported exceptionalism is built. Some heuristic theoretical propositions have stemmed from this literature. Godin and Chafer's is one of them. According to this proposition French exceptionalism is intertwined with the concepts of Enlightenment and the French Revolution, to the extent that France prides itself on being the 'repository of values inherited from the Enlightenment and the French Revolution' and 'bearing the mission to diffuse them universally' (Godin and Chafer 2005: xvi). This proposition underlies three aspects of exceptionalism. The first is that the French exception, as a discourse, is embedded in the idea of progress. Enlightenment philosophy, which clearly opposes obscurantism, assumes and advocates the responsibility of humans to escape from their subordination to nature through the use of reason. It also values movement as a condition of progress, of which the French Revolution constitutes to a large extent a paradigmatic symbol. The second aspect consists in the *relational* dimension of French exceptionalism. Similar to the logic of identity, affirmation of exceptionalism requires the introduction into the map of an 'Other' (be it a nation, a people or a larger constituency) – even an unidentified one – as a body of comparison. The Other is constructed as it is invoked in this discourse. The third aspect of exceptionalism consists in inferring the duty of responsibility for – or tutelage over – the Other, whose life project is to be defined and organised out of themselves. In this regard, France, as an exceptional entity, is invested with the mission to diffuse the core elements of its exceptionalism beyond its cradle. Through this mission, exceptionalism becomes automatically associated with leadership and superiority.

Both the construction of the Other by the dominant group and the claim of a responsibility towards them are basically narratives about the former as well as the latter. Indeed, by stating its exceptionalism, France not only establishes its own status and position but also, conversely, those of the Other. In so doing, the possibility is created for the Other to become not only an object but a subject of discourse as well. Such a dynamic makes the discourse on French exceptionalism an identity narrative. Yet, following the Hegelian approach, any identity discourse is dialogical, in other words, it requires acknowledgement by the Other, all the more so as it takes place in a dominant/subordinate framework. Africans come into play with respect to the issue of French exceptionalism since they embody the figure of the Other whose (re)appropriation of their own identity implies, in the first instance, that they reassess the narrative of exceptionalism.

In the light of the previous discussion, Godin and Chafer's contribution to the understanding of French exceptionalism provides an invaluable theoretical point of departure if we are to sketch a sound understanding of Africans' reception of this discourse. However, we need to complement it by stressing the relation between this discourse and a wide array of means, resources, channels, etc. that guarantee its efficiency and embody it. To do so, Bourdieu's contribution to social theory will be of great use (Bourdieu 1991). His analysis of the power of language shows that to bring an idea into existence by the simple magic of uttering it owes much to a composite apparatus that has to be mobilised during this process. Among many elements, this apparatus consists of the legitimacy of the one who utters this idea to do so, the physical location in which this is done, and various fetishes and means that are to be displayed during this process (for instance a wig, a sceptre, a robe, etc.). A close examination of Bourdieu's argument would convincingly result in the postulate that the contribution of this apparatus in the power of language may lead those upon whom the effect of this power is exerted to equate this power with each of the components of this apparatus. The inclination in France of organised protest groups for justice and democracy to gather in the Place de la Bastille, the Place de la Concorde or the Parvis de l'Assemblée Nationale, provides evidence of the equation of channels of the power of language – of which the mentioned sites are examples – with the power of language itself. My point through this example is simply to stress that the French exception is to a large extent expressed in symbols and metaphors. As a result, to analyse Africans' discourses on the exceptionalism of France consists in tracking first, and giving meaning afterwards, to metaphorical and symbolic expressions of French subordination of, or leadership over, Africans. I would like, in the wake of this argument, to hypothesise that Africans' reception of the French exception is revealed through Africans' understanding of the institutions, instruments, means, or channels symbolising or metaphorising the purported superiority of France. Due to space constraints, my analysis will dwell unevenly on two metaphors of French exceptionalism in particular: the civilising mission and the French language.

The 'civilising mission' as a metaphor of French exception

The claim to a French exception is strongly equated with the project of the 'civilising mission' in the writings of French political figures and/or organic intellectuals as well as in those of African thinkers. This equation has traversed a wide body of French literature for at least two centuries. As early as in the writings of some craftsmen of the French Revolution, France was vested with the privilege of representing the *horizon* of human achievement, due to the supposed origin of its revolution in Enlightenment philosophy (Majumdar 2005; Schor 2001). It is thus asserted, in effect, that the French Revolution crystallises the best and universal values, rights, and ideas for which each human being would or should long. This idea of the superiority and even completeness of France's culture or civilisation was implied in the Revolution era notion of regeneration as used by Abbé Grégoire; a notion that entails France's power and capacity to improve the state of the Other (Sepinwall 2005). Historian Jules Michelet, another authoritative figure of the French intelligentsia, stated flatly that: 'The Frenchman wants above all to print his personality on the defeated peoples, not as his, but as a type of *good* and *beautiful*: that is his naive belief. He believes himself that he can do nothing more profitable for the world than to give his ideas, his mores, his habits' (Michelet, quoted by Seck 1993: 50. My translation and underlining).[2] The colonial enterprise would eventually tap into this belief. Indeed, the colonial mission had operated on the basis of the bipolarisation of humanity. In addition, it had emphasised the *relational* characteristic of the idea of exceptionalism by underlining the duty of the 'superior' people towards the Other, whom the former must lead to betterment, in brief to civilisation.[3]

This idea of the civilising mission has triggered reactive discourses among African writers. These discourses have never been homogeneous. They sometimes reveal contradictions, or internal conflicts in the writings of the same author, not to mention those showing through the comparison of several authors. The existence of such contradictions or conflicts is to be understood in the light of the internal characteristic of the civilising mission which relies on a promise to deliver, and an instrument to carry it out: respectively the elevation of African people in particular to the level of Frenchmen with whom they would equally share rights and duties attached to French-ness, and the transmission of the French language. Though to uneven extents, both the promise and the method are likely to be consensual as well as conflictual.

Senghor's writings are relevant ones through which Africans' reception of the French civilising mission can be assessed, for they epitomise the contradictions and conflicts aforementioned. To a large extent, Senghor's prose and poetry echo the idea of French exceptionalism, especially the hierarchisation – obviously favourable to France – of the peoples and cultures that it conveys. The texts are filled with oppositional characterisations of French-ness on the one hand and African-ness on the other: thus respectively the 'light' opposed to 'fog' in his poem *The Death of the Princess* (Towa 1971: 94); the 'reason' opposed to the 'intuition'; 'the requirement of intelligibility' as opposed to the African 'sense of concreteness' (Towa 1971: 104). This dichotomy inspires, or fuels, Senghor's advocacy of the politics of cultural *métissage* (crossbreeding), a close examination of which reveals the Senegalese thinker's debt to Abbé Grégoire's concept of regeneration. Indeed, Senghor's concept of *métissage*, like Grégoire's regeneration, suggests a hierarchy. They are both grounded, or at least carry on the belief, in the superiority of the French contribution to humanity. As in Grégoire's writing, so in Senghor's, France is viewed as the exclusive fertiliser of other nations and peoples, while she does not (have to) expect anything from them in return, perfect as she is. The individuals or the people who are likely to turn into cultural *métis* in Senghor's view are African, not French. Accordingly, he encourages Africans to assimilate the spirit of the French civilisation. As if to demonstrate his self-compliance with his own recommendation, Senghor seized every opportunity to emphasise his pride and delight in being a cultural *métis*, thus extending to France the honour to assess the superiority of its culture.

However, an extensive review of Senghor's poetry and prose shows clearly that the Senegalese thinker is inhabited by opposite views, so much so that his adherence to, and praise of, the French civilising mission appear to be neither systematic nor unconditional. The same writer who lyrically lauds French civilisation happens conversely to look down on it as he assesses the methods in which the civilising mission is grounded as well as the results of the promise it bore. He sometimes casts doubts on the superiority and the perfection of France's cultural values and civilisation. This country's claim to stand as a role model is called into question. Its betrayal of its promises of equality and solidarity with its dark subjects and of its own principle of respect of human life, as well as its extensive use of physical violence against the colonised people, make it finally as imperfect as many civilisations. As an indirect witness of the massacre at Camp Thiaroye – a military base located in the suburbs of Dakar, in Senegal, where, during the night of December 1st, 1944, a group of demobilised African soldiers arriving from the war front who dared to claim payment of their salaries before returning to their respective homelands were shot dead by the French army on the pretence that they disobeyed the military hierarchy;[4] and as a direct witness of the sacrificial use, without either acknowledgment or gratitude, of the Senegalese soldiers for the survival of the Republic by the same French political and intellectual establishment,[5] Senghor renounces his belief in the superiority of French civilisation, and the need for Africans to appropriate it. Thus, alluding to the French colonial undertaking in Africa, he cries out in his poem *Snow in Paris*:

> They tore down the black forest to build a railroad
> They cut down Africa's forests to save Civilisation
> Because they needed human raw materials. (Senghor 1991: 13)

As abstract as Senghor's poetry may appear to many commentators, the purpose is clear in the previous verses: French civilisation is largely perceived as anthropophagic; it sacrifices the black forest, that is by analogy the most valid members of the African community, to perpetuate its existence.[6] Turning towards African values viewed as a benchmark that is set in opposition to those of the French nation, Senghor implores in the poem *To the Music of Koras and Balaphon*:

> Austere earth, land of purity, cleanse me of all
> My petty desires and the contamination of being civilised (Senghor 1991: 17)

Through various metaphors and symbols as shown in these verses, Senghor intends to underline that the civilisation that French politicians and revolutionaries, and even contemporary intellectuals,[7] have praised for being the quintessential achievement of France and the major contribution to the evolution of mankind, is much less a cure than a germ of which humans are better being purged. Hence his use of the medical metaphor 'contamination', for this civilisation, instead of feeding humanity, feeds itself with human flesh; instead of promoting humanity, it annihilates it.

The internal conflict and ambiguity *vis-à-vis* the French civilising mission that springs up in Senghor's thought is not specific to the president-poet. They define, on the contrary, the attitude of most of the colonial generation of African writers. Alioune Diop's articles in *Présence africaine* testify in their own way to this intellectual's adherence to France's superiority, but in parallel question it. Better, Ch.H. Kane's novel, *L'aventure ambiguë* (*Ambiguous Adventure*), offers one of the starkest illustrations of the double reception of French exceptionalism in African literature. On the one hand, the indigenous aristocracy's decision to flock to the French school, dragging the masses with them in search of the tools for their country's survival, is in many regards the acknowledgment of France's leadership and the superiority of its culture. However, the reflection of Grande Royale, a major character in the novel, with regards to France's domination over the dark peoples constitutes a point worth dwelling upon. Indeed, her question as to how is victory possible if it is not grounded in reason (*'comment vaincre sans avoir raison'*), stands as an implicit, none the less radical, critique of French civilisation (Kane 2001: 47). This question asks – sketchily maybe – how a civilisation that prides itself on being built on the core component of the Enlightenment, viz *Reason* – according to Touraine (1995: 9ff) – conceives of its own expansion (or diffusion) at the expense of that very *Reason*.

Unlike colonial writers whose reception of the French colonial mission has never departed from such an ambiguity – put aside authors of systematic critique of this enterprise such as Cheikh Anta Diop and Mongo Beti – post-colonial writers have been mostly concerned with downplaying any French exceptionalism with regards to its civilising mission.[8] A significant illustration of this, among many, has been the reception by African thinkers of president Sarkozy's speech in Senegal. On 26 July, 2007, in this hour-long speech that is now popularly referred to as the '*Discours de Dakar*' and was delivered in the flossiest amphitheatre of Cheikh Anta Diop University, President Sarkozy, gazing down at an audience of more than 100 African students, professors and political authorities, lectured them on the meaning of being Black/African as he engaged in a review of the aftermaths of France's colonial presence in Africa. Warning his hosts that he intended to address this issue with 'frankness and sincerity' (Sarkozy 2007e), Sarkozy marvelled first at what he believes to be 'the first mystery of Africa', which consists, according to him, in African people's ability to consider each other as brothers in spite of their linguistic, religious and customary differences, to rally around the same identity banner of African-ness while they still fight and hate each other. Later on, the French president praised the 'colonial *oeuvre*' of France in Africa by listing the purportedly innumerable positive contributions it brought to the continent, for instance the principle of human rights and medical and economic infrastructures. In the same breath he updated the 1789 revolutionaries' assumption that French culture in particular, and European culture in general, are calls for 'liberty and emancipation', 'justice and equality', 'reason and collective conscience'. Sarkozy then continued by disclosing to his hosts his belief that the 'tragedy of Africa' resides not in its past experience of the slave trade and colonisation, but in that the 'African man has not sufficiently entered into history' ('*l'homme africain n'est pas assez entré dans l'histoire*'). Breaking down his thesis, he then urged Africa to rise to some challenges: 'to get down more into history', 'to emancipate itself from the myth of the eternal return', 'to learn to view its accession to the universal not as a renunciation of what it is, but as an accomplishment', 'to learn to feel itself as the inheritor of what exists as universal in all human civilisations' (Sarkozy 2007e). Reading Sarkozy's speech, and following the critical approach adopted by Ch.A. Diop – who was eager to demonstrate the superiority and precedence of black Egyptian civilisation (Diop 1974: 1979) – Makhily Gassama takes heed to underline the hidden, if not subtle, thesis in the '*Discours de Dakar*'. In keeping with most of the contributors to his book, he begins by arguing that the French president's speech is basically nothing but an updating of the thesis of the 'white man's burden', the Frenchman to be specific. For Gassama, through its most prominent representative, namely Sarkozy, France is reiterating the old conviction of its grandeur, of the pre-eminence of its contribution to world civilisation, and, in addition, its patronising attitude *vis-à-vis* African people, whose cultural contribution to the achievement of mankind is almost downplayed in the '*Discours de Dakar*' as soon as it is underlined. Thus he writes: 'When we listen to him [Nicolas Sarkozy], we have the impression that "le nègre" [the negro], in order to get any better, to edge his way towards the human, to "get down into history", for his "accomplishment", that is for his salvation, needs to rub shoulders biologically and culturally with the White, the white European above all' (Gassama 2008: 29).

On the one hand, Gassama points out Sarkozy's acknowledgment of Africa's contribution to the renewal of artistic creation in Europe in the 20th century, thanks to its consideration for the ecological system, but notes that right after the French president demeans such a quality as a cause of Africa's backwardness. On the other, Gassama is quick to reassess Sarkozy's assertion of the exteriority of the idea of universalism with regard to Africa and the origin of this idea in the French Revolution. Thus he writes: 'Nicolas Sarkozy speaks, with a stunning smugness, of the necessity of our "accession to the universal" as if he himself and his own were already comfortably settled in it' (Gassama 2008: *ibid*). Drawing mostly from oral history, and minimising France's claim to the paternity of this civilising principle as a simple act of usurpation, Gassama argues that prior to the elaboration of a human rights charter by 1789 revolutionaries, the Malian emperor Soundjata Keïta had already, as early as 1222, designed 'a similar charter' extending these rights even to non-members of his empire (Gassama 2008: 31). Assuming thereby France's debt to African civilisation, Gassama means to stress that the rationale for France's civilising mission in Africa is unfounded, and, as a consequence, its claims to superiority and leadership null and without foundation.

The French language as the embodiment of French exceptionalism

The idea of the French exception proves to be linked to the issue of the French language. Indeed, the latter turns out to be a key instrument of the civilising mission. If not, it is indistinguishable from French culture, as Glissant contends (Glissant 2003: 105). One of the characters in *The Ambiguous Adventure*, Pierre-Louis puts it quite blatantly, as he posits that its language, along with its law, is the 'very texture' of the 'genius' of France (Kane 2001: 144). What's more, France's language is flatly asserted, in the French literature and political speeches, to be one of its most valuable contributions to the evolution of mankind in general, and of Africans in particular. Rivarol's well-known dissertation on the 'reasons for the universality of the French language', in which the French language is asserted to be the communication tool with men, whereas German is to be used with horses, Italian with women, Spanish with God and English with merchants, expresses a stunning hierarchy of languages that, as expected, favours France[9] (Calvet 1998). In the wake of 18th century writers, many 20th century French politicians and intellectuals have been quick to reiterate the exceptionalism of the French language. The late president Pompidou made the case for what former French colonies owe to France for their elevation.

Out of Africans' writings stem various forms of the reception of this narrative. Veneration of the colonisers' language – synonym of power for Bourdieu (1991) – is expected among colonised African-descended people. Two writers of different styles, Leon Gontran Damas (1977: 15), the Guyanese-born poet, and oft-times forgotten component of the Négritude movement triumvirate, and Frantz Fanon, the famous psychiatrist from Martinique who distinguished himself through his support and justification for the armed option of the Algerian independence fighters (1967: 18ff), provide evidence for this. Senghor, however, offers the most overt illustration thereof in his essays, so much so that he has been nicknamed 'the black Rivarol' (Midiohouan 1994: 25). Priding himself on mastering the French language better than his mother tongue, the poet praises French for its suitability for scientific demonstration, better than any language, especially its contemporary rival, English, which according to him borrowed two thirds of its vocabulary from Latin, Greek and, more often French itself. Moreover, for its nuanced suppleness, grace, clarity, and rich vocabulary, French proves to be the ideal idiom for the composition of prose and poetry (Senghor 1977: 81; Senghor 1988: 170–1), and even 'the language of communication *par excellence*' (Senghor 1977: 19).

Such an explicit acknowledgment of the linguistic superiority of France has been cohabiting with the questioning of this very idea in Africans' writings. Two responses have resulted. The first consists in a trivialisation of the qualities of the French language. If many writers are worthy of mention, two among them come to mind for their significant contribution to this debate. One is Cheikh Anta Diop, the Senegalese historian and Egyptologist, author of *Nations nègres et culture* (partly translated in English as *The African Origin of Civilisation: Myth or Reality*), arguably the book by an African that has been most influential among educated Africans in Africa, not to mention its impact in some milieus of the Black

Diaspora.[10] At the present stage of this analysis, the section of the book that is worth dwelling on is the appendix. In this section, the Senegalese historian, who held also a university degree in science (nuclear physics to be specific), engages in the translation of Einstein's theory of relativity into Wolof, Senegal's dominant language. In so doing, his main purpose was, on the one hand, to demonstrate the inherent ability of African languages to support a highly sophisticated scientific discourse, and on the other, to suggest that the exclusive assignation to the French language of the power to express an organised and orderly discourse, as Senghor expressed it, is grounded in ideology rather than facts (Diop 1979). The second African writer who is to be mentioned here is Boubacar Boris Diop. Contemporary of Cheikh Anta Diop, although much younger than him, this Senegalese academic and, most notably, novelist undertook the unprecedented effort of writing a novel in Wolof. *Doomi Golo* (*Son of the Monkey*), an existential reflection on death, life and mental insanity, is the story of an old man, Ngiraan Faye, who on the verge of dying writes to his son, an immigrant in a Western country, a seven-chapter letter in which confidence, lessons about life and advice alternates. During a short-lived movement of valorisation of Wolof in the 1970s and 1980s, *Doomi Golo* sprung out an avant-gardist consciousness of the necessity to dispel the idea of the inferiority of African languages, and conversely that of the superiority of French. In this regard, the novel appears to be consistent with the trivialisation of French.

The questioning of the superiority of the French language results, most importantly, in a reversal of the hierarchy between this language and African languages. This is most of the time conveyed in novels and poetry. The fictional works by the late Ivoirian-born award-winning novelist, Ahmadou Kourouma, the late Senegalese award-winning filmmaker and also novelist, Ousmane Sembène, the deceased Congolese playwright, poet and novelist, Sony Labou Tansi and, to a lesser extent, the works of the younger generation of African fiction writers, carry the subtle assertion that the future of the French language depends on its fertilisation by African languages in particular. The shake-up of the grammatical structure of the French language is thereby becoming a common theme in Francophone African literature. Kourouma and Tansi are unarguably amongst the precursors of this literary dynamic. Kourouma, for instance, who partly owed to it his title of the most original Francophone African writer for decades, had taken heed to batter the so widely praised French concise style and graciousness, to quote Senghor, by imposing upon it the grammatical rules of his mother tongue, Malinké. Reflecting on his techniques and methods of writing, Kourouma made clear the necessity of the 'inbreeding' of the French language with African languages so as not only to allow African writers to channel the richness and complexity of their culture through the French language, but also so as better to provide the French language with other world views that sometimes prevent it from being able to express the full complexity of human imagination, especially when it is African. He thus wrote:

> The French language is the second language in my country; it is officially my national language. French is a disciplined language, refined by writing [...]. My mother tongue, the language in which I think, doesn't know anything but the large freedom of oral language ['*oralité*' in the original text]. [...] I struggle in a great confusion of terminologies with the French expressions. Let me give an example. The law in my motherland would condemn to several years of imprisonment those who confessed to having eaten the soul of a deceased person. To eat the soul of a deceased person is an unusual expression in French, it makes one smile because in the French culture we cannot eat the soul. [...] I must rethink, take up again, re-conceive of fiction in the French language in which it is written, that is 'africanising' French in order that the work could preserve the essence of its qualities. (Kourouma 1997: 115–17)

The necessity of 'africanising' French advocated by Kourouma in this excerpt is a subtle critique of the French language. It reverses the long-established order according to which this language has everything to provide Africans and nothing to receive from theirs. Yet Kourouma suggests through his systematic introduction of African words and expressions the idea of the deficiency of the French language which would be unable to capture the complexity of the world imaginaries (Kourouma 1981). Senghor, himself – who occasionally reiterates his idea of the linguistic exceptionalism of France, and may fail to be cognisant of his own contradictions – stated once that his mission within the French Academy would be to fertilise the French language.

Conclusion

As the previous lines have demonstrated, French exceptionalism is a discourse of self-identification. In light of the logic of identity politics as a relational enterprise (Taylor 1994), it appears to be also a narrative on the Other. Through the discourse of French exceptionalism, France sends to other people or societies the message that they are ordinary

entities. As a consequence, it imposes on them only two options: either
to acknowledge and subscribe to, or to refuse, its superiority and leadership. If Africans are a special group from whose perspective the understanding and reception of this discourse outside France's boundaries
can legitimately be assessed, it is partly because the purported French
exceptionalism has decisively contributed to the 'invention of Africa',
to quote Mudimbe (Mudimbe 1988). It is also because this exceptionalism is fed at the same time by the representation of Africa it conveys.
The idea of the 'civilising mission' hallows the superiority and leadership of French culture and civilisation as much as it downgrades the
culture of Africans on whom it is imposed. Consequently, to restore or
craft the image and identity of Africa equates for Africans to debating
the notion of French exceptionalism. The result of this situation is an
ambiguous reception of French exceptionalism by many Africans: praise
for the standard of the French language as well as for the benefits of
the colonial mission cohabit with a diminution, or at least a trivialisation,
of the cultural achievement of France.

Notes

1   For the sake of stylistic simplicity, I will use the term Africans when I refer
    to the aforementioned group of Africans after this sentence.
2   The original version of the citation reads as follows: 'Le Français veut surtout
    imprimer sa personnalité aux vaincus, non comme siennes mais comme type
    du bon et du beau: c'est sa croyance naïve. Il croit, lui, qu'il ne peut rien faire
    de profitable au monde que de lui donner ses idées, ses mœurs, ses modes'. As
    presented, this excerpt from Michelet's book *Introduction à l'histoire universelle*,
    could suggest that Michelet distances himself from this belief. Yet the rest
    of the citation suggests the contrary. Indeed, the French historian and pur-
    portedly artisan of modern France was also a true believer and advertiser of
    the superiority of France, as these words show: 'Our [France's] history is com-
    plete. This [history] is the tradition that makes the history of France that of
    humanity as a whole' (Michelet, quoted by Hewlett 2005: 5).
3   If evidence needs to be provided that Michelet's idea of France has expanded
    far beyond the Revolution era to shape the thought of some artisans of the
    colonial enterprise, the writings of Hubert Deschamps, who held a double
    legitimacy as a scholar for having authored a Ph.D. dissertation and as a col-
    onial administrator and governor of the French colonies, would be a good illus-
    tration. Not only does Deschamps never query the rationale of 'the historical
    responsibility of France in matters of civilising the backward populations of
    which she is in charge' but he stated that 'the education of the new indige-
    nous societies is our essential task', echoing thus the conclusion of his own
    1938 dissertation that: 'the mistake would appear to be to hinder them [the
    Africans], to keep them in childhood, to push them back to the Middle Ages
    or to prehistory. [...] Let us be good educators and prepare good Europeans'
    (quoted by Seck 1993: 54).

4   This event has been memorialised in 1988 in the eponymous film, *Camp de Thiaroye* by the late Senegalese film-maker, writer and former soldier enrolled in 1942 in the 'Senegalese *tirailleurs*' military unit, Ousmane Sembène. Interestingly, the film has been censored for many years in France.

5   Enrolled in the French army and eventually held prisoner in a concentration camp by the Nazi army, Senghor had been in direct contact with the horror perpetrated on Black African soldiers by the enemies at the same time that he captured the French military authorities' decision to send these people to the front lines where they were more likely to be the first victims of the Nazi war machine.

6   The forests, I believe, symbolise the bodies of Africans, bodies which, Césaire wrote, served as the crosspieces of the railroads built in the colonies (Cesaire 2000), an allusion to the number of African workers who lost their lives during the realisation of this gigantic enterprise.

7   The topicality of this idea is evidenced by recent statements made by politicians and intellectuals, including President Sarkozy's highly-controversial 'Discours de Dakar' (www.elysee.fr/documents/index.php?mode) in which he praised the colonial record of France; the bill voted by the French Parliament in February 2005 to officialise France's recognition of 'the positive aspects of French colonialism', and finally the interview given on 18 November 2005 to the Israeli daily newspapers, *Haaretz*, by the well-known philosopher, Alain Finkielkraut, in which he emphasised the ingratitude of the French black community towards France, a country that had done its best to civilise the 'savages' that their ancestors were.

8   For a more detailed account of this issue, see Gueye (2001).

9   One may counterargue that the association between Spanish and God contradicts the thesis of the superiority of the French language in Rivarol's dissertation. Yet, although apparently more positive, the association between God and Spanish proves nonetheless to be downplaying this language, as Rivarol was under the influence of Enlightenment philosophy, in which the superiority of *Reason* (associated with Man) over *Belief* (associated with God) is unquestionable. Besides, Rivarol is quick to distinguish the language of women from that of men so as to express the inequality between men and women. It is well-known that womanhood has been a condition of inferiority in 18th century thought; a biological difference impossible to overcome or delete according to Abbé Grégoire, and so much so that even the Egalitarian Revolution found itself unable to elevate women to a status equal to men and therefore confined them outside the margins of citizenship (Scott 2005: 16). On, the contrary, man/male as an abstract entity, that is one deprived of all its particularities, symbolises the universal. But, as Sartre unveils it in his Black Orpheus, the male in question is male because first and foremost he is white (Sartre 1977).

10 *Nations nègres et culture* led Cheikh Anta Diop to be awarded the prize for 'the writer who has most influenced black thought in the twentieth century'. The award was made at the First World Festival for Negro Arts held in Dakar in 1966. It propelled him as well into the realm of the canonical figures of the Black community, so much so that a 'Dr. Cheikh Anta Diop Day' is celebrated every 4 April – also the anniversary of the assassination of Martin Luther King – in the American city of Atlanta. Lastly, the book, reprinted four

times in its original language, is known to be a best-seller of the historiography in French by Black African scholars. To a certain extent, its reputation is at odds with its trajectory. Indeed, it has been facing manifold criticisms by scholars since its publication, and above all was rejected by a French academic committee – to which it was submitted under the form of a doctoral dissertation – who judged as unfounded the overarching argument of the book, that is, the Nubian origin of the Pharaonic civilisation.

Section VI

Conclusion: French Exceptionalism Reconsidered

13
French Exceptionalism and the Sarkozy Presidency

Tony Chafer and Emmanuel Godin

In this volume the notion of French exception has been defined both as a set of politically loaded discourses as well as an analytical tool that can be used to decipher specific socio-economic, political and cultural issues that form what is now commonly referred to as the French model. That some political and electoral rewards can be gained in presenting the French model as exceptional, either because of its virtues or its archaism is clear enough. That this 'French model' actually remains transfixed into a parody of its *dirigiste*, Jacobin or republican self as if it were immune to global, European and domestic pressures, has amply been questioned in this volume. In some respect, France may have changed more rapidly than the discourses about France. Whether such cumulative changes amount to a rupture with the French model and whether such a rupture lead to the normalisation of France – the end of the French exception – are two questions that this concluding chapter seeks to address.

The French exception

Most contributors in this volume agree that the notion of exceptionalism is difficult to define and to use. First, an exception only exists in opposition to a general rule or norm and it is not obvious what the norm ought to be. Whether a departure from the norm constitutes an exception rather than specificity or a variance is equally problematic. Usually, in most political discourses, France is defined as an exception to the neo-liberal Anglo-Saxon model. The 2008 financial and economic crisis has led to questioning of the intrinsic value of the neo-liberal model as the norm (*Alternatives économiques* 2009). Equally, now that Barack Obama has succeeded George Bush in the White House, opportunities to demonise arrogant Anglo-Saxon posturings have been partly undercut (Roger 2002; Colombani 2009): the Obamania which swept France in November 2008 was followed by much soul-searching about France's inability to promote ethnic minorities (Bui 2008). However, the truce may not extend to the cultural sphere, given the entrenched fear from left to right, about the Americanisation of French culture, as is well explained by Dauncey in this volume. Finally, it should not be assumed that a virtuous Anglo-Saxon model is the only alternative to a deficient French model. Sue Milner, for instance, has shown that in the field of family policy reforms, the Scandinavian model is a great source of inspiration both for France and Britain and for the EU. Second, there is a risk that a feature of the French exception had been greatly exaggerated in the past leading to its 'surprising' demise today: in this volume, Helen Drake, for instance, warns against the supposedly 'golden age of France's influence in Europe which never quite existed'. Such a belief, however, is not without consequence – Drake argues – as it acts as a 'drag on France's current ability to adapt to a changing world'. In the same vein, Vince has shown that the notion of *laicité*, has been largely reconceptualised over the past 20 years with an attempt to crystallise it into an exceptional and unchanging feature of French republicanism: invariably conflicts emerge when debates are opened about the possibility to review the working of this very recent tradition.

Sue Collard reminds us 'the debate about the "French exception" and its proclaimed demise' has come 'to permeate public discourse in France in a way that has not been reproduced anywhere else'. Here lies what is exceptional about France and what crucially defines the process through which it is constructing its national identity. This identity has become both politicised and polarised. Over the past 15 years or so, *la pensée unique*, whose logic and development has been well defined by Sue Collard, has been challenged by parties and movements with a radical voice. Today, such radicalism is a mix of old and new tendencies. In that respect, three points are worth making: first, a revolutionary culture is still very much at work in France and its influence is felt well beyond the confines of a rejuvenated extreme left, as David Bell explains. By European standards, the electoral success of the French extreme left is not negligible and there is enough evidence to trace its influence in a variety of new social movements contesting the logic and the devastating consequences of global capitalism. Second, at a time when the extreme right has become a common feature of most European democracies (Hainsworth 2008), it appears to be in relative decline in France. Hewlett and Schain have shown how Sarkozy has skilfully integrated some radical elements of Le Pen's programme into his own, demonstrated as Minister of the Interior he could effectively implement them and subsequently managed to siphon away a substantial number of FN voters. Third, references to the republican model as a powerful, radical alternative to *la pensée unique*, seem to have lost the radicalism they acquired in the previous decade. This is particularly visible in the changing nature of the criticism levelled against the European Union, as demonstrated in this volume by Harmsen: both left-wing Jacobinism, well symbolised by Chevénement, and the 'universalist Gaullist aspirations of the republican model', have lost their political attractiveness and been displaced respectively by the alternativist movement on the left and a traditional particularist defence of the French national way of life on the right.

The debate about the enduring exceptionality of the republican model is also questioned by some contributors. There seems to be a major contrast between a stifled republican discourse and a more flexible republican practice. For instance Vince shows that Republican values still maintain a 'talismanic status' in France. Likewise, Drake insists on how traditional, republican principles have often formatted French strategic choices at the European level, sometimes with a degree of dogmatism that has puzzled France's partners. Yet, Vince also shows that there is no such thing as a stable and eternal republican model: in the case of *laicité*, the concept has evolved with time. At critical junctures, political and ideological reasons have provided *laicité* with an aura of exceptionality which is difficult to establish empirically. Likewise Martin Schain warns us against the danger of reifying the republican model. A comparison between the French republican and Anglo-Saxon, multicultural models of immigration unravels some enduring myths about their respective virtues. Schain also demonstrates that in practice the French republican model has been able to make compromises with multiculturalism and introduce anti-discrimination measures based on the Anglo-Saxon experience, whereas the Anglo-Saxon model has found in centrally defined civic integration a source of inspiration. This nuanced and comparative approach shows that there is a certain degree of practical flexibility in the way republican principles are implemented. It also highlights a degree of adaptation to external constraints as much as its ability to provide inspiration for the reform of other models. Hugh Dauncey also stresses this point when he shows that the 'French state has partly tamed its *dirigiste* approach to culture with the inclusion of neo-liberal recipes', 'the rising commercial importance of the cultural industries worldwide is making other governments such as that of the UK pay greater attention to the active role they should play in supporting their own cultures of film, music, video and television'.

It is thus worth considering that a degree of convergence between Western countries does not necessarily point towards a neo-liberal model.

The weight of external constraints has been recurrently used to explain the decline of the French state in its traditional *dirigiste* guise. Drake and Sue Milner both explain how the EU has provided tactical opportunities for successive governments of both left and right to scale down the public ownership of economic and industrial resources. Likewise, welfare reforms, Milner argues, have been on the agenda for a long time and substantial reforms have been engaged well ahead of Sarkozy's electoral victory to respond to a mixture of demographic changes, financial external pressures, and the increasing normative power of the EU which tends to favour productivist rather than welfarist social policies. Such conditions affect all European nations and 'in such a policy environment, it is difficult for countries to remain exceptional'. Yet, common pressures do not necessarily lead toward convergence, as Milner points out: the robustness of existing institutions and the strength of veto actors within the domestic political system mean that common pressures are processed differently in different national settings. In this volume, contributors have brought to the fore the crucial role played by veto actors in resisting change, whether it be the 'medical establishment and pharmaceutical companies' described by Milner or Dauncey's *'intermittents du spectacle'*. For Harmsen, resistance to external pressures can also be explained by the salience of a common referent across the French political spectrum: protectionism. Harmsen argues that it implies not only 'the protection of a model of state economic intervention or social welfare provision, but also more intangibly the protection of a "way of life" or a sense of cultural community'. If this protectionism provides a defining element of a French political culture, then Europeanisation and globalisation are essentially viewed as a threat rather than an opportunity and this stance provides a marked contrast with the previous confidence that France had in its universal destiny.

France's universal destiny is a central theme of this volume and has become a highly contested subject both within and outside France, whether in terms of France's *rayonnement culturel* (Dauncey and Gueye), relations to Europe (Harmsen and Drake) or Africa (Chafer, Majumdar and Gueye). Drake and Gueye in particular insist on how France's attempt to define as universal its relations to European construction and the African *pré carré* have been essential in delineating its national identity. Yet, French exceptionalism, as a discourse of self-identification, has lost some of its potency. Analysing the discourse of French exceptionalism 'outside the ethnic boundaries of Frenchness', Gueye explains how its reception has changed with time. From one generation to the other, the trend has been from praising the cultural benefits of France's colonial mission to a trivialisation of its cultural achievement. The shift certainly reflects a greater confidence in the construction of a post-colonial African identity and a growing uneasiness in France about the way the country ought to manage its colonial past and define its rank and role in the world. Yet, from the attempt to introduce a revisionist version of colonial history in 2005 to Sarkozy's discourse on *l'homme africain* in Dakar in July 2007, there is evidence that a colonial mind is still part of the national psyche, as Chafer and Majumdar have shown. Despite Sarkozy's willingness to present himself as a man from a new generation with a new approach to Africa, his message and his references hark back to the period of French colonial rule. In the same vein, France's claim to be the standard bearer of a European (non-Anglo-Saxon) model has often been greeted as the particularist defence of its national interests and perceived as an expression of arrogance, a point made both by Harmsen and Drake. To the genuine surprise of the French elite, France's *exemplarité* in an enlarged Europe does not appear to be as attractive to its neighbours as it thought it would be. In that respect, the two first years of the Sarkozy presidency demonstrate a willingness to make Europe a core element of France's narrative about its own identity, as Drake has shown, and to recapture its European rank that previous expressions of self-doubt had dented. The French presidency of the EU (July–December 2008) was certainly presented by Sarkozy's communication team as a major step in that direction (Cornudet 2009): whether Sarkozy's leadership would enable France to break away from 'the prison walls' of its political culture remains, of course, a matter of debate, as Drake has argued.

What is clearer is that France's political culture makes it particularly difficult to embrace a European and global culture which appear to be at odds with its own values. At home, there is evidence that policy makers seek to avoid overt forms of cultural and linguistic 'nationalism', which would invariably have led to the fossilisation of French culture. Tensions around the development of a videogame industry illustrate this point and, as Dauncey shows, French policy makers are not always reluctant to endorse new values and new working methods. Support for cultural diversity and a degree of openness to global values go hand in hand with more flexible state support, greater freedom from regulation, and crucially, enhanced commercial rewards. Abroad, accusations of cultural arrogance and neo-colonialism have also prompted France, not without reluctance, to revise the role it intends to play on the European and international stage. France's self-justification as a standard bearer of universal values has evolved. Dauncey has shown how, in a global context, France does not vindicate the exceptionality (superiority) of its own culture in the way that it once did. Rather it seeks to portray itself as the defender of cultural pluralism against the uniformity of the Anglo-Saxon global steamroller. Likewise, Chafer and Majumdar have highlighted how France has attempted to overcome accusations of 'neo-colonialism' by revising its discourse about Africa and 'multilateralising' its interventions on the continent. Yet again, there is ample evidence that this process is fraught with tensions: Sarkozy's chequered launch of the Union for the Mediterranean, for instance, illustrates France's ambiguous commitment to multilateralism in the same way as his lukewarm support for Franco-phonie indicates a departure from the rhetoric of multipolarity promoted, most notably, by Jacques Chirac. As Chafer and Majumdar argue, the underlying theme of Sarkozy's foreign policy is to restore France to great-ness, an objective which owes more to the Gaullist legacy than the new president's electoral motto: *la rupture tranquille*. In this perspective, it seems apt to evaluate the extent to which the Sarkozy presidency heralds the end of the French exception.

The French exception and the Sarkozy presidency

What is *le Sarkozysme*? Does it represent a new form of the right in France? Is it a unique French phenomenon? In this volume, Nick Hewlett explains that if there is anything such as *le Sarkozysme*, then it is an ambiguous mixture between a long French tradition – Bonapartism – and a neo-liberal right which, hitherto, had made few inroads into French politics. What is clear is that Sarkozy belongs to a new generation of right-wing politicians whose historical and ideological references – and also electoral support (Fourquet 2009) – are different from the classical, Gaullo-Chiraquist right (Nielsberg and Sahuc 2006; Levy *et al* 2008). It is also characterised by an initial willingness to put an end to the French excep-tion with a direct assault on the 'French model' (Jarreau 2008). In this volume, Sue Collard has explained how *déclinistes*, locate the origin of the French decline in a reluctance to embrace an economic liberal culture (Bavarez 2003b) and have provided Sarkozy's generation with enough ammunition to assail the French administrative and political elite, who over the past 30 years have failed to undertake the 'necessary' reforms, that is, to align the French model with a neo-liberal, Anglo-Saxon one (Sarkozy 2006). Profit is not a dirty word and the love of money is not considered to be shameful (Mossuz-Lavau 2007). Sarkozy's Rolex watches, rich friends and *bling-bling* style, the 172 per cent pay rise he granted himself a few months after he took office and the tax shield (*bouclier fiscal*) he immediately introduced to protect richer households from further taxation, but above all, his campaign motto '*travailler plus, pour gagner plus*' ('work more to earn more'), are all symbolic of this new rapport with money. In this respect, Sarkozy's presidential style points to other ruptures with the French model of politics.

One immediately senses that under Sarkozy's leadership, the tendency has been to concentrate rather than redistribute power. The Fifth Republic has shifted power away from parliament to the executive, and provided the president with substantial constitutional powers and a clear political legitimacy. Over the past decade or so, debates about the French executive have been focused on the effects of *cohabitation* and the possibility for the prime minister to regain a degree of autonomy *vis-à-vis* the president, with a return to a constitutional text purged of its Gaullist interpretation (Elgie 2001; Bell 2002; Clift 2005). However, since 2007, after three relatively weak consecutive presidential terms, France seems to be returning to a strong presidency (Levy and Skach 2008). Deriding his predecessors as *rois fainéants* Sarkozy himself asserts his willingness to occupy the entire policy space (*être omnipresent*), both on the domestic and foreign fronts, thus inaugurating what has been commonly termed the *hyperprésidence* (Badinter 2008). In this context, the core of the debate has shifted to the continuing relevance of the prime minister (Auffray and Guiral 2007), with François Fillon himself initially casting doubt on the relevance of his own job (Willsher 2007) and some pundits still wondering why, for the sake of coherence, the 2008 constitutional reforms did not do away with the Prime Minister (Julliard 2009). The fact that Nicolas Sarkozy and Claude Guéant, Secrétaire Général de l'Elysée, initially organised meetings with the most influential members of the government without inviting the Prime Minister, indicates rather clearly the preference given to appointed advisers over the leader of the parliamentary majority and serves to renew the criticisms against the monarchic evolution of the institutions. Yet, the constitutional reform voted 23 July 2008 following most of the recommendations of the Balladur Committee (National Assembly 2008), is rather ambiguous and does not lead to an overt presidentialisation of the regime *à l'américaine* (Ghevontian, R. 2009). However, it does provide parliament with new powers (such as a greater share in the definition of the parliamentary agenda) and equally seeks to limit – very slightly – some presidential prerogatives (notably the power to nominate). But the overall logic of the reform is not aimed at reducing or halting the presidentialisation of the regime, but rather at strengthening counter powers to this very presidentialisation: a stronger parliament as a counter point to a stronger president.

One of the most symbolic features of the 2008 constitutional reform is that once a year it allows the president to address the Congress assembled in Versailles, in a way reminiscent of the American State of the Union address. The ceremony has a certain regalian aura and if its usefulness can be questioned, it fits well with the desire of French public opinion to see a strengthening of the presidential function (Strudel 2007). Its first occurrence in June 2009 may have contributed to invert the initial image associated with the first two years of the Sarkozy presidency: his brash and abrasive personality, his willingness to adopt a confrontational style, his association with the world of glamour and show business, his real or cultivated 'non-intellectualism' contrast sharply with the images of his predecessors (Vaulerin 2007; Marmande 2009). Experts in communication, who have noticed that public opinion, and in particular a substantial segment of his own electoral base, did not react positively to the debasing of the presidential function (Kraus and Zumsteeg 2008; Sarkozy 2009b) are now geared to create an image of Sarkozy as a competent statesman of international stature. The appointment of Frédéric Mitterrand as Minister of Culture in June 2009 goes a long way to redress the image of a presidency tarnished by a suspicion of philistinism. More perilous is the management of the president's public/private image. Raymond Kuhn in this volume has shown that the division between public and private, once a clear French feature protected by a strong legal apparatus, is becoming blurred as the result of three different types of change: the growing importance of political communication and marketing, the economic imperative for news media to chase audiences and changing relations between journalists and politicians, with the development of a less deferential and more aggressive journalistic style, more commonly found in Anglo-Saxon countries. Collusion between journalists, politicians and readers to expose the private life of public figures has brought the French experience more in line with other comparable democracies. In 2004, Jean-Marie Charon noted that if there was still no French translation for 'spin-doctors',[1] the sort of 'media management' that the term implies was already at work, albeit in a less intense and public form than in Blair's Britain (Charon 2004). Yet there is evidence that political communication is now central to Sarkozy's presidency: the presidential appointment of television and radio directors, made possible by the 2009 *loi audiovisuelle*, increases the already cosy relations between the president and major media keyplayers, whereas the desire to control the political agenda and to release a permanent flow of information may make it more difficult for journalists to pursue their critical role (Padis 2007).

Far more unusual has been Sarkozy's *ouverture*: the promotion of prominent members of the opposition to a variety of positions within or outside the government. Here is a real rupture. *Ouverture* as a strategy does not seem contingent upon specific electoral results: it was announced early in Sarkozy's electoral campaign and pursued after the 2009 European elections that witnessed the success of the UMP lists. Unlike Mitterrand in 1988, Sarkozy has a large majority in the National Assembly which does not make it vital for him to seek support in the opposite camp, a fact that angered some of his supporters, notably Jean-François Coppé. Likewise, the 1988 *ouverture* brought under the same roof personalities whose ideological differences, or at least political itineraries, were not entirely incompatible: an alliance between socialists and centrists was not ideologically difficult to conceive. The promotion of left-wing personalities within *la droite décomplexée* is far more surprising and, in contrast to the 1988 *ouverture*, they have been given major responsibilities: Bernard Kouchner as Foreign Secretary or Eric Besson heading the newly created immigration and national integration ministry are hardly in charge of purely technical administrations. Prominent left-wing figures – Michel Rocard, Jacques Attali, Jack Lang – have been asked to chair prestigious commissions or been assigned specific missions whereas Sarkozy supported and finally secured the appointment of Dominique Strauss Kahn as the IMF director general.

A statesmanlike posture requires presidents to reach beyond the natural limits of their own political family: in France, reaching out to the opposition in such a systematic manner is unusual. The *ouverture* is first of all an attempt to disorganise and demoralise the left at a time when its leadership is weak and its confidence in its own ideas is low. It also serves to deprive the centrist leader, F. Bayrou, of one of his main proposals: to turn the centre into the natural place to organise the debate between left and right standpoints. In reality, it is difficult to assess the impact of left-wing ministers on the policies introduced and implemented by what remains a right-wing government (Revault d'Allones 2007). Yet *ouverture* is more than an electoral trick: it is also a political strategy aimed at redefining the terms of the political debate, an attempt to blur the line between left and right and to redistribute political roles. For instance, during the presidential campaign Sarkozy's references to Jaurès and Blum were easily derided by the left, but his subsequent promotion to the government of personalities from ethnic minority backgrounds (Rachida Dati, Rama Yade and Fadela Amara) has been far more disarming for the left, whose own failure to undertake such promotions only serves to highlight its conservatism on such issues. There has been a deliberate choice to push forward and mediatise policies which clearly expose the ideological weakness of the PS and divide its ranks,[2] such as the banning of advertising on public TV channels (Bacqué and Chemin 2008). The objective is not quick electoral gain, but to redefine the terms of the debate. Thus, the political *bric à brac* which makes up *la droite décompléxée* should not hide its hegemonic purpose. As Nicolas Sarkozy declared: '*Au fond, j'ai fait mienne l'analyse de Gramsci: le pouvoir se gagne par les idées. C'est la première fois qu'un homme de droite assume cette bataille-là*' ('In the end, I agree wholeheartedly with Gramsci's analysis: power is won by ideas. It is the first time that a right-wing leader has undertaken this battle') (Sarkozy 2009b). Given the weakness of the French Socialist party, in terms of leadership, values and programmatic offering (Grunberg 2009), Sarkozy's task may be facilitated. A stronger extreme-left is electorally more problematic for the PS than it is for the UMP. With an *ouverture* ranging from the PS to the ultra-conservative Villieristes, the most potent political opposition to the president is more likely to come from the UMP's own ranks.

If the political opposition has been partly tamed, social conflicts are still rife. Sarkozy famously declared in July 2008 that '*désormais, quand il y a une grève en France, personne ne s'en aperçoit*'. (From now on, every time there is a strike in France, no one notices) and it is true that the introduction in July 2007 of the minimum service law in public transport and schools has contributed to limiting the immediate impact of some social movements (Guiral 2008). Rather than the number of demonstrations or the intensity of strikes, what is remarkable is the radicalisation of social movements, often outside the remit of established trade unions. Facing redundancy, a number of French factory workers have threatened to blow up their factory, sequestrated their bosses or vandalised public buildings. Used as a way to attract media attention, it reveals the difficulty that French trade unions have in leading social protests and managing negotiations (Roux 2009). Such movements remain fairly unknown in other countries and even if they do not represent the majority of social conflicts, they nevertheless convey a radicalisation rather than a normalisation of social relations. They also highlight the fact that Sarkozy's electoral pledge to give people the opportunity 'to work more to earn more' is particularly difficult to honour during an economic recession.

It may be too early to evaluate the extent to which the Sarkozy presidency represents a *rupture* with the French model and whether such *rupture* can be qualified as *tranquille* or not. A series of specific policies seems to point towards a clear break with the past. Sarkozy's initial willingness to challenge the 'French model' and explicit intention to smash a number of traditions and dogma point indeed towards a *rupture tranquille*. Does this herald the end of the French exception? In some limited cases, new policies have been introduced to respond to traditional clientelist demands, which must be immediately satisfied after an electoral victory: the introduction of *le bouclier fiscal* (tax shield) falls into this category. Conversely, continuity rather than rupture may well prevail. Policies which have been initiated by previous administrations are given a sharper political presentation and a higher level of media exposure: the level of attention paid to political communication often represents the major innovation. There is no doubt that, depending on the policy sectors under review and the yardstick used to evaluate the nature and extent of change, the diagnostic will differ. For instance, in terms of European and foreign policy, it is not easy to evaluate whether Sarkozy's initiatives are innovative because they mark a return to a more orthodox Gaullist tradition or because they accelerate France's normalisation. In any case, a stronger leadership at the helm of the state does not necessarily lead to an increased ability to deliver the substantial *ruptures* Sarkozy promised during his campaign, especially in an adverse financial and economic environment. Indeed, in another national context, R.A.W. Rhodes (2007) has shown that in Britain the centralisation of power at No. 10 Downing Street, under the 'Blair presidency', did not always lead to policy making success, despite a clear policy agenda. Rather, it revealed the resilience of a complex and opaque policy making process which remained highly fragmented. Sarkozy's hyperpresidency may well serve to mask the fact that under such *tournis*, there is no major *tournant* (Mongin, Fœssel and Padis 2007: 9). On the other hand, for Nick Hewlett, Sarkozy's strategy reflects developments which are at work in many other advanced capitalist countries. It is a highly ideological enterprise: the personalisation and presidentialisation of power and the trivialisation of politics are now the usual and common traits of a capitalist society. *Le Sarkozysme* is thus not an exceptional phenomenon, even if its political form is partly shaped by France's political culture. Its enduring effects on what constitutes the French exception – polarisation, role of the state, republican model and universal mission – as much as its ability to manipulate the discourses about the French exception – its archaism and its exemplarity – should be evaluated in the long term.

Notes

1 Charon offers as a translation, '*docteurs folimage*'.
2 And to a lesser extent, to challenge part of his own majority, as is the case with the law extending the possibility to work on Sunday (*le travail dominical*) or the HADOPI law (Haute Autorité pour la Diffusion des Œuvres et la Protection des droits sur Internet) aimed at protecting artists against the abusive downloading of their work.

Bibliography

Adams, D.K. and van Minnen, C. (eds) 1994. *Reflections on American Exceptionalism* (Keele: Ryburn).

Adda, J. and Smouts, M.C. 1989. *La France face au sud. Le miroir brisé* (Paris: Karthala).

Addi, L. 2006. En Algérie, du conflit armé à la violence sociale, *Le Monde diplomatique*, April, pp. 6–7.

Aeschimann, E. and Riche, P. 2006. De Saint-Simon à la République, *Libération*. 18 September. www.liberation.fr/grand-angle/010160670-de-saint-simon-a-la-republique

Alba, R. and Foner, N. 2009. 'Entering the precincts of power: Do national differences matter for immigrant-minority political participation?', in J. Hochschild and J. Mollenkopf (eds) *Bringing Outsiders In: Transatlantic Perspectives on Immigrant Political Incorporation* (Ithaca: Cornell University Press).

Algalarrondo, H. 2008. Conseillers, amis, experts ou fidèles du président. Le vrai gouvernement de la France, *Nouvel Observateur*, November 20.

Allemand, S. 2004. 'Une France en déclin?', in *L'Exception française: mythe ou réalité?*, special issue no. 46 of *Sciences humaines*. www.scienceshumaines.com/-0aune-france-en-declin–0a_fr_13704.html

Alternatives économiques 2009. Le modèle français face à la crise, July, no. 282.

Anderson, P. 2004a. Dégringolade, *London Review of Books,* 2 September.

Anderson, P. 2004b. Union sucrée, *London Review of Books,* 23 September.

Anderson, P. 2005. *La Pensée tiède. Un regard critique sur la culture française,* followed by Nora P. *La Pensée rechauffée* (Paris: Seuil).

Andolfatto, D. 2005. *PCF de la mutation à la liqudation* (Paris: Editions du Rocher).

Anwar, M. 2001. The participation of ethnic minorities in British politics, *Journal of Ethnic and Migration Studies* 27(3): 533–49.

Appleton, A. 2009. 'France the unexceptional', in Appleton, A., Brouard, S. and Mazur, A. (eds) *The French Fifth Republic at Fifty* (London: Palgrave Macmillan).

Armingeon, K. 2006. *The Politics of Post-Industrial Welfare States: Adapting Post-War Social Policies to New Social Risks* (London: Routledge).

Artufel, C. and Duroux, M. 2006. *Nicolas Sarkozy et la communication* (Paris: Edition Pepper).

ATTAC 2005. *Cette «Constitution» qui piège l'Europe* (Paris: Éditions Mille et Une Nuits).

Aubry, E. and Pleynet, M. 2006. *Pas de deux à l'Élysée* (Paris: Éditions Héloïse d'Ormesson).

Audier, S. 2008. *La Pensée anti-68. Essai sur une restructuration intellectuelle* (Paris: La Découverte).

Auffray, A. and Guiral, A. 2007. A quoi sert Fillon? Le Premier ministre cherche à exister au côté d'un Président hyperactif, *Libération*, 28 June.

Austin, J.L. 1975. *How to Do Things with Words* (Oxford: Clarendon Press).

Bacqué, R. 2006. Pour qui roulent les déclinologues?, *Le Monde,* 24 February.

Bacqué, R. and Chemain, A. 2008. Et Sarkozy zappa la pub de la télévision publique, *Le Monde*, 12 February.

Badinter, R. 2008. Non à l'hyperprésidence, *Le Monde*, 20 July.

Badiou, A. 2008. *Sarkozy. De quoi est-il le nom?* (Paris: Lignes).

Baehr, P. (ed.) 2004. *Dictatorship in History and Theory: Bonapartism, Caesarism and Totalitarianism* (Cambridge: Cambridge University Press).

Bahri, F. 2008, May 14. L'Algérie et le Maroc se disputent l'autorité sur les musulmans de France. Retrieved February 14 2009 from www.afrik.com/article14281.html

Bainbrigge, S. 2001. L'exception française? Utopia and dystopia in the debate on parity, *French Cultural Studies*, 12: 193–206.

Bancel, N., Blanchard, P. and Vergès, F. (2003) *La République coloniale: essai sur une utopie*. (Paris: Albin Michel).

Barou, J. 1994. *Processus de segregation et ethnicisation de l'espace* (Paris: final report to DPM, October).

Barret-Kriegel, B. 1989. *La République incertaine* (Paris: Presses Universitaires de France).

Baubérot, J. 2004. *Laïcité 1905–2005 – entre passion et raison* (Paris: Seuil).

Baubérot, J. 2007. Existe-t-il une religion civile républicaine?, *French Politics, Culture and Society,* 25(2): 3–18.

Bavarez, N. 2003a. Le déclin français?, *Commentaire*, no. 102, Summer, pp. 299–315.

Bavarez, N. 2003b. *La France qui tombe, Un constat clinique du déclin français* (Paris: Perrin).

Bavarez, N. 2006 *Nouveau monde, Vieille France* (Paris: Perrin).

Baverez, N. 2007. *Que faire? Agenda pour 2007* (Paris: Perrin).

Beaugé F. and Bernard, P. 2005. Le général Schmitt est à nouveau accusé de torture en Algérie, *Le Monde,* 19 March.

Beauhair, J. 2008. *Olivier Besancenot* (Paris: Respublica).

Bedouelle, G. and Costa, J-P. 1998. *Les laïcités à la française* (Paris: PUF).

Beer, S.H. and Ulam, A.B. 1958. *Patterns of Government: The Major Political Systems of Europe* (New York: Random House).

Begag, A. 2007. *Le Mouton dans la baignoire* (Paris: Fayard).

Bell, D. 2002. *French Politics Today* (Manchester: Manchester University Press).

Bell, D. 2002. *Presidential Power in the Fifth Republic* (Oxford: Berg).

Bell, D. 2005. 'French communism: An exceptional orthodoxy', in E. Godin and T. Chafer (eds) *The French Exception*, pp. 47–60 (Oxford: Berghahn).

Bélot, C. and Cautrès, B. 2004. 'L'Europe invisible, mais omniprésente', in B. Cautrès and N. Mayer (eds) *Le nouveau désordre électoral: Les leçons du 21 avril 2002*, pp. 119–41 (Paris: Presses de Sciences Po).

Benoît, B. 1997. *Social-Nationalism: An Anatomy of French Euroscepticism* (Aldershot: Ashgate).

Bergounioux, A. and Werkoff-Leloup, C. 2006. *Les Habits neufs de la droite française* (Paris: Plon).

Bertrand, R. 2006. *Mémoires d'empire. La controverse autour du 'fait colonial'* (Bellecombe-en Bauges: Editions du croquant).

Besancenot, O. 2003. *Révolution! 100 mots...* (Paris: Flammarion).

Bezat, J.-M. and Chombeau, C. 2001. Droite et gauche s'opposent à Jean-Marie Messier sur l'exception culturelle, *Le Monde*, December 29.

Bezat, J.-M. 2003. Sarkozy, le préfet musulman et le philosophe, *Le Monde*, 17 March.

Blendon, R.J., Schoen, C., DesRoches, C.M., Osborn, R., Scoles, K.L. and Zapert, K., 2002. Inequities in health care: A five-country survey, *Health Affairs*, 21(3): 189–91.

Body-Gendrot, S. 1993. *Ville et Violence: l'irruption de nouveaux acteurs* (Paris: PUF).

Bonoli, G. 2000. *The Politics of Pension Reform. Institutions and Policy Change in Western Europe* (Cambridge: Cambridge University Press).

Bossuat, G. 2003. French development aid and co-operation under de Gaulle, *Contemporary European History*, 12(4): 431–56.

Bossuat, G. 2005. Faire l'Europe sans défaire la France (Brussels: Peter Lang).

Bourdieu, P. 1991. *Language and Symbolic Power,* translated by Gino Raymond and Matthew Adamson (Cambridge: Polity Press).

Bové, J. 2007. *Un autre monde est en marche.* Accessed 10 October 2008 at www.fluctuat.net/3938-Programme-de-Jose-Bove.

Bowen, J.R. 2007. *Why the French Don't Like Headscarves: Islam, the State and Public Space* (Princeton: Princeton University Press).

Bozo, F. 1995. 'France and security in the new Europe: Between the Gaullist legacy and the search for a new model', in G. Flynn (ed.) *Remaking the Hexagon: The New France in the New Europe*, pp. 213–32 (Boulder, Colorado: Westview Press).

Bozo, F. 2008. *Alliance Atlantique: la fin de l'exception française?* (Document de travail) (Paris: Fondation pour l'innovation politique)

Bozzo, A. 2005. 'Islam et République: une longue histoire de méfiance', in P. Blanchard *et al* (eds) *La Fracture coloniale*, pp. 75–82 (Paris: La Découverte).

Brochier, J.-C. and Delouche, H. 2000. *Les nouveaux sans culottes* (Paris: Grasset).

Brossat, A. 2007. *Bouffon Impérator* (Paris: Politis).

Brouard, S., Appleton, A. and Mazur, A. (eds) 2008. *French Fifth Republic at Fifty* (Basingstoke: Palgrave Macmillan).

Bruckner, P. 1990. *La Mélancolie démocratique* (Paris: Seuil).

Brunel, S. 1993. *Le Gaspillage de l'aide publique* (Paris: Seuil).

Büchs, M. 2007. *New Governance in European Social Policy. The Open Method of Coordination* (Basingstoke: Palgrave).

Bui, D. 2008. Un président noir, vous imaginez! Cherche Obama français désespérément...*Le Nouvel Observateur*, No. 2274, 5 June.

Cabanne, P. 1981. *Le Pouvoir culturel sous la Ve République* (Paris: Olivier Orban).

Calvet, L.-J. 1998. *Language Wars and Linguistic Politics,* translated by Michel Petheram (Oxford: Oxford University Press).

Caron, M. 1990. Immigration, intégration et solidarité, *Regards sur l'actualité*, No. 166, December.

Caron, R. 1989. *L'Etat et la culture* (Paris: Economica).

Carton, D. 2003. *Bien entendu... c'est off* (Paris: Albin Michel).

Cerny, P. 1980. 'The new rules of the game', in P. Cerny and M. Schain (eds) *French Politics and Public Policy*, pp. 26–47 (New York: St. Martin's).

Cesaire, A. 2000. *Discourse on Colonialism,* translated by Joan Pinkham (New York: Monthly Review Press).

Cesari, J. 2005a. 'Introduction', in J. Cesari and S. McLoughlin (eds) *European Muslims and the Secular State*, pp. 1–7 (UK and US: Ashgate).

Cesari, J. 2005b. 'Islam, secularism and multiculturalism after 9/11: A transatlantic comparison', in J. Cesari and S. McLoughlin (eds) *European Muslims and the Secular State*, pp. 39–51 (UK and US: Ashgate).

Chafer, T. 2002. Franco-African relations: No longer so exceptional?, *African Affairs*, 101: 343–63.

Chafer, T. 2005. Chirac and 'la Françafrique': No longer a family affair, *Modern and Contemporary France*, 13(1): 7–23.

Chafer, T. 2008. 'From confidence to confusion: Franco-African relations in the era of globalisation', in M. Maclean and J. Szarka (eds) *France on the World Stage: Nation State Strategies in the Global Era*, pp. 37–56 (Basingstoke: Palgrave Macmillan).

Chafer, T. and Evans, M. 2008. 'France and her African empire: The second world war and the colonial imagination', in M. Riera and G. Schaffer (eds) *The Lasting War*, pp. 248–68 (Basingstoke: Palgrave Macmillan).

Chambeau, C. 2005. Le Pen dans le texte des autres, *Le Monde*, 27 December.

Charbonneau, B. 2008a. *France and the New Imperialism* (Aldershot: Ashgate).

Charbonneau, B. 2008b. Dreams of empire. France, Europe and the new interventionism in Africa, *Modern and Contemporary France*, 16(3): 279–95.

Chardon, J.-M. and Lensel, D. (eds) 1998. *La Pensée unique. Le vrai procès* (Paris: Editions Economica).

Charon, J.-M. 2004. Les Spin docteurs au centre du pouvoir, *Revue internationale et stratégique*, 56(4): 99–108.

Chemin, A. and Catalano, G. 2005. *Une famille au secret* (Paris: Stock).

Chesnault, V. 1990. Que faire de l'Afrique?, *Le Monde*, 28 February.

Chevènement, J-P. 1992. *Une certaine idée de la République m'amène à…* (Paris: Albin Michel).

Chevènement, J-P. 2006. *La faute de M. Monnet* (Paris: Fayard).

Chipman, J. 1989. *French Power in Africa* (Oxford: Blackwell).

Chirac, B. 2001. *Conversation: Entretiens avec Patrick de Carolis* (Paris: Plon).

Chirac, J. 2004. Discours de M. Jacques Chirac, Président de la République à l'occasion du 60ème anniversaire du Débarquement en Provence, 15 August, Accessed 12 June 2009 from: www.elysee.fr/elysee/francais/interventions/ discours_et_declarations/2004/aout/discours_de_m_jacques_chirac_president_de_la_republique_a_l_occasion_du_60eme_anniversaire_du_debarquement_en_provence.22053.html

Choisel, F. 1987. *Bonapartisme et Gaullisme* (Paris: Albatros).

Chopin, T. 2008. *France-Europe. Le Bal des Hypocrites* (Paris: Éditions Saint-Simon).

Clancy-Smith, J. 1998. 'Islam, gender and the making of French Algeria, 1830–1962', in J. Clancy-Smith and F. Gouda (eds) *Domesticating the Empire: Race, Gender and Family Life in French and Dutch Colonialisms*, pp. 154–74 (Charlottesville and London: University of Virginia Press).

Clift, B. 2005. 'Dyarchic presidentialisation in presidential polity: The French V republic', in T. Poguntke, P. Webb (eds) *The Presidentialisation of Parliamentary Democracies*, pp. 221–41 (Oxford: OUP).

Cohen, R. 1997. France vs US: Warring versions of capitalism, *New York Times*, 20 October.

Cole, A. 1998. *French Politics and Society* (London: Prentice Hall).

Collard, S. 2006. 'Une Europe Franglaise?', in Cahiers Charles V. (Université Paris 7 – Denis Diderot) no. 41, special issue on 'La Grande Bretagne et l'Europe', pp. 205–33.

Colley, L. 1992. *Britons: Forging the Nation* (New Haven, CT: Yale University Press).

Colombani, J-M. 2009. Survivance de l'anti-americanisme, *Revue internationale et stratégique*, 74(2): 15–17.

Colombani, J.-M. 1998. *Le Résident de la République* (Paris: Stock).

Conseil d'Etat 1987. *December 8, 1978 (G.I.S.T.I.., C.F.D.T., et C.G.T.-Rec. Lebon)*.

Cornudet, C. 2009. Sarkozy érige la présidence française de l'Union européenne en modèle, *Les Echos*, 5 May.

Corsani, A. and Lazzarato, M. 2008. *Intermittents et précaires* (Paris: Editions Amsterdam).

Costa-Lascoux, J. 1989. *De l'immigré au citoyen* (Paris: La Documentation Française).

Council of the European Union 2004. *Justice and Home Affairs, Press Release*, 2618th Council Meeting, 19 November 2004, pp. 19–24.

Cour des comptes 2007. *Rapport public annuel* (Paris: Cour des Comptes/La Documentation Française).

Courtois, S. and Lazar, M. 1995. *Histoire du Parti communiste français* (Paris: PUF).

Crespy, A. 2008. Dissent over the european constitutional treaty within the French Socialist party: Between response to anti-globalization protest and intra-party tactics, *French Politics*, 6(1): 23–44.

Creton, L., Palmer, M. and Sarrazac, J.-P. 2005. *Arts du spectacle, métiers et industries culturelles. Penser la généalogie* (Paris: La Sorbonne Nouvelle).

Crettiez, X. and Sommier, I. 2002. *La France rebelle* (Paris: Michalon).

Cross, G. 1983. *Immigrant Workers in Industrial France: The Making of a New Laboring Class* (Philadelphia, PA: Temple University Press).

Crozier, M. 1970. *La société bloquée* (Paris: Editions du Seuil).

Crozier, M. 1964. *The Bureaucratic Phenomenon* (Chicago: The University of Chicago Press).

Culpepper, P.D., Hall, P.A. and Palier, B. (eds) 2006. *Changing France: The Politics that Markets Make* (Basingstoke: Palgrave Macmillan).

Cumming, G. 2001. *Aid to Africa* (Aldershot: Ashgate).

D'Epenoux, C. and Hoche, C. 1979. Giscard l'Africain, *L'Express*, 22 December, pp. 34–8.

Dakhi, L., Maris, B., Sue, R. and Vigarello, G. 2007. *Gouverner par la peur* (Paris: Fayard).

Damas, L.-G. 1977. 'Hoquet', in L.S. Senghor (ed.) *Anthologie de la poésie nègre et malgache*, pp. 15–17 (Paris: PUF).

Dauncey, H. and Le Guern, P. (eds) 2008. *Stéréo. Sociologie comparée des musiques populaires, France/UK* (Paris: IRMA/Mélanie Séteun).

Debray, R. 1989. *Que vive la République* (Paris: Odile Jacob).

Delwitt, P. (ed.) 2004. *Où va la social-démocratie européenne?* (Brussels: ULB).

Dewhurst, M. 2007. *The Boundaries of the Republic: Migrant Rights and the Limits of Universalism in France, 1918–1940* (Stanford: Stanford University Press).

Diop, C.A. 1979. *Nations nègres et culture*, vol. 2 (Paris: Présence Africaine).

Diop, C.A. 1974. *The African Origin of Civilization: Myth or Reality*, translated by Mercer Cook (New York: Lawrence Hill Books).

Dolek, C. 2008. From Françafrique to Eurafrique with Sarkozy: Not much of a difference?, *Journal of Turkish Weekly*, 11 March, accessed 23 August 2008 from www.turkishweekly.net/

Domain, V. 2006. *Entre le cœur et la raison* (Paris: Fayard).

Drake, H. 2005. 'Perspectives on French relations with the European Union: An introduction', in H. Drake (ed.) *French Relations with the European Union*, pp. 1–20 (London: Routledge).

Drake, H. 2006. France: An EU founder member cut down to size?, *Journal of European Integration*, 28(1): 89–105.

Drake, H., 2009. What difference did a (French) Presidency Make? *FPEU08 and EU Foreign Policy, CFSP Forum*, 7(1): 1–4, accessed 16 February 2009, at www.fornet.info

Drake, H. and Lequesne, C. 2009. 'France: From rejection to return?', in M. Carbone (ed.) *National Politics and European Integration: From the Constitution to the Lisbon Treaty* (Cheltenham: Edward Elgar).

Dubois, J.P. 2008. *Une démocratie asphyxiée. L'état des droits de l'homme en France, édition 2008* (Paris: La Découverte).

Duhamel, A. 1985. *Le Complexe d'Astérix* (Paris: Gallimard).

Duhamel, A. 1989. *Les Habits neufs de la politique* (Paris: Flammarion).

Duhamel, A. 2005. Le non, complice de l'Europe libérale, *Libération*, 23 March.

Duhamel, A. 2009. *La marche consulaire* (Paris: Plon).

Duhamel, A., Duhamel, O. and Jaffré, J. 1984. Consensus et dissensus français, *Le Débat*, 30: 4–26.

Duhamel, O. 1993. *Aux urnes, citoyens!* (Paris: Éditions du May).

Dupin, E. 2007. *A Droite toute* (Paris: Fayard).

Dupont-Aignan, N. 2008. *Le Coup d'État simplifié* (Paris: Éditions du Rocher).

Dupuy, F., Thoenig, J.-C. 1985. *L'Administration en miettes* (Paris: Fayard).

Duverger, M. 1988. *La Nostalgie de l'impuissance* (Paris: Albin Michel).

Elgie, R. 2001. 'Cohabitation: Divided government french-style', in R. Elgie (ed.) *Divided Government in Comparative Perspective*, pp. 106–26 (Oxford: Oxford University Press).

Erhel, C., Mandin, L. and Palier, B. 2005. 'The leverage effect. The open method of coordination in France', in J. Zeitlin, P. Pochet (eds) *The Open Method of Coordination in Action*, pp. 217–48 (Brussels: Peter Lang).

Espaces 89, 1985. *L'Identité française* (Paris: Editions Tiercé).

Esping-Andersen, G. 1990. *The Three Worlds Of Welfare Capitalism* (Princeton: Princeton University Press).

Eurobarometer 2005. The European constitution: Post-referendum survey in France, *Flash Eurobarometer* 171 (June). Accessed 1 October 2008 at europa.eu.int/comm/public_opinion/flash/fl171_en.pdf

European Union 2007. *Employment in Europe Report. Annex 2: Key Employment Indicators* (Brussels: EU).

Exit Poll 2005. *Le Monde*, 30 May.

Fanon, F. 1970. *Toward the African Revolution*, translated by Haakon Chevalier (Harmondsworth: Penguin).

Fanon, F. 1967. *Black Skin, White Masks*, translated by Charles Lam Markmann (New York: Grove Press).

Farbiaz, P. and Mamère, N. 2009. *Petits Arrangements entre amis* (Paris: Jean-Claude Gawsewitch).

Farchy, J. 1999. *La fin de l'exception culturelle* (Paris: CNRS Editions).

Fauroux, R. 1986. Interview by Patrick Fridenson, 'L'industriel et le fonctionnaire', *Le Débat*, 40: 159–84.

Feldblum, M. 1993. Paradoxes of ethnic politics: the case of Franco-Maghrebis in France, *Ethnic and Racial Studies*, Vol. 16, No. 1, January 1993, pp. 52–74.

Femme en burqa: Ni putes ni soumises et le FN satisfaits de l'arrêt du Conseil d'Etat. 2008, July 13. *Le Monde*.

Ferenczi, T. 1989. *Défense du consensus* (Paris: Flammarion).

Ferrari, S. 2005. 'The secularity of the state and the shaping of Muslim representative organisations in western europe', in J. Cesari and S. McLoughlin (eds) *European Muslims and the Secular State*, pp. 11–23 (UK and US: Ashgate).

Fetzer, J.S. and Soper, J.C. 2005. *Muslims and the State in Britain, France and Germany* (Cambridge: Cambridge University Press).

Finkielkraut, A. 1987. *La défaite de la pensée* (Paris: Gallimard).

Floch, J. 2004. *Rapport d'information sur la présence et l'influence de la France dans les institutions européennes* (Paris, Assemblée nationale, 12 May, rapport no. 1594), retrieved 1 January 2010 from www.assemblee-nationale.fr/12/europe/rap-info/i1594.asp

Flood, C. 2005. 'French Euroscepticism and the politics of indifference', in H. Drake (ed.) *French Relations with the European Union*, pp. 42–63 (London: Routledge).

Flynn, G. 1995. 'French identity and post-Cold War Europe', in G. Flynn (ed.) *Remaking the Hexagon. The New France in the New Europe*, pp. 213–32 (Boulder, Colorado: Westview Press).

Forcari, C. 2007. Le Pen, plus dure est la chute. *Libération*, 23 April.

Formesyn, R. 1984. 'Europeanisation and the pursuit of national interests', in V. Wright (ed.) *Continuity and Change in France*, pp. 219–43 (London: Allen and Unwin).

Fourquet, J. 2007. *L'échec de Jean-Marie Le Pen à la présidentielle de 2007: les causes d'une hémorragie*. Accessed: 28 June 2007, from www.cevipof.msh-paris.fr/bpf/analyses/Fourquet_Le%20pen2007.pdf

Fourquet, J. 2008. 'L'Érosion électorale du lepénisme', in P. Perrineau (ed.) *Le vote de rupture*, pp. 213–35 (Paris: Les Presses de Sciences).

Fourquet, J. 2009. 1995–2007: Une redefinition géographique du clivage gauche-droite, *Problèmes Politques et Sociaux*, 958, pp. 38–40.

Frank, T. 1998. Vue des Etats-Unis. Cette impardonnable exception française, *Le Monde diplomatique*, April.

Fressoz, F. 2009. François Bayrou se pose en procureur du sarkozysme, *Le Monde*, 30 April.

Fries, F. 2004. *Propositions pour développer l'industrie du jeu vidéo en France* (Paris: Ministère de l'industrie/Documentation française).

Friot, B. 2004. 'Resource regime reforms and worker status', in B. Clasquin, N. Moncel, M. Harvey and B. Friot (eds) *Wage and Welfare: New Perspectives on Employment and Social Rights in Europe*, pp. 75–100 (Brussels: Peter Lang).

Front National 2007. *Programme de Gouvernement de Jean-Marie Le Pen*. Accessed on 13 January 2008 at: www.lepen2007.fr/pdf/Programmejmlp2007.pdf

Fumaroli, M. 1991. *L'Etat culturel: essai sur une religion moderne* (Paris: Editions Fallois).

Furet, F. 1978. *Penser la Révolution française* (Paris: Gallimard).

Furet, F. 1983. La Révolution dans l'imaginaire politique français, *Le Débat*, 26: 173–81.

Furet, F., Julliard, J. and Rosanallon, P. 1988. *La République de centre. La fin de l'exception française* (Paris: Calmann-Lévy).

Fysh, P. and Wolfreys, J. (2003). *The Politics of Racism in France* (Basingstoke: Palgrave Macmillan).

Gassama, M. 2008. 'Le piège infernal', in M. Gassama (ed.) *L'Afrique répond à Sarkozy: Contre le discours de Dakar*, pp. 13–52 (Paris: Philippe Rey).

Gattegno, H., 2006. *L'irresponsable* (Paris: Stock).

Gauchet, M. 1985. *Le Désenchantement du monde* (Paris: Gallimard).

Gauchet, M. 1998. *La religion dans la démocratie. Parcours de la laïcité* (Paris: Gallimard).

Gauzy, F. 1998. *L'Exception allemande* (Paris: Armand Colin).

Geddes, A. 2003. *The Politics of Migration and Immigration in Europe* (London: Sage).

Gellner, E. and Ionescu, G. (eds) 1969. *Populism* (London: Macmillan).

Genestar, A. 2008. *Expulsion* (Paris: Bernard Grasset).

Ghevontian, R. 2009. La révision de la Constitution et le Président de la République: l'hyperprésidentialisation n'a pas eu lieu, *Revue française de droit constitutionnel*, 77(1): 119–33.

Giddens, A. 2007. *Europe in the Global Age* (Cambridge: Polity Press).

Giesbert, F.-O. 2006. *La Tragédie du président* (Paris: Flammarion).

Gildea, R. 1994. *The Past in French History* (London: Yale UP).

Girardet, R. 1993. Des Français en terre algérienne 1830–1962, *Historia*, 556, pp. 76–84.

Glissant, E. 2003. 'The French language in the face of Creolization', in T. Stovall, J. Van Den Abbeele (eds) *French Civilization and its Discontents: Nationalism, Colonialism, Race*, pp. 105–14 (Oxford: Lexington Books).

Godin, E. 1996. Le néo-liberalise à la française: une exception?, *Modern and Contemporary France*, ns 4, 1, pp. 61–70.

Godin, E. and Chafer, J. 2005. 'Introduction', in E. Godin and T. Chafer (eds) *The French Exception*, pp. xiii–xxiv (Oxford: Berghahn).

Godin, E. and Chafer, T. 2005. *The French Exception* (Oxford: Berghahn).

Gordon, P.H. and Meunier, S. 2001. Globalisation and French cultural identity, *French Politics, Culture and Society*, 19(1): 22–41.

Gorrillot, B. 2008. Francis Ponge et l'exception française: une politique gaullienne de l'écriture, *Contemporary French and Francophone Studies*, 12(3): 403–12.

Grillo, R.D. 1985. *Ideologies and Institutions in Urban France* (London: Cambridge University Press).

Grossman, E. 2007. Introduction. France and the EU: From opportunity to constraint, *Journal of European Public Policy* 14(7): 983–91.

Grunberg, G., Mayer, N. and Sniderman, P. (eds) 2002. *La démocratie à l'épreuve* (Paris: Presses de sciences Po).

Grunberg, G. 2009. Le danger qui guette le PS, c'est que l'on n'attende plus rien de lui, qu'on ne l'écoute plus, *Le Monde*, 27 July.

Guaino, H. 2009. L'audit du modèle français, *L'Expansion*, 1 June.

Guénif-Souilamas, N. 2006. The other French Exception: Virtuous Racism and the war of the sexes in postcolonial France, *French Politics, Culture and Society* 24(3): 23–41.

Gueye, A. 2001. *Les intellectuels africains en France* (Paris: L'Harmattan).

Guillot, J.-P. 2004. *Pour une politique de l'emploi dans le spectacle vivant, le cinéma et l'audiovisuel* (Paris: Ministère de la culture et de la communication/ Documentation française).

Guiral, A. 2008. Sarkozy décrète la grève invisible et nargue les syndicats, *Libération*, 7 July.

Guyomarch, A., Machin, H., Hall, P. and Hayward, J. 2001. *Developments in French Politics 2* (Basingstoke: Palgrave).

Guyomarch, A., Machin, H. and Ritchie, E. 1998. *France and the European Union* (Basingstoke: Macmillan).

Hague, R. and Harrop, M. 2001. *Comparative Government and Politics* (Basingstoke: Palgrave).

Hainsworth, P. 2006. France says no: The 29 May 2005 referendum on the European constitution, *Parliamentary Affairs*, 59(1): 98–117.

Hainsworth, P., O' Brien, C. and Mitchell, P. 2004. 'Defending the nation: The politics of Euroscepticism on the French right', in R. Harmsen and M. Spiering (eds) *Euroscepticism: Party Politics, National Identity and European Integration*, pp. 37–58 (Amsterdam: Rodopi).

Hainsworth, P. 2008. *The Extreme Right in Western Europe* (London: Routledge).

Halimi, S. 2005. *Les nouveaux chiens de garde* (Paris: Raisons d'Agir).

Hall, P.A. 2006. 'Introduction: The politics of social change in France', in P.D. Culpepper *et al*, *Changing France. The Politics that Markets Make*, pp. 1–26 (Basingstoke: Palgrave).

Hamon, H. and Rotman, P. 1982. *La Deuxième gauche: Histoire intellectuelle et politique de la CFDT* (Paris: Eds Ramsay).

Hare, G. 2003. 'Popular music on French radio and television', in H. Dauncey and S. Cannon (eds) *Popular Music in France: from Chanson to Techno*, pp. 57–76 (Aldershot: Ashgate).

Hargreaves, A. 1995. *Immigration, 'Race' and Ethnicity in Contemporary France* (London: Routledge).

Harmsen, R. 2005. L'Europe et les partis politiques nationaux: Les leçons d'un «non-clivage», *Revue internationale de politique comparée*, 12(1): 77–94.

Harmsen, R. 2007. 'Is British Euroscepticism still unique? National exceptionalism in comparative perspective', in J. Lacroix and R. Coman (eds) *Les résistances à l'Europe: Cultures nationales, idéologies et stratégies d'acteurs*, pp. 69–92 (Brussels: Éditions de l'Université de Bruxelles).

Harmsen, R. 2008. The evolution of Dutch European discourse: Defining the 'Limits of Europe', *Perspectives on European Society and Politics*, 9(3): 316–41.

Harmsen, R. and Spiering, M. 2004. 'Introduction: Euroscepticism and the evolution of European political debate', in R. Harmsen and M. Spiering (eds) *Euroscepticism: Party Politics, National Identity and European Integration*, pp. 13–35 (Amsterdam: Rodopi).

Hassenteufel, P. 2008. 'Welfare policies and politics', in A. Cole, P. Le Galès and J. Levy (eds) *Developments in French Politics*, pp. 227–42 (Basingstoke, New York: Palgrave Macmillan).

Hassenteufel, P. and Palier, B. 2005. Le trompe-l'oeil de la gouvernance dans l'assurance maladie, *Revue Française d'Administration Publique*, 113, 13–28.

Hauser, P. 2008. Forces politiques et ordre policier, *Lignes*, 25, 21–31.

Hay, C. and Rosamond, B. 2002. Globalisation, european integration and the discursive construction of economic imperatives, *Journal of European Public Policy*, 9(2): 147–67.

Hayward, J. 1988. 'From trend-setter to fashion-follower in Europe: The demise of French exceptionalism', in J. Howorth and G. Ross (eds) *Contemporary France: A Review of Inter-disciplinary Studies*, vol. 2 (London: Frances Pinter).

Hayward, J. 2007. *Fragmented France: Two Centuries of Disputed Identity* (Oxford: Oxford University Press).

Hazan, E. 2007. *Changement de propriétaire. La guerre civile continue* (Paris: Seuil).

Hewlett, N. 2005. 'France and exceptionalism', in E. Godin and T. Chafer (eds) *The French Exception*, pp. 3–15 (Oxford: Berghahn Books).

Hewlett, N. 1998. *Modern French Politics: Analysing Conflict and Consensus since 1945* (Cambridge: Polity Press).

Hewlett, N. 2003. *Democracy in Modern France* (London: Continuum).

Hewlett, N. 2007. Nicolas Sarkozy and the legacy of Bonapartism. The French presidential and parliamentary elections of 2007, *Modern and Contemporary France*, 15(4): 405–23.

Hill, C. and Smith, K. (eds) 2000. *European Foreign Policy: Key Documents* (Oxford: Routledge).

Hoang-Ngoc, L. 2008. *Sarkonomics* (Paris: Grasset).

Hoffmann, S. 1967. 'Heroic leadership: The case of modern France', in L. Edinger, (ed.) *Political Leadership in Industrialized Societies: Studies in Comparative Analysis*, pp. 108–54 (New York: John Wiley).

Hoffmann, S. *et al*, 1963. *In Search of France* (New York: Harper and Row).

Hollifield, J. and Ross, G. 1991. *Searching for the New France* (London: Routledge).

Houziaux, A. (ed.) 2004. *Le voile que cache-t-il?* (Paris: Editions ouvrières).

Howarth, D. and Varouxakis, G. 2003. *Contemporary France: An Introduction to French Politics and Society* (London: Arnold).

Imbert, C. 1989. The end of French exceptionalism, *Foreign Affairs*, 68(4): 48–60.

INSEE 2005. *Enquête emploi de 2005* (Paris: Insee).

IPSOS Public Affairs 2006. *Associated Press International Affairs Poll*, May.

Ivaldi, G. 2006. Beyond France's 2005 referendum on the European constitutional treaty: Second-order model, anti-establishment attitudes and the end of the alternative European utopia, *West European Politics*, 29(1): 47–69.

J.P. 2008. *Une démocratie asphyxiée. L'état des droits de l'homme en France, édition 2008* (Paris: La Découverte).

Jarreau, P. 2008. *La droite contre l'exception française* (Paris: Plon).

Jazouli, A. 1992. *Les années banlieues* (Paris: Seuil).

Jeambar, D. 2005. *Accusé Chirac, levez-vous* (Paris: Éditions du Seuil).

Jobert, B. (ed.) 1994. *Le Tournant néo-libéral en France* (Paris: L'Harmattan).

Julliard, J. 2009. L'impromptu de Versailles, *Le Nouvel Observateur*, 25 June, p. 23.

Julliard, J. 1988. Droite, gauche, centre. L'exception française: fin ou recommencement?, *Le Débat*, no. 52, pp. 4–10. (Reproduced in the 2nd edition of *La République du centre*, 1988, which includes a press review of the book and a postface by Pierre Rosanvallon).

July, S. 1986. *Les Années Mitterrand. Histoire baroque d'une normalisation inachevée* (Paris: Grasset and Fasquelle).

Kahn, J.-F. 1995. *La Pensée unique* (Paris: Fayard).

Kane, C.H. 2001. *L'aventure ambiguë* (Paris: éditions 10/18).

Keenan, J.H. 2006. Security and insecurity in North Africa, *Review of African Political Economy*, 108: 269–96.

Keese, A. 2007. First lessons in Neo-colonialism: The personalisation of relations between African politicians and French officials in sub-Saharan Africa, 1956–66, *Journal of Imperial and Commonwealth History*, 35(4): 593–613.

Keiger, J. 2001. *France and the World since 1870* (London: Arnold).

Kemp, A. 2009. Marianne d'aujourd'hui?: The figure of the *beurette* in contemporary French feminist discourses, *Modern and Contemporary France*, 17(1): 19–33.

Kergoat, J. 1999a. Tribune libre, *L'Humanité*, 30 June.

Kergoat, J. 1999b. La fin de la Fondation Saint-Simon vue par Jacques Kergoat, *L'Humanité*, 30 June.

Kesselman, M. 1991. 'La nouvelle cuisine en politique: la fin de l'exceptionnalité française', in Y. Mény (ed.) *Idéologies, partis politiques et groupes sociaux*, pp. 159–73 (Paris: Presses de la FNSP).

King, A. (ed.) 2002. *Leaders' Personality and the Outcomes of Democratic Elections* (Oxford: Oxford University Press).

Klausen, J. 2005, *The Islamic Challenge: Politics and Religion in Western Europe* (Oxford: Oxford University Press).

Koch. F. 1999 *La vraie nature d'Arlette* (Paris: Seuil).

Kopecký, P. and Mudde, C. 2002. The two sides of Euroscepticism: Party positions on European integration in East Central Europe, *European Union Politics*, 3(3): 297–326.

Kourouma, A. 1997. Écrire en français, parler dans sa langue maternelle, *Études françaises*, 33(1): 115–18.

Kourouma, A. 1981. *Suns of Independence*, translated by A. Adams (London: Heinemann).

Kramer, S.P. 1994. *Does France Still Count? The French Role in the New Europe* (Washington: Praeger, Washington Papers, no. 164).

Kraus, F. and Zumsteeg, S. 2008. Nicolas Sarkozy: la fin de l'état de grâce, IPSOS-Le Point, January. Accessed 10 October 2008 at: www.ipsos.fr/CanalIpsos/articles/2414.asp

Kuhn, R. 2004. 'Vive la différence?' The mediation of politicians' public images and private lives in France, *Parliamentary Affairs*, 57(1): 24–40.

Kuhn, R. 2007. The public and the private in contemporary French politics, *French Cultural Studies*, 18(2): 185–200.

Kuisel, R. 2001. The Gallic rooster crows again: The paradox of French anti-Americanism, *French Politics, Culture and Society*, 19(3): 1–16.

Kvist, J. and Saari, J. (eds) 2007. *The Europeanisation of Social Protection* (Bristol: The Policy Press).

La burqa, obstacle à la nationalité française. 2008, July 12. *Le Figaro*.

Lacroix, J. 2002. Le 'national-souverainisme' en France et en Grande-Bretagne, *Revue internationale de politique comparée*, 9(3): 391–408.

Langellier, J.P. 2005. Une occasion inespérée pour M. Blair et son programme libéral, *Le Monde*, 7 June.

Laurence, J., 2005. From the Elysée salon to the table of the republic: State-Islam relations and the integration of Muslims in France, *French Politics, Culture and Society*, 23(1): 37–64.

Laurence, J., Vaisse, J., 2006. *Integrating Islam: Political and Religious Challenges in Contemporary France* (Washington: Brookings Institution Press).

Laurent, V. (pseudonym of L. Bonnelli) 1998. Enquête sur la Fondation Saint-Simon. Les architectes du social-libéralisme. *Le Monde diplomatique*, pp. 1 & 26–7. September.

Lavabre, M.-C. and Platone, F. 2003. *Que reste-t-il du PCF?* (Paris: Autrement).

Lazar, M. 1999. La gauche communiste plurielle, *Revue Française de Science Politique*, 49(4–5): 605–705.

Lazar, M. 2002. *Le communisme une passion française* (Paris: Perrin).

Lazar, M. 2003. Le discours de la gauche extrême, *Le Débat*, 127 (Nov–Dec), pp. 176–9.

Le Boucher, E. 2005. La bataille de Lisbonne: une Europe 'à l'anglaise' ou 'à la française'?, *Le Monde*, 19 March.

Le Diberder, A. and Le Diberder, F. 2002. *La création de jeux vidéo en France* (Paris: Ministère de l'industrie/Documentation française).

Le Figaro. 2008. Dossier spécial: La présidence française de l'UE, 1st July.

Le Monde Dossiers et Documents, special issue 'Le déclin de la France en débat', 328, February 2004.

Le Monde 2002. 'Dossier spécial: L'exception française', 15 April.

Le Point 1993. 28 August, quoted in J.A. McKesson 1994. Concepts and realities in a multiethnic France, *French Politics and Society*, 12(1): 30.

Le Roy Ladurie, E. 1990. *Entrer dans le XXIe siècle. Essai sur l'avenir de l'identité française* (Paris: La Découverte/La Documentation française).

Lecaussin, N. 2008. *L'absolutisme efficace. Enquête sur la présidence de Nicolas Sarkozy* (Paris: Plon).

Leclerc, H. 2008. 'Sécurité, justice, prisons: éloge de la répression', in J.P. Dubois (ed.) *Une démocratie asphyxiée. L'état des droits de l'homme en France*, édition 2008, pp. 29–44 (Paris: La Découverte).

Lecoutre, D. and Kambudzi, A. 2006. Vers un divorce entre Paris et le continent africain?, *Le Monde diplomatique*, June, pp. 6–7.

Lequesne, C. 2008. *La France dans la nouvelle Europe. Assumer le changement d'échelle* (Paris: Presses de Sciences Po).

Les déclarations de Nicolas Sarkozy sur les religions, Retrieved February 14 2009 from the Toulon *Ligue des droits de l'Homme* website: www.ldh-toulon.net/spip.php?article2474

Levy, J. 2001. Partisan politics and welfare adjustment: The case of France, *Journal of European Public Policy*, 8(2): 265–85.

Levy, J., Cole, A. and Le Galès, P. 2008. 'From Chirac to Sarkozy: A new France?', in A. Cole, P. Le Galès and J. Levy (eds) *Developments in French Politics*, pp. 1–20 (Basingstoke: Palgrave Macmillan).

Levy, J. and Skach, C. 2008. 'The return to a strong presidency', in A. Cole, P. Le Gales and J. Levy (eds) *Developments in French Politics 4*, pp. 111–26 (Basingstoke: Palgrave Macmillan).

Leymarie, P. 2006. Ingérence à l'ancienne au Tchad, *Le Monde diplomatique*, June, pp. 6–7.

Ligue Communiste Révolutionnaire 2006. *Le monde doit changer de base.* Accessed on 23 June 2007 at: www.fluctuat.net/articles/IMG/Manifeste_LCR_fevrier_ 2006.pdf

Ligue des Droits de l'Homme, n.d. 'Histoire et colonies: Le discours de Sarkozy à Dakar', documents accessed 2 February 2010 at www.ldh-toulon.net/spip.php?rubrique131.

Lindenberg, D. 2002. *Rappel à l'ordre: Enquête sur les nouveaux réactionnaires* (Paris: Seuil).

Lipovetsky, G. 1983. *L'Ere du vide* (Paris: Gallimard).

Lipset, S.M. 1996. *American Exceptionalism: A Double-Edged Sword* (New York: Norton).

Looseley, D. 1995. *The Politics of Fun: Cultural Policy and Debate in Contemporary France* (Oxford/Washington: Berg).

Lorcerie, F. 1994. Les ZEP 1990–1993 pour mémoire, *Migrants-formation*, No. 97, June, 1994, 30–48.

Losurdo, D. 2007. *Démocratie ou bonapartisme. Triomphe et décadence du suffrage universel*, translated from the Italian by J.M. Goux (Paris: Le Temps des Cerises).

Lovecy, J. 1999. The end of French exceptionalism, *West European Politics*, 22(4): 205–24.

Lutaud, L. and Dromard, T. 2006. *Les Dessous de la presse people* (Paris: Éditions de la Martinière).

Maclean, M. 2002. *Economic Management and French Business. From De Gaulle to Chirac* (Basingstoke: Palgrave).

Madsen, D.L. 1998. *American Exceptionalism* (Edinburgh: Edinburgh University Press).

Maigret, E. 2008. *L'Hyperprésident* (Paris: Armand Colin).

Majumdar, M. 2005. 'Exceptionalism and universalism: The uneasy alliance in the French speaking world', in Godin, E. and Chafer T. (eds) *The French Exception*, pp. 16–29 (Oxford: Berghahn).

Majumdar, M.A. 2004. 'Exceptionalism and universalism: The uneasy alliance', in E. Godin and T. Chafer (eds) *The French Exception*, pp. 16–29 (Oxford/New York: Berghahn).

Mandin, C. and Palier, B. 2005. 'The politics of pension reform in France: The end of exceptionalism?', in G. Bonoli, T. Shinkawa (eds) *Ageing and Pension Reform Around the World. Evidence from Eleven Countries*, pp. 74–93 (Cheltenham: Edward Elgar).

Marmande, F. 2009. M'sieur l'résident... , *Le Monde*, 1 April.

Martelli, R. 2008. *L'Archipel communiste. Une histoire électorale du PCF* (Paris: Editions Sociales).

Martin, G. 1982. Africa and the ideology of Eurafrica: Neo-colonialism or pan-Africanism?, *Journal of Modern African Studies*, 20(2): 221–38.

Martin, L. 2005. *Le Canard enchaîné* (Paris: Nouveau Monde).

Martucci, F. 2005. La Constitution eurpéenne est-elle libérale?, Fondation Robert Schuman, *Supplément de la Lettre* no. 209, 25th April.

Marx, K. 1968. 'The eighteenth Brumaire of Louis Bonaparte', in F. Engels and K. Marx, *Selected Works*, pp. 96–179 (First published in 1852) (London: Lawrence and Wishart).

Mathy, J.-P. 2008. 'Refonder l'universalisme: Bourdieu, Balibar et l'exception' philosophique française', *Contemporary French and Francophone Studies*, 12(3): 357–64.

Mattelart, A. 2007. *Diversité culturelle et mondialisation* (Paris: La Découverte).

Maus, D. 2005. 'La fin de l'exception constitutionnelle française?', *Revue Politique et Parlementaire*, 107(1034): 103–7.

Mayer, N. 2002. *Ces français qui votent Le Pen* (Paris: Flammarion).

Mayer, N. 2007. Comment Nicolas Sarkozy a rétréci l'électorat Le Pen, *Revue française de science politique*, 57(3/4): 429–45.

Mehl, D. 1996. *La télévision de l'intimité* (Paris: Éditions du Seuil).

Mellah, S. and Rivoire, J.-B. 2005. Enquête sur l'étrange 'Ben Laden du Sahara', *Le Monde diplomatique*, February, pp. 4–5.

Menger, P.-M. 2005. *Les intermittents du spectacle: Sociologie d'une exception* (Paris: Editions EHESS).

Menon, A. 2008. *Europe: The State of the Union* (London: Atlantic Books).

Meny, Y. and Surel, Y. 2002. *Democracies and the Populist Challenge* (Basingstoke: Palgrave Macmillan).

Messier, J.-M. 2001. Vivre la diversité culturelle, *Le Monde,* 10 April.

Métaoui, F. 2005. Après les déclarations de Bouteflika sur les massacres du 8 mai 1945, polémique entre Alger et Paris, *El Watan,* 12 May. Accessed 12 April 2009 from: www.elwatan.com

Michelet, J. 1963. *Histoire de France* (Paris: Editions J'ai Lu).

Midiohouan, G.O. 1994, *Du bon usage de la francophonie: essai sur l'idéologie de la francophonie* (Porto Novo: éditions CNPMS).

Miller, M. 1981. *Foreign Workers in Europe: An Emerging Political Force* (New York: Praeger).

Milner, H. 2006. 'Yes to the Europe I want; No to this one': Some Reflections on France's rejection of the EU constitution, *PS: Political Science and Politics,* 39(2): 257–60.

Milner, S. 2004. 'For an alternative Europe: Euroscepticism and the French left since the Maastricht treaty', in R. Harmsen and M. Spiering (eds) *Euroscepticism: Party Politics, National Identity and European Integration,* pp. 59–82 (Amsterdam: Rodopi).

Milner, S. 2005. 'Protection, reform and political will: France and the European social model', in H. Drake (ed.) *French Relations with the European Union,* pp. 105–23 (London, New York: Routledge).

Milner, S. 2007. Paths to retirement: The French life-course regime and the regulation of older workers' employment, *French Politics,* 5(3): 229–52.

Minc, A. 1994. *La France de l'an 2000* (Commissariat général du Plan. Paris: Editions Odile Jacob).

Missika, J.-L. 2006. *La fin de la télévision* (Paris: Éditions du Seuil).

Mitterrand, F. 1962. *Le Coup d'état permanent* (Paris: Plon).

Modood, T. 2002. 'The place of Muslims in British secular multiculturalism', in N. AlSayyad and M. Castells (eds) *Muslim Europe or Euro Islam: Politics, Culture and Citizenship in the Age of Globalisation,* pp. 113–30 (Maryland: Lexington).

Money, J. 1999. *Fences and Neighbors: The Political Geography of Immigration Control* (Ithaca: Cornell University Press).

Mongin, O., Fœssel, M. and Padis, M-O. 2007. Retour au politique ou nouvelles illusions?, *Esprit,* November, 339, pp. 8–13.

Monterny, E. de. 2009. Je lis 'La Princesse de Clèves', *Le Figaro,* 19 March.

Montesquieu, C.L. Baron de 1961. *De l'esprit des lois* (Paris: Garnier).

Moreau, J. 2003. *Les socialistes français et le mythe révolutionnaire* (Paris: Hachette).

Mossuz-Lavau, J. 2007. *L'argent et nous* (Paris: La Martinière).

Mouvement pour la France 2007. *Un projet pour la France.* Accessed 16 April 2007 at www.pourlafrance.fr/projetpresidentiel.php

Mudimbe, V.Y. 1988. *The Invention of Africa: Gnosis, Philosophy and the Order of Knowledge* (Bloomington: Indiana University Press).

Musso, P. 1999. Saint-Simon libéré, *Libération,* 6 July.

Musso, P. 2008. *Le Sarkoberlusconisme* (Paris: Editions de l'Aube).

National Assembly 2008. *Constitution of 4 October 1958*, accessed 23 January 2009, at: www.assemblee-nationale.fr/english/8ab.asp)

Neveu, E. 2005. Politicians without politics, a polity without citizens: The politics of the chat show in contemporary France, *Modern & Contemporary France*, 13(3): 323–35.

Nielsberg, J. and Sahuc, S. 2006. Le 'sarkozysme', nouvelle étape de la mutation de la droite; synthèse idéologique et adaptation neoconservatrice, *Nouvelle Fondation* (Fondation Gabriel Péri), 1(1): 12–23.

Noiriel, G. 1988. *Le Creuset Francais* (Paris: Editions du Seuil).

Non Socialiste 2005. *Pourquoi au nom de l'Europe, cette fois c'est Non*. Accessed 12 June 2007 at: www.nonsocialiste.fr

Nora, P. 1984–92. *Les Lieux de mémoire*, 3 vols (Paris: Gallimard).

Nord, P. 1955. *L'Eurafrique: notre dernière chance* (Paris: Fayard).

Nougayrède, N. 2008. La fin du gaullisme? *Le Monde*, 6 May.

OECD 2006. *International Migration Outlook* (Washington DC: OECD).

OECD 2005. *Ageing and Employment Policies: France* (Paris: OECD).

OECD 2008a. *Social Expenditure Statistics*. Accessed 28 November 2008 at stats.oecd.org/brandedviewpilot/default.aspx?datasetcode=socx_ref).

OECD 2008b. *Growing Unequal? Income Distribution and Poverty in OECD countries* (Paris: OECD).

Ould Mohamedou, M. 2005. Variation sur l'usage du coup d'Etat en Mauritanie, *Le Monde diplomatique*, November, pp. 8–9.

Ozouf, M. 1983. Peut-on commémorer la Révolution française?, *Le Débat*, 26: 161–72.

Padis, M.O. 2007. Manipulation ou saturation médiatique?, *Esprit*, November, 339: 43–51.

Palier, B. 2006. 'The long goodbye to Bismarck? Changes to the French welfare state', in P.D. Culpepper, P.A. Hall and B. Palier (eds) *Changing France. The Politics that Markets Make*, pp. 107–28 (Basingstoke: Palgrave).

Palier, B. 2008. Les transformations du modèle social français hérité de l'après-guerre, *Modern and Contemporary France*, 16(4): 437–50.

Palier, B. and Petrescu, L. 2007. 'France: Defending our model', in J. Kvist and J. Saari (eds) *The Europeanisation of Social Protection*, pp. 61–76 (Bristol: The Policy Press).

Palou, A. 2007. *Allô, c'est Jean-Edern* (Paris: Michel Lafon).

Parsons, C. 2000. Showing ideas as causes: The origins of the European Union, *International Organization*, 56(1): 47–84.

Parsons, C. 2003. *A Certain Idea of Europe* (Ithaca, New York: Cornell University Press).

Parti Communiste Français 2007. *Quatre engagements pour une politique de gauche qui change vraiment la vie*. Accessed 30 September 2007 at www.pcf.fr/IMG/pdf/brochure_programme_mail.pdf?var_recherche=programme%20pr%C3%A9sidentiel

Pedder, S. 1999. The grand illusion, *The Economist* (US edition), 5 June.

Pelissier, N. and Lacroix, C. (eds) 2008. *Les Intermittents du spectacle: De la culture aux médias* (Paris: L'Harmattan).

Perrineau, P. 2005. 'Le Référendum du 29 mai 2005: L'irrésistible nationalisation d'un vote européen', in P. Perrineau (ed.), *Le vote européen 2004–2005: De l'élargissement au référendum français*, pp. 229–44 (Paris: Presses de Sciences Po).

Pew Global Attitudes Project 2006, July 22.

Pew Research Center 2006. *The Great Divide: How Westerners and Muslims View Each Other* (Washington D.C.: Pew Global Attitude Project, June).

Picq, F. 2002. Parité, la nouvelle exception française, *Modern and Contemporary France,* 10: 13–23.

Pierson, P. (ed.) 2001. *New Politics of the Welfare State* (Oxford: Oxford University Press).

Pingeot, M. 2005. *Bouche cousue* (Paris: Julliard).

Plan B. (2008) La grande Peur des sociaux-libéraux, 20 September. Accessed 13 January 2009 at leplanb.org/La-grande-peur-des-sociaux.html

Platone, F. and Ranger, J. 2000 Les adhérents du Parti communiste français en 1997, *Cahiers du CEVIFOP*, no. 27 (March).

Poguntke, T. and Webb, P. (eds) 2005. *The Presidentialization of Politics* (Oxford: Oxford University Press).

Poulet, B. 1999. A gauche de la gauche, *Le Débat no.* 103 (Jan–Feb), pp. 38–59.

Priest, D. 2005. Help from France key in covert operations, *Washington Post,* 3 July.

Private Lives in France, *Parliamentary Affairs*, 57(1): 24–40.

Ramonet, I. 1995. La pensée unique, *Le Monde diplomatique*, January.

Ramonet, I. 1999/ 2007. *La tyrannie de la communication* (Paris: Gallimard).

Refus de nationalité lié à la burqa: le CFCM regrette l'imprécision de la décision. 2008, July 16. *Agence France Press.*

Rémond, R. 1982. *Les Droites en France* (Paris: Aubier).

Renard, M. 2000. 'L'impossible separation. Administration coloniale, élus et religieux musulmans face à 'l'indépendance du culte musulman' en Algérie (1947–1959)', in *La Guerre d'Algérie au miroir des décolonisations françaises* colloque organisé par la Société française d'Histoire d'Outre-Mer en l'honneur de C.-R. Ageron, pp. 57–86 (Paris: SFHOM).

Renaut, A. and Touraine, A. 2005. *Un débat sur la laicité* (Paris: Stock).

Revault d'Allones, D. 2007. Opération ouverture, *Esprit*, 339, November, pp. 62–71.

Reynié, D. 2005. *Le vertige social nationaliste: La gauche du Non* (Paris: La Table Ronde).

Reynié, D. (ed.) 2007. *L'Extrême gauche, moribonde ou renaissante* (Paris: PUF).

Rhodes, R.A.W. 2007. 'Blair governance', in R. Koch and J. Dixon (eds) *Public Governance and Leadership: Political and Managerial Problems in Making Public Governance Changes the Driver for Re-Constituting Leadership*, pp. 95–116 (Wiesbaden: Deutscher Universitäats-Verlag).

Rigby, B. 1991. *Popular Culture in France: A Study of Cultural Discourse* (London/ New York: Routledge).

RMC Sondage sur la Culture 2007. Accessed 10 October 2008, at http://manifeste. rmc.fr/

Robert, A.-C. 2007. L'Afrique au kärcher, *Le Monde diplomatique*, September, p. 32.

Roberts, H. 2003. *The Battlefield: Algeria 1988–2002. Studies in a Broken Polity* (London/New York: Verso).

Rochefort, F. 2007. Religions, genre et politiques laïques en France, XIXe-XXe siècles, *French Politics, Culture and Society*, 25(2): 19–33.

Rodwin, G.W. 2003. The health care system under French national health insurance: Lessons for health reform in the United States, *American Journal of Public Health*, 93(1): 31–7.

Roger, P. 2002. *L'Ennemi américain: Généalogie de l'antiaméricanisme français* (Paris: Seuil).

Roman, J., Ferry, L. and Mongin, O. 1990. Le retour de l'exception française, *Esprit*, no. 164, September, pp. 65–6.

Rosanvallon, P. 2004. *Le Modèle politique français* (Paris: Seuil).

Ross, G. 2006. Danger, one EU crisis may hide another: Social model anxieties and hard cases, *Comparative European Politics*, 4: 309–30.

Roux, G. 2009. Mouvements radicaux: Peu de chances de généralisation, *Le Figaro*, 30 July.

Roy, O. 2005. *La laïcité face à l'islam* (Paris: Stock).

Royal, S. 2007. *Pacte présidentiel*. Accessed 28 April 2007 www.desirsdavenir.org/index.php?c+sinformer_dossier&id=870&dossier

Rozenberg, O. 2007. 'La faute à Rousseau? Les conditions d'activation de quatre idéologies critiques de la construction européenne en France', in J. Lacroix and C. Ramona (eds) *Les résistances à l'Europe: Cultures nationales, idéologies et stratégies d'acteurs*, pp. 129–53 (Brussels: Éditions de l'Université de Bruxelles).

Rozès, S. 2007. Epuisement d'un compromis social et contournement politique, *La Revue socialiste*, 29.

Sabato, L.J. 2000. *Feeding Frenzy: Attack Journalism and American Politics* (Baltimore: Lanahan).

Saint-Etienne, C. 1992a. *L'Exception française: pour un nouveau modèle démocratique de croissance* (Paris: Armand Colin).

Saint-Etienne, C. 1992b. Moderniser l'exception française, *Le Débat*, no. 71, pp. 66–71.

Sandier, V., Paris, V. and Polton, D. 2004. *Healthcare Systems in Transition: France* (Copenhagen: WTO).

Sarkozy, N. 2006. *Témoignage* (Paris: XO Editions).

Sarkozy, N. 2007a. *Ensemble tout devient possible*. Consulted at: www.sarkozy.fr/lafrance/

Sarkozy, N. 2007b. Le vrai sujet, ce sont les valeurs, *Le Figaro*, 18 April.

Sarkozy, N. 2007c. Discours de Bercy, 29 April 2007. Accessed 13 January 2009 at: www.u-m-p.org/.../discours/nicolas_sarkozy_a_bercy

Sarkozy, N. 2007d. Speech on Sunday 6 May, Salle Gaveau, Paris, *Le Monde*, 8 May, pp. 4–5.

Sarkozy, N. 2007e. Allocution de M. Nicolas Sarkozy, Président de la République, prononcée à l'Université de Dakar le 26 juillet 2007. Accessed 28 April 2009 from www.elysee.fr/elysee/elysee.fr/francais/interventions/2007/juillet/allocution_a_l_universite_de_dakar.79184.html

Sarkozy, N. 2007f. Victory speech, 6 May. Accessed 23 August 2008 from www.u-m-p.org/site/index.php/ump/s_informer/discours/je_serai_le_president

Sarkozy, N. 2007g. Discours de Nicolas Sarkozy devant le Congrès des Etats-Unis, 7 November. Accessed 13 January 2009 at www.elysee.fr/download/index.php?mode=edito&id=23

Sarkozy, N. 2009a. Le modèle français a de nouveau sa chance, *Le Monde*, 24 June.

Sarkozy, N. 2009b. J'ai commis des erreurs, *Le Nouvel Observateur*, 7 July.

Sartre, J.-P. 1977. 'Orphée noir', in L.S. Senghor (ed.) *Anthologie de la poésie nègre et malgache*, pp. ix–xliv (Paris: PUF).

Sauger, N. 2005. Sur la mutation contemporaine des structures de la compétition partisane en France. Les partis de droite face à l'intégration européenne, *Politique européenne*, 16: 103–26.

Schain, M. 1985. 'Immigrants and politics in France', in J. Ambler (ed.) *The French Socialist Experiment*, pp. 176–81 (Phila: ISHI Press).

Schain, M. 1994. Ordinary politics: Immigrants, direct action and the political process in France, *French Politics and Society*, no 2–3. Spring–Summer, 5–38.

Schain, M. 2006. The extreme-right and immigration policy-making: Measuring direct and indirect effects, *West European Politics*, 29(2): 270–89.

Schmidt, V. 2006. *Democracy in Europe: The EU and National Polities* (Oxford: Oxford University Press).

Schmidt, V. 2007. Trapped by their ideas: French elites' discourses of European integration and globalization, *Journal of European Public Policy*, 14(7): 992–1009.

Schmitt, J. 1986. *Fin de la France? Histoire d'une perte d'identité* (Paris: Nouvelles Editions Debresse).

Schnapper, D. 2002. 'Making citizens in an increasingly complex society: Jacobinism revisited', in S. Hazareesingh (ed.) *The Jacobin Legacy in Modern France* (Oxford: Oxford University Press), pp. 196–216.

Schnepf, S. 2004. *How Different are Immigrants? A Cross-Country and Cross Survey Analysis of Educational Achievement*, IZA (Institute for the Study of Labor)/ Bonn, DP# 1398, November.

Schonfield, A. 1973. *Europe. Journey to an Unknown Destination* (London: Penguin).

Schor, N. 2001. The crisis of French universalism, *Yale French Studies*, 100: 43–64.

Scott, J. 2007. *The Politics of the Veil* (Princeton: Princeton University Press).

Scott, J.W. 2005. *Parité!: Sexual Equality and the Crisis of French Universalism* (Chicago: University of Chicago).

Seaton, J. 2003. Public, private and the media, *The Political Quarterly*, 74(2): 174–83.

Seck, P.I. 1993. *La stratégie culturelle de la France en Afrique* (Paris: L'Harmattan).

Seferdjeli, R. 2004. *'Fight with us, women, and we will emancipate you': France, the FLN and the struggle over women in the Algerian War of National Liberation, 1954–1962*. Unpublished doctoral dissertation, LSE, London.

Séguin, P. 1992a. *Discours pour la France* (Paris: Bernard Grasset).

Séguin, P. 1992b. Séguin-la-nation contre Léotard-l'Europe, *Nouvel Observateur*, 7–13 May.

Séguin, P. 1993. *Ce que j'ai dit* (Paris: Grasset).

Senghor, L.S. 1977. *Liberté III* (Paris: Seuil).

Senghor, L.S. 1988. *Ce que je crois* (Paris: Grasset).

Senghor, L.S. 1991. *The Collected Poetry*, translated by M. Dixon (Charlottesville: University of Virginia).

Sepinwall, G.A. 2005. *The Abbé Grégoire and the French Revolution: The Making of Modern Universalism* (Berkeley: University of California Press).

Sieburg, F. 1991. *Dieu est-il français?* (Paris: Grasset).

Silber, M. 2008. Le monde culturel manifeste son inquiétude, *Le Monde*, 2 March.

Silverman, M. 1992. *Deconstructing the Nation* (London, New York: Routledge).

Silverstein, P.A. (2004). *Algeria in France. Transpolitics, Race, and Nation* (Bloomington/Indianapolis: Indiana University Press).

Sonntag, A. 2008. 'The burdensome heritage of prestige politics', in M. Maclean and J. Szarka (eds) *France on the World Stage: Nation State Strategies in the Global Era*, pp. 77–90 (Basingstoke: Palgrave).

Soubie, R. 1991. *Dieu est-il toujours français?* (Paris: Editions de Fallois).

Sour Sarkozy Storms Out of TV Interview 2007. Accessed October 29, 2007, from the *Times* Online website: www.timesonline.co.uk/tol/news/world/europe/article 2763277.ece

Spire, A. 2005. *Etrangers à la carte: l'administration de l'immigration en France (1945–1975)* (Paris: Grasset).

Stanyer, J. and Wring, D. 2004. Public images, private lives: The mediation of politicians around the globe, *Parliamentary Affairs*, 57(1): 1–235.

Starke, P., Obinger, H. and Castles, F. 2008. Convergence towards where: In what ways, if any, are welfare states becoming more similar? *Journal of European Public Policy*, 15 (7): 975–1000.

Statham, P. 2005. Forging divergent and 'path dependent' ways to Europe? Political communication over European integration in the British and French public spheres, *European Political Communication Working Papers Series*, 11/05 (University of Leeds: Centre for European Political Communication). Available at www.eurpolcom.eu/exhibits/paper_11.pdf

Strudel, S. 2007. L'électorat de Nicolas Sarkozy: « rupture tranquille » ou syncrétisme tourmenté? *Revue française de science politique*, 57(3/4): 459–74.

Subileau, F. 2001. 'Abstentionnisme', in P. Perrineau and D. Reynié (eds) *Dictionnaire du vote*, pp. 1–14 (Paris: PUF).

Taggart, P. 1998. A touchstone of dissent: Euroscepticism in contemporary west European party systems, *European Journal of Political Research*, 33(3): 363–88.

Taggart, P. 2006. Questions of Europe: The domestic politics of the 2005 French and Dutch referendums and their challenge for the study of European integration, *Journal of Common Market Studies*, 44 (Annual Review): 7–25.

Taggart, P. and Szczerbiak, A. 2002. The party politics of Euroscepticism in EU member and candidate states, *Sussex European Institute Working Paper* no. 51. Available at: www.sussex.ac.uk/Units/SEI/pdfs/wp51.pdf

Taguieff, P.A. 2002. *Résister au bougisme: démocratie forte contre mondialisation technophobe* (Paris: Fayard).

Taylor, Ch. (ed.) 1994. *Multiculturalism and the Politics of Recognition* (Princeton: Princeton University Press).

Tepe, M. 2006. Some empirics on the concept of path dependence in comparative welfare politics, *Working Paper*, Freie Universität Berlin.

Teyssière, D. 2006. *La France singulière* (Paris: Bourin Editeur).

Tocqueville, A. de 1928. *L'Ancien régime et la révolution* (Paris: Calmann-Lévy).

Tocqueville, A. de 1966. *De la démocratie en Amérique* (London: Macmillan/ St. Martin's Press).

Touraine, A. 1995. *Critique de la modernité* (Paris: Librairie Générale Française).

Towa, M. 1971. *Léopold Sédar Senghor: Négritude ou servitude?* (Yaoundé: éditions Clé).

Unesco 2001. *Universal Declaration on Cultural Diversity* (Paris: Unesco).

Vail, M. 2008. From 'welfare to work' to 'buttressed liberalization': The shifting dynamics of labor market adjustment in France and Germany, *European Journal of Political Research*, 47: 334–58.

Vaulerin, A. 2007. Et si le gouvernement avait oublié de penser? *Liberation*, 23 July.

Vedel, T. 2007. *Comment devient-on Président/e de la République? Les Stratégies des candidats* (Paris: Laffont).

Védrine, H. and Moïsi, D. 2000. *Les Cartes de la France à l'heure de la mondialisation* (Paris: Fayard).

Verschave, F.-X. 1998. *La Françafrique. Le plus long scandale de la République* (Paris: Stock).

Verschave, F.-X. 2000. *Noir Silence. Qui arrêtera la Françafrique?* (Paris: Les Arènes).

Viet, V. 1998. *La France immigrée: Construction d'une politique 1914–1997* (Paris: Fayard).

Villiers de, P. 1992. *Notre Europe sans Maastricht* (Paris: Albin Michel).

Volpi, M. 1979. La democrazia autoritaria. Forma di governo bonapartista e V Repubblica francese (Bologna: il Mulino).

Weil, P. 1991. *La France et ses Etrangers* (Paris: Calman-Lévy).

Weil, P. 2004. *Qu'est-ce qu'un français?* (Paris: Folio).

Wieviorka, M. 2002. 'Race, culture and society: The French experience with Muslims', in N. AlSayyad and M. Castells (eds) *Muslim Europe or Euro Islam: Politics, Culture and Citizenship in the Age of Globalisation*, pp. 131–45 (Maryland: Lexington).

Wihtol de Wenden, C. 1988. *Les Immigrés et la politique* (Paris: Presses de la Fondation Nationale des Sciences Politiques).

Wihtol de Wenden, C. 1992. Les associations 'beur' et immigrés, leurs leaders, leurs stratégies, *Regards sur l'actualité*, no. 178, February.

Willaime, J-P. 2007. Religion et politique en France dans le contexte de la construction européenne, *French Politics, Culture and Society*, 25(3): 37–61.

Williams, P. 1964. *Crisis and Compromise: Politics in the Fourth Republic* (London: Longmans, Green and Co. Ltd.).

Willsher, K. 2007. Francois Fillon shows Gallic indifference to role, *The Sunday Telegraph*, 8 July.

World Health Organization, 2005. *Make Every Mother and Child Count* (Copenhagen: WTO).

World Health Organization, 2006. *Highlights on Health: France* (Copenhagen: WTO).

Wright, V. 1992. *The Government and Politics of France* (London: Routledge).

Wyplosz, C. 2000. Vices hexagonaux, *Libération*, 27 November.

Yost, D. 2006. France's new nuclear doctrine, *International Affairs*, 82(4): 701–21.

Index